CELEBRATING HERBS

Cooking Arts Collection™

CREDITS

About the Author

Patsy Jamieson is a freelance food writer and recipe developer based in Burlington, Vermont. She specializes in healthy cooking and contributes articles to *Cooking Pleasures*, *Vegetarian Times*, *Cooking Light* and *Tufts University Health & Nutrition Letter*. She has conducted cooking classes and demonstrations across the country, and has appeared on numerous television shows, including ABC's "Good Morning America," NBC's "Today Show," CNN's "On the Menu" and the Television Food Network's "Chef du Jour." She is a graduate of La Varenne Ecole de Cuisine in Paris.

CELEBRATING HERBS

Printed in 2011.

Laura Hunter, Vice President Product Marketing and Creative Development
Jennifer Weaverling, Managing Editor
Julie Cisler, Senior Book Design and Production
Wendy Holdman, Cover Design and Production
Bill Lindner Photography, Commissioned Photography
Abby Wyckoff, Food Stylist
Pegi Lee, Susan Telleen, Assistant Food Stylists

Special thanks to: Kathy Bauwens, Denise Bornhausen, Marcia Brinkley, Terry Casey, Jessica Doboszenski, Pat Durkin, Mike Hehner, Cindy Jurgensen, Bea Krinke, Jason Lund, Ruth Petran, Todd Schwiekert, Martha Zeimer and Betsy Wray.

On Cover: No-Cook Summer Tomato Sauce, page 168.
Herbed Goat Cheese Spread, page 61.
Southwestern Hominy Soup, page 76
Peach-Blackberry Compote With Basil Syrup, page 145

1 2 3 4 5 / 15 14 13 12 11
ISBN 13: 978-1-58159-498-0
© 2011 Cooking Club of America

Cooking Club of America
12301 Whitewater Drive
Minnetonka, MN 55343
www.cookingclub.com

All rights reserved. No part of this publication may be reproduced, stored in an electronic retrieval system or transmitted in any form or by any means (electronic, mechanical, photocopying, recording or otherwise) without the prior written permission of the copyright owner.

TABLE OF CONTENTS

INTRODUCTION...4

HERB ESSENTIALS 6

HERB GLOSSARY..20

RECIPE POTPOURRI 48

SOUPS, SALADS & SIDES...70

PASTA, GRAINS & BEANS...92

MEAT, POULTRY, FISH & SEAFOOD.................112

DESSERTS & BEVERAGES......................................138

SAUCES & CONDIMENTS.......................................154

RECIPE INDEX 172

GENERAL INDEX 173

INTRODUCTION

Fragrant, attractive and sometimes mysterious, herbs are perhaps the most seductive of all the ingredients used in cooking. While seldom featured as primary ingredients, herbs impart an essential flavor dimension to a dish and give it a distinctive personality.

Herbs have become more prominent on the North American culinary scene and, happily, more accessible to the home cook. Today's supermarkets stock a good selection of fresh herbs throughout the year. During the growing season, garden centers offer a dazzling array to tempt the kitchen gardener. As this book demonstrates, you can grow your own herbs. And thanks to overnight shipping, you can purchase some of the more exotic herbs, such as angelica and lovage, by mail order.

When I left for Paris to study cooking about 25 years ago, my exposure to herbs was limited to curly parsley and dried seasonings from a bottle. At La Varenne cooking school, I was introduced to the classic pairing of fresh tarragon and chicken, and learned to love the tart flavor of sorrel in soup or in sauce for fish. In spring and summer, there was always a generous supply of fresh chervil to garnish salads. During winter, we bundled parsley stems, dried thyme sprigs and bay leaves into fat *bouquet garnis* to flavor the hearty braises and stocks that simmered constantly at the back of the *fourneau* (stove).

My formal training is in classic French cooking, but in the years since my stint in Paris, I have enjoyed traveling and learning about the cuisines from many places. While exploring ethnic cooking, I have discovered some particularly interesting and effective uses of herbs. I have always been charmed by the way Southeast Asian cooks finish a salad or soup with a generous shower of vibrant cilantro, mint or basil. In Greek cooking, *avgolemono* — a mixture of egg, lemon juice and dill — adds a magical touch to soups and stews. Navigating the world of herbs provides a fascinating opportunity for a global taste tour.

In addition to developing more adventurous dining habits, many of us have become more concerned with eating healthfully. Relying on herbs for flavor is one of the easiest and

most delicious ways to enjoy a healthier diet. In this collection you will find numerous recipes that are inherently healthful because they derive their complex flavor from herbs rather than fat- and sodium-laden ingredients. The recipes are not stingy with beneficial fats, such as olive oil and nuts, but use a minimum of saturated fat. When it comes to creating flavorful — yet healthful — food, not only are herbs a cook's best friends, they are strategic allies as well.

The art of cooking with herbs ranges from a suggestion to a bold statement. Lavender, for example, is exquisite when used subtly, offering just a hint of its presence. Basil, on the other hand, can be used with abandon and happily asserts itself in pesto sauce and tomato salads. The recipes in *Celebrating Herbs* illustrate these principles. My goal is to show you how to use herbs in varied and exciting ways, in dishes ranging from appetizers and breads to main courses and desserts.

The fresh taste of herbs is something to celebrate. As you learn more about these valuable seasonings, I hope you will experiment with some unfamiliar herbs in your cooking and enjoy everyday herbs in delicious and sometimes surprising ways.

Introduction

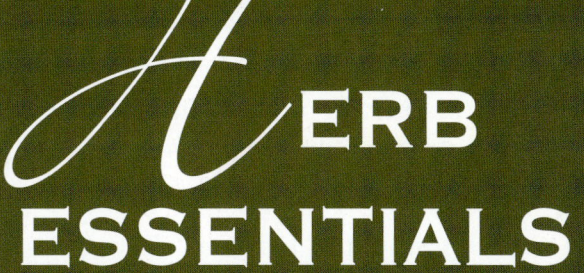

Herb Essentials

What is the best way to store herbs? How can you preserve herbs? When should you add them to a recipe? In this chapter, you will find answers to these questions, plus many interesting tricks, such as how to turn a lemongrass stalk into a skewer for grilling.

Edible Flowers, page 17

Tips and Techniques for Preparing Herbs

Cooking creatively with herbs starts with proper cleaning, storage and preparation techniques. Here are the secrets.

STORING SHORT-TERM

In an ideal world, you would always harvest herbs just before using them. But in real life, you will often need to store bunches of herbs in the refrigerator for a few days. Here are several options:

Bouquet of Flowers Method. Leafy, tender herbs — such as parsley and dill — are well-suited to this method. Trim stem ends, place herb stems in a container of water, cover loosely with a plastic bag and refrigerate. Most herbs will keep for up to 1 week; change water every 2 days.

Plastic Food Bag Method. Supermarket herbs are often subjected to produce misting to keep them looking good in the store. But because moisture promotes rotting, it is a good idea to wrap herbs in paper towels to absorb moisture before enclosing in a plastic food-storage bag. Herbs protected in this way and stored in the vegetable crisper should keep for up to 4 days, depending on freshness and type of herb. Plastic bags specially designed for extending the storage time of fruits and vegetables are useful for fresh herbs. These reusable, breathable bags are processed with the mineral oya, which absorbs ethylene gas. They can be found in health food stores.

Note that basil turns black when refrigerated. Use as soon as possible after harvesting or purchasing.

CLEANING

Sturdy herbs and some packaged herbs require just a thorough rinse under cold water and patting dry with a paper towel. But large bunches of parsley, basil, cilantro and dill may harbor grit, so wash them carefully as you would salad greens. Strip leaves from stems. Place leaves in a salad spinner basket and set it in the basin of a salad spinner. (Or use a colander set in a large bowl.) Fill the basket with cold water and swish. Let soak for a few minutes, then lift out the basket. Repeat the process until no trace of grit remains in the basin. Spin herbs dry. It is important to dry herbs thoroughly before storing or chopping.

STRIPPING LEAVES FROM STEMS

In most cases, it is the leaves you want to use in cooking. For herbs like parsley, cilantro, basil and dill, grasp the stems and pull off the leaves. To strip leaves from thyme, oregano, savory and tarragon, grasp sprigs at the top and run your fingers along the stem toward its base.

TEARING

Tender herbs, such as basil and chervil, are lovely when simply torn into small pieces. This casual approach is appropriate for dishes such as tomato salads and green salads.

SNIPPING

Kitchen scissors are convenient for snipping tender herbs like chives and chervil into attractive casual slivers.

SLIVERING

Tender herbs used for garnish — such as basil, mint and cilantro — are often more attractive when cut into chiffonade. Stack about 6 leaves on a cutting board and, if the leaves are large enough, roll them up. Using a sharp chef's knife or snippers, cut the roll crosswise into thin slivers.

CHOPPING

Pile herb leaves on a cutting board. Securing the tip of a sharp chef's knife with your free hand, use a rocking motion to chop herbs as finely as you wish. If you are chopping a large quantity of herbs, you can pulse them in a food processor. Make sure the blade is very sharp. For a small quantity of herbs, use a mini food processor rather than a large model.

USE QUICKLY

Once chopped, herbs quickly lose their flavor. Wait until just before using them to chop, tear or snip herbs. If you are entertaining and would like to get some of the preparation out of the way in advance, strip herb leaves from stems, wash and dry carefully. Enclose the leaves in a plastic food-storage bag and refrigerate until you are ready to chop.

Herb Essentials

PRESERVING HERBS

Whether you have a single pot of herbs on the deck or an extensive garden, access to homegrown herbs makes cooking a pleasure during the summer. But at the end of the growing season, you may want to capture the flavor of summer and prepare for winter cooking by preserving your herbs. Here's how.

HARVESTING

When preserving herbs, gather them when they are at their peak, just before they start to flower. Choose a sunny day and pick herbs midmorning after the dew has evaporated, but before the sun causes them to wilt. Discard any bruised or blemished leaves.

STOCKING UP ON HERB SAUCES

One of the most practical ways to preserve herbs is to make sauces and compound butters for the freezer. Make up a large batch of *Traditional Basil Pesto* (page 157) or *Parsley-Walnut Pesto* (page 162). Divide the pesto among containers and freeze for up to 6 months. Just thaw in the refrigerator and toss with pasta for a quick meal. Herb-flavored butters are another good option. You can use the recipe for *Shallot-Mustard Herb Butter* (page 163) or one of its variations as a guideline. Form butter into cylinders, wrap in plastic wrap and freeze for up to 6 months. Slice off pieces of butter as needed.

FREEZING

Tender leaf herbs, such as basil, chives, cilantro, dill, mint and parsley, are good candidates for freezing. There are a number of techniques for freezing herbs, but based on my testing, I have found that blanching herbs prior to freezing produces far superior results.

Freezing Herbs by Blanching Method. Trim stems from herb sprigs. Wash leaves. Bring a large saucepan of water to a boil. Place a bowl of ice water and a tray lined with a clean kitchen towel or paper towels beside the stove. Drop leaves *briefly* (just a few seconds) into the boiling water. With a slotted spoon,

transfer leaves to ice water to chill quickly, and then pat dry with towels. Spread herbs in a single layer on a wax paper-lined baking sheet and place in the freezer about 1 hour or until solid. Transfer to plastic food-storage bags; seal, label and freeze for up to 4 months. Frozen herbs are fine for flavoring, but are not suitable for garnishes. Chop frozen herbs with a knife or in your food processor.

Making Herb Ice Cubes. Place about 1 tablespoon chopped fresh herbs in each compartment of an ice cube tray. Add enough boiling water to cover herbs (boiling water replaces blanching) and freeze about 5 hours or until solid. Unmold ice cubes into a plastic food-storage bag and freeze for up to 4 months. This is the simplest method for freezing herbs. Herb ice cubes are handy for seasoning sauces and stews.

DRYING

This is the age-old method for preserving herbs. Sturdy herbs, such as rosemary, thyme, oregano and sage, are good candidates for drying. A food dehydrator, which provides uniform air circulation and controlled low heat, is the most efficient way to dry herbs, but they can also be simply hung to dry.

Drying Herbs in a Dehydrator. Wash and thoroughly dry herbs, then strip leaves from stems. Line dehydrator screens with cheesecloth so leaves won't fall through the screen. (Leaves will shrink as they dry.) Place herb leaves on screens and place trays in dehydrator. Dehydrate at low (90°F) 12 to 24 hours or until herbs crumble easily between your fingertips. Unless herbs will be used in a mixture, such as *herbes de Provence*, dry only one kind of herb at a time to prevent flavors from mingling.

Drying Herbs by Hanging. Do not remove stems. Rinse herb sprigs and pat dry thoroughly. Tie small bunches together at stems. Punch holes in a brown paper bag with a hole punch or skewer. Place leafy ends in the prepared bag. (The bag will protect herbs from dust and minimize light.) Secure bag around stems with a string or elastic band. Hang bag, stem-ends up, in a well-ventilated place until leaves crumble easily between your fingers. This will take 5 to 10 days.

Herb Essentials

Storing Dried Herbs. Trim stems, if necessary, and place herb leaves in a clean jar. Secure lid and store in a cupboard away from heat-producing appliances for up to 6 months. Just before using, crumble dried leaves with your fingertips to release their fragrance.

HERB-INFUSED VINEGAR

Herb-flavored vinegars allow you to enjoy the subtle flavor of herbs in your salads throughout the year. Herbs that complement salads — such as tarragon, burnet, dill, mint and basil — are good candidates for herb-infused vinegar.

Making Herb Vinegar. Wash and thoroughly dry 1 cup of herb sprigs, discarding any damaged leaves. Lightly bruise the herb sprigs to release their fragrance. (A mortar and pestle works well.) Place herbs in a sterilized wide-mouth 1-pint glass jar. In small saucepan, heat 2 cups white wine vinegar or rice vinegar until almost simmering. Pour vinegar over herbs. Cover and let steep overnight. Place a clean and dry herb sprig in a sterilized decorative bottle. Pour infused vinegar through a cheesecloth or coffee filter-lined funnel into the bottle. Cork or secure lid on the bottle and store vinegar in a cupboard away from heat-producing appliances. Use within 1 year.

Caution On Herb-Infused Oil. Despite serious health risks, I continue to see dangerous recipes for herb-infused oils in recently published cookbooks. This is disturbing because when executed incorrectly, the procedure of infusing herbs (and garlic and other aromatics) can lead to botulism, a serious and potentially fatal form of food poisoning. A container of oil is an anaerobic environment. When herbs (which are likely to have some soil contamination) are added, the result is an environment favorable to the growth of *botulinum* bacteria. Blanching herbs in boiling water does not kill the spores of *Clostridium botulinum*. However, acid does prevent the growth of these spores.

To make a safe infused oil, take the following precautions. Wash and dry herbs carefully. Be sure to add 1 tablespoon of an acidic ingredient, such as vinegar or lemon juice, at a ratio of 1 tablespoon per cup of oil. Store infusion in the refrigerator for no longer than 1 week.

CLASSIC HERB COMBOS

Here are some time-tested and classic ways to combine herbs.

BOUQUET GARNI

This herb bundle is used to flavor French-braised and long-simmered dishes. Tie the whole sprigs together securely so the bouquet can easily be removed before serving. Sprigs of parsley, thyme and bay leaf are standard. But a celery rib, leek leaf and strip of orange peel may also be included. To make a standard *bouquet garni*, gather together about 8 sprigs of fresh parsley, 8 sprigs of fresh or dried thyme and 1 bay leaf. Wrap butcher's twine up and down the length of the bundle and tie securely. Or enclose herbs in a double layer of cheesecloth and secure tightly with twine. When using *bouquet garni* ingredients to flavor stocks and other dishes that will be strained, don't bother to tie components together. If you will be using chopped parsley to finish the dish, reserve leaves for that purpose and make the *bouquet garni* with parsley stems only.

FINES HERBES

This French quartet includes chopped fresh parsley, tarragon, chervil and chives, combined in equal proportions. Only fresh herbs are used. A delicate mixture, you can use it in salads, egg dishes and light sauces. Always add *fines herbes* at the end of cooking.

Herb Essentials **13**

HERBES DE PROVENCE

This popular mixture of dried herbs typifies the seasonings widely used in the south of France. It may include some or all of the following: rosemary, thyme, savory, sage, basil, marjoram, bay leaf, lavender and anise. The specific mix, however, may vary according to preferences of the cook. You can find commercial jars of *herbes de Provence* in specialty stores, but they are expensive and may not be as fresh as you would like. For the most flavorful blend, combine your own, preferably from home-dried herbs. I recommend staying with herbs that stand up well when dried.

Here's how to blend your own *herbes de Provence*. In a small jar with a tight-fitting lid, mix 1 tablespoon dried thyme, 1 tablespoon dried rosemary, 1 tablespoon dried oregano and 1 tablespoon dried savory. If desired, add a pinch of dried lavender and crushed anise seed. If you have a quantity of these dried herbs you would like to preserve for winter and plan to use the mixture within 6 months, follow the basic proportions and make a larger batch.

GREMOLADA

A simple mixture of parsley, lemon peel and garlic, gremolada is used in Italian cooking, most notably as a garnish for the famous Milanese dish, *osso bucco* (braised veal shanks). It is also a delicious way to finish lamb, seafood, vegetable stew or seafood risotto. The fresh-tasting parsley and lemon rind counter the garlic's pungency. For a good balance, use a ratio of 1/3 cup chopped fresh parsley, 1 teaspoon freshly grated lemon peel and 2 medium minced garlic cloves. Just toss the mixture together shortly before using, and sprinkle over hot dishes; heat releases the fragrance.

PERSILLADE

In France, chopped fresh parsley flavored with minced garlic is known as persillade. It is stirred into quick sautés of meat, fish or vegetables at the last minute.

ZATAR

This blend from the Middle East is often served with flatbreads. Zatar is the Arabic word for wild thyme. To make a zatar herb blend, grind 2 tablespoons dried thyme, 2 tablespoons toasted sesame seeds and 1/4 teaspoon salt in a spice grinder. Transfer to a small bowl or jar and stir in 1/2 teaspoon ground sumac. Sumac, a spice with a slightly tart flavor, is made from dried berries of the sumac bush. You can find it in Middle Eastern markets. Store zatar, tightly covered, in the refrigerator for several months. Mix with a little extra-virgin olive oil and serve as a dip for warm pita breads.

Herb Garnishes

Herbs are the quintessential garnish. You just cannot go wrong embellishing a plate with sprigs of an herb featured in the dish. But in addition to the straight-forward herb sprig or sprinkle of slivered herbs, there are some fun and interesting ways to garnish with herbs.

CHIVE "RIBBONS"

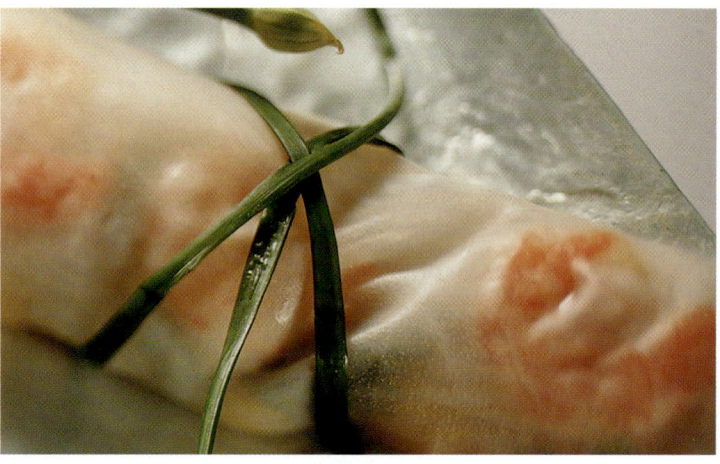

A long chive ribbon is an attractive way to secure and decorate a bouquet of herb sprigs, bundle of vegetables, spring roll or beggar's purse (an appetizer made by enclosing a spoonful of caviar and a dollop of *crème fraîche* in a crepe wrapper). To make chives pliable enough to tie, blanch them in boiling water for a few seconds, then place in a bowl of ice water and pat dry.

HERB BOUQUETS

A bouquet of assorted herb sprigs is an appealing way to garnish an appetizer tray or roast turkey. Sage, rosemary, thyme and bay leaves make an attractive grouping. Tie stems together loosely with a chive ribbon and place them on the platter.

FRIED PARSLEY

This is a classic garnish for fried fish and other fried foods. In this case, curly parsley is a better choice than Italian parsley. To prepare fried parsley, trim sprigs, leaving about 1 inch of stem. Wash parsley and dry thoroughly. (Just a little moisture will cause the oil to splatter.) Place about 1 inch vegetable or olive oil in a deep fryer or heavy saucepan; heat to 375°F. Carefully drop a handful of parsley sprigs into the hot oil and turn with a skimmer. Fry 10 to 15 seconds or until crisp but not colored. Lift sprigs out with skimmer and drain on a paper towel. Sprinkle lightly with salt and serve immediately.

FROSTED HERB SPRIGS

Herb sprigs coated with glistening sugar make interesting and attractive garnishes for desserts and pastries. Herbs with stubby, thick leaves (such as rosemary, lemon verbena and lemon thyme) work best. Frosted rosemary sprigs, accompanied by frosted cranberries, are festive-looking and are a lovely way to decorate a *bûche de Noël* (Yule log) or holiday cheesecake. To frost herbs, rinse sprigs and dry thoroughly. In small bowl, stir 1 pasteurized egg white briskly with a fork. Set a bowl of superfine sugar beside it. Place a wire rack over a sheet of parchment paper or a baking sheet. Holding on to the stem, dip an herb sprig into the egg white and shake off the excess. Dip into sugar, turn to coat, and sprinkle again with sugar. Place on rack and let dry 1½ to 2 hours.

Note that because of food safety, use only pasteurized egg whites. You can find pasteurized dried egg whites, such as Just Whites, and refrigerated pasteurized liquid egg whites, such as All Whites, in most supermarkets.

EDIBLE FLOWERS

A few herbs, such as chives and borage, produce edible flowers that make great garnishes for salads. Nasturtium flowers have a delightful peppery taste that is welcome in salads. For sweet dishes, pansies, violas and rose petals make lovely decorative finishes. Be sure to avoid any flowers that may have been sprayed with pesticides.

Herb Essentials 17

Tips for Cooking with Herbs

Here are a couple of tips for cooking creatively — and deliciously — with herbs.

Timing. As a general rule, dried herbs and sturdy fresh herbs, such as rosemary, thyme, oregano and bay leaf, are added at the beginning of cooking. Delicate herbs, such as parsley, basil, dill, cilantro and tarragon, should be used as seasonings at the end of cooking.

Herb Infusions. A subtle infusion of herbs is effective in both savory and sweet dishes.

The infusion technique is useful when you are making soups. Simmering canned broth with rosemary sprigs and garlic for about 20 minutes is a great trick for adding depth of flavor to a canned product. A tea infuser is handy for containing the flavorings because it can be simply lifted out when the infusion is ready. (Or broth can be passed through a strainer.)

A subtle herbal infusion gives a magical quality to fruit desserts. To infuse milk for a custard or sugar syrup for a fruit salad or sorbet, add herb sprigs to the hot liquid and let it steep for about 30 minutes, then strain out the herbs.

To release maximum fragrance, lightly bruise the herbs before infusing them in vinegar or cold fruit juice. To bruise: Place herb sprigs in a medium bowl. Using a wooden mortar or large wooden spoon, crush herbs until you notice the fragrance.

GRILLING WITH HERBS

Herbs add life and flavor to your grilling creations. Here are some ideas.

Add Aroma to the Fire. If you have an abundant supply of herbs, toss a few sprigs of a sturdy herb (such as rosemary, thyme or bay leaf) that complements the food you are grilling onto the coals or grid over a gas flame.

Herbal Protection. Use herbs to protect meat, chicken or fish from the grill's searing heat. Lightly oil food, then stick whole sage or mint leaves onto meat surfaces before placing on the grill. The herbs will also impart a subtle flavor.

Creative Kabobs. Thread whole sage leaves or bay leaves (soaked in water, if dried) between pieces of food when assembling skewers.

Lemongrass Skewers. Edible skewers made from lemongrass stalks add an extra dimension and interesting presentation to Southeast Asian-flavored kabobs. To prepare a stalk of lemongrass for use as a skewer, trim the stem end and enough of the leafy end so the stalk is about 10 inches long. Remove outer leaves so the stalk is between 1/4- and 1/2- inch thick. Using a small and sharp knife, whittle the stem end into a sharp point. Wrap the stalk in plastic wrap and freeze 1 hour or until firm. When you are ready to assemble kabobs, first use a metal skewer to pierce a hole through the food, then thread onto lemongrass skewers.

Herb Essentials

Herb Glossary

Herb or spice? Dried herbs and spices share space on the spice racks of North American kitchens. But few cooks know the subtle distinctions between these two flavoring agents.

"Herb" generally refers to a plant from which the fragrant leafy parts (and sometimes stems) are used for culinary, cosmetic or medicinal purposes. Most herbs can be cultivated in temperate zones and typically do not have woody stems. Fresh herbs are often preferred, but sturdier ones can be dried for longer storage. "Spices," on the other hand, come from the seeds, roots and barks of plants. Most spices (but not all) come from tropical regions. They are generally used in dried form.

Although there are countless plants that may meet the botanical definition of an herb, the focus in this book is herbs for culinary purposes. The following is a guide to 25 of the most useful kitchen herbs.

Angelica

DESCRIPTION

With a taste and fragrance as delicate and lovely as its name, angelica is an uncommon herb that is definitely worth seeking out. A member of the parsley family, this herb resembles celery — but it is much larger. At maturity, angelica can reach a towering height of 6 feet. It is native to Europe and Asia but is easily cultivated in North America. Angelica is generally considered a biennial. Its distinctive flavor is reminiscent of licorice, vanilla and celery.

TRADITIONAL USES

Although you may not be aware of it, you may be familiar with the taste of angelica if you enjoy herb liqueurs. The roots and seeds contribute a delicate flavor to Benedictine and Chartreuse, while the roots are used to flavor gin. Perhaps angelica is best known for its stems, which are traditionally candied. European pastry chefs use candied angelica to decorate cakes, pastries and puddings. Angelica has a long-term relationship with rhubarb. It mellows the tartness and astringency, and contributes a delicate herbal fragrance to rhubarb dishes. Cooking rhubarb with angelica allows you to reduce sugar slightly.

PREPARATION AND COOKING TIPS

The stems are the most useful part in cooking. Add a few tablespoons of finely diced angelica stems to a rhubarb pie or compote (see *Rhubarb Fool*, page 148).

STORAGE

Enclose stalks in a plastic food-storage bag and refrigerate up to 4 days. The traditional method of preserving angelica is to candy the stems in sugar syrup. This somewhat complicated process involves first blanching angelica and then submerging and boiling repeatedly in sugar syrup of specific densities, and finally, drying.

COMPLEMENTS

Angelica works well with rhubarb and other tart fruits such as gooseberries or damsen plums.

GROWING ANGELICA

Angelica archangelica

Plant type—Biennial or short-lived perennial.

Size—4 to 8 feet tall, 3 feet wide.

Light—Light shade.

Soil—Humus-rich, moist.

Propagation—Sow fresh seed outdoors in early autumn. Keep moist but do not cover, as seed requires light to germinate. Seed loses viability in 3 months, but it will keep up to a year if refrigerated in an airtight container. Thin to 3 feet apart. If seeds are not sown in place in the garden the previous autumn, transplant to the permanent site in mid-spring.

Care—Remove flowers as they develop to prolong the life of the plant. Let flowers develop on at least one plant to provide seed for new plants. Spray aphids or spider mites with horticultural soap.

asil

DESCRIPTION

Although supermarkets now stock this leafy herb year-round, fragrant basil epitomizes the sweet taste of summer. Basil is native to India, Africa and Asia but has been long valued as a culinary herb in Mediterranean regions. The flavor is sweet, with a hint of pepper and undertones of mint and cloves.

VARIETIES

In addition to common sweet basil, there are numerous varieties to explore. Here are a few interesting options: Bush basil is a dwarf variety with tiny leaves. Opal basil and purple ruffles basil have attractive dark maroon-colored leaves and look stunning in an herb vinegar. Thai basil offers distinctive anise tones and is appropriate for Thai and Vietnamese dishes. Cinnamon basil and lemon basil offer slight variations on the basil theme.

TRADITIONAL USES

Basil is a fine salad herb and has a much-appreciated affinity with tomatoes. Basil, of course, is the dominant flavoring in the classic Italian sauce, pesto. In Asia, basil flavors curries and adds life to salads and soups.

PREPARATION AND COOKING TIPS

Fresh is best; dried basil just doesn't compare. To preserve the flavor of basil, use it raw or add it to a dish at the end of cooking. Because basil tends to turn black when bruised, tear leaves into smaller pieces before adding to a rustic salad or sauce, or use a sharp knife to cut leaves into chiffonade (page 9). Scatter torn basil leaves over fresh tomato salads, stir into tomato sauce or finish a vegetable sauté or soup with slivered basil. Add torn leaves to green salads and layer in sandwiches instead of lettuce. Basil is also good in sweet dishes.

STORAGE

Because the recommended temperature for holding basil is 48° to 50°F (colder than room temperature, warmer than a refrigerator), storing basil is difficult. It turns black when subjected to temperatures below 48°F and wilts quickly at warmer temperatures. So purchase or harvest basil the day you plan to use it. If you are a gardener or frequent farmers' markets, you will certainly want to preserve some of the late-summer abundance for winter. One of the best ways to do this is to make a large batch of pesto and freeze in small containers for up to 6 months. You can also freeze basil. For best results and optimum flavor, blanch it as directed on page 10.

COMPLEMENTS

Use basil with garlic, tomatoes and other summer vegetables such as zucchini, bell peppers, eggplant and corn.

GROWING BASIL
Ocimum basilicum

Plant type—Tender annual.

Size—1 to 3 feet tall, 1 to 2 feet wide.

Light—Full sun.

Soil—Humus-rich, moist, well-drained.

Propagation—Start seed indoors 4 weeks before the last frost, planting 1/8-inch deep and with 75°F bottom heat; germination takes about 3 days. Set out when all danger of frost is past and night temperatures are above 65°F. Seed can also be sown directly into the garden at this time. Space plants 12 to 18 inches apart. The basils easily adapt to containers filled with a fast-draining potting mix. Feed monthly with a balanced fertilizer according to the manufacturer's directions.

Care—Fertilize at 6-week intervals during the growing season with a balanced organic fertilizer. Remove the flower spikes as they emerge to keep the plant bushy and producing new leaves.

Herb Glossary

Bay Leaf

DESCRIPTION

One of the most indispensable herbs in European and North American cooking, bay leaves slowly release their pungent, somewhat piney aroma to numerous soups and stews. This herb is also known as bay laurel, laurel leaf or sweet bay. It comes from a perennial evergreen shrub that thrives in the Mediterranean region, although it can be grown in North America. In colder areas, it survives best in a container that can be brought indoors for the winter. Dried bay leaves are essential seasonings in any pantry. Some supermarkets now sell fresh bay leaves. These are shinier and a deeper green than the familiar dried leaves.

VARIETIES

Of the two main varieties, Turkish bay and California bay, the more subtly flavored Turkish leaves are preferred for cooking.

TRADITIONAL USES

Along with parsley and thyme, bay leaf is a key ingredient in the *bouquet garni* used to flavor classic French stocks and braises. Bay leaves are routinely added to meat dishes, cream sauces, potatoes and rice pilafs for a subtle infusion of fragrance during cooking.

PREPARATION AND COOKING

Keep fresh or dried leaves whole and always remove them from the dish before serving to avoid any possibility of choking. Don't overdo it with bay — too much will make a dish bitter. One leaf is generally enough to flavor a dish for 4 to 6 people. In addition to stews, stocks, pilafs and sauces, bay will perk up your cooking in a variety of ways: For example, drop a leaf into the water used for boiling seafood or potatoes. You can also thread bay leaves between chunks of meat, poultry or seafood to make attractive and flavorful kabobs (see *Swordfish Souvlaki*, page 130). Try flavoring desserts with fresh bay leaves; you can infuse the milk for sweet custards or sugar syrup for poaching fruit with subtle scent of bay.

STORAGE

Store fresh bay leaves in a plastic food-storage bag in the refrigerator. They will keep for several days. Remember that dried bay leaves lose their fragrance over time. Try to use within 6 months.

COMPLEMENTS

Bay works well with strong flavors like meat, poultry and seafood, but also enhances delicate cream sauces.

GROWING BAY

Laurus nobilis

Plant type—Woody, evergreen shrub or tree.

Size—Up to 50 feet when grown year-round outdoors; 5 to 10 feet in containers.

Light—Full sun to light shade.

Soil—Humus-rich, well-drained.

Propagation—Difficult to start from seed, but if you're feeling adventurous, try them indoors with 75°F bottom heat; germination takes 4 weeks. Cuttings are much more reliable, but still a slow process. Take cuttings in the fall from young shoots; rooting may take 6 to 9 months.

Care—Except where hardy, grow bay in containers filled with a fast-draining potting mix and overwinter indoors. Fertilize in the spring with a balanced fertilizer according to the manufacturer's directions. Pinch out tip growth to encourage branching. Bay is very susceptible to scale. Control with sprays of horticultural soap or a summer horticultural oil.

BURNET

DESCRIPTION

This hardy perennial was commonly used by Europeans as far back as the 15th century. Sadly, this old-fashioned herb is seldom used in contemporary cooking. Native to Europe, it is also known as salad burnet. It has very pretty fern-like foliage, and the delicate leaves have a refreshing cucumber-like flavor. If you would like to brighten your salads with burnet, you will probably have to grow your own. In mild climates, it may stay green year-round.

TRADITIONAL USES

Burnet has long been enjoyed in salads and is used to flavor wine and beverages.

PREPARATION AND COOKING TIPS

Use only tender young leaves, as old ones may be tough and bitter. Rinse sprigs and pat dry. Strip leaves from stems; leave whole or chop. Add whole burnet leaves to salad greens. Flavor cream cheese spreads and yogurt (or sour-cream) dips with chopped burnet. Use whole leaves to garnish cold soups and sprigs in wine coolers.

STORAGE

This is an herb to enjoy fresh from the garden. It loses its cucumber flavor when dried. To preserve the delicate taste of burnet for the winter, use it in an herb vinegar (page 12).

COMPLEMENTS

Burnet goes well with salad greens, fresh cheeses, yogurt and sour cream.

GROWING BURNET

Sanguisorba officinalis

Plant type—Herbaceous perennial.

Size—2 to 4 feet tall, 2 feet wide.

Light—Full sun.

Soil—Moist, well-drained soil.

Propagation—Propagate by seed or by dividing established clumps. Sow seeds in March and thin out to 9 inches apart. You can also propagate by dividing roots in autumn so that they become well-established before the next summer's dry weather sets in.

Care—Pick off the flowers when they appear; you use only the stem and leaves of the herb. Burnet was originally used medicinally to help stop bleeding.

Herb Glossary

Chervil

DESCRIPTION

Chervil is not well-known in North America, but it is highly appreciated by French cooks. It has feathery green leaves that resemble parsley, and its delicate flavor also recalls parsley, but it is distinguished by a hint of anise. Because you are unlikely to find cut fresh chervil at food markets, you will probably have to grow your own. This hardy annual is easy to grow from seed in a garden or container.

TRADITIONAL USES

Chervil is one of the herbs used in the classic French *fines herbes* mixture (page 13).

PREPARATION AND COOKING TIPS

This herb loses its delicate charm when heated. Use chervil to embellish salads or add it to a soup or sauce just before serving. Use chopped chervil in *fines herbes* (page 13). You can also coarsely snip or tear the tender leaves and toss with greens for a refreshing salad. The lacy sprigs make an especially attractive garnish.

STORAGE

This is an herb to enjoy fresh; dried chervil is not acceptable. Chervil wilts quickly after picking. However, you may store it in a plastic food-storage bag in the refrigerator for a day or so. For long-term storage, your best bet is to make up a batch of *Shallot-Mustard Herb Butter* (page 163) for the freezer.

COMPLEMENTS

Try chervil with eggs, fish and green salads.

GROWING CHERVIL

Anthriscus cerefolium

Plant type—Annual.

Size—12 to 18 inches tall, 12 inches wide.

Light—Light shade.

Soil—Humus-rich, moist, well-drained.

Propagation—Chervil does not readily transplant, so it is best to sow the seed directly into the garden about four weeks before the last frost. Make a furrow 1-inch deep and sprinkle in the seed but do not cover. Mist the area lightly each day. Germination takes about 10 days and is best with fresh seed. Thin to 6 inches apart. Chervil makes an excellent container plant, and for growing outdoors.

Care—Chervil tends to bloom quickly. To ensure a continued harvest, sow seed every 2 weeks until June. Begin sowing seeds again in late summer for an autumn crop.

CHIVES

DESCRIPTION

Chives belong to the (*allium*) onion family. The flavor is reminiscent of onion but with less bite because chives contain much less sulphur. The grass-like hollow leaves are the most useful part of the plant for cooking, but the light purple flowers are edible. This hardy perennial is a staple in any herb garden.

VARIETIES

The most common chives are onion chives, but garlic chives are also widely available at garden centers. Garlic chives, also known as Chinese chives, have flat leaves and white flowers. As the name implies, they have a mild garlic flavor.

TRADITIONAL USES

An essential ingredient in *fines herbes* (page 13), chives blend well with other herbs. They are used for both flavoring and decoration.

PREPARATION AND COOKING TIPS

Use scissors to snip chives. Alternatively, slice crosswise with a sharp knife; do not chop or mince. Use chives to flavor cheese spreads and salads. Add them to hot dishes at the last minute. Garnish cream soups and sauces with snipped chives. Sprinkle edible chive flowers over salads or use them to flavor vinegar. For an interesting decorative effect, use chives as herb "ribbons" to wrap around small bundles of vegetables or bouquets of mixed herbs (page 16).

STORAGE

Enclose chives in a plastic food-storage bag and refrigerate up to 4 days.

COMPLEMENTS

Chives work well with eggs, delicate fish such as sole, fresh cheeses, potatoes and green salads.

GROWING CHIVES

Allium schoenoprasum

Plant type—Perennial.

Size—12 to 18 inches tall, 12 to 18 inches wide.

Light—Full sun.

Soil—Humus-rich, well-drained soil.

Propagation—Sow seeds indoors 8 weeks before the last spring frost, placing 1/4-inch deep. At temperatures between 60° and 70°F, seeds will germinate in 2 to 3 weeks. It's much easier to buy plants in the spring or get a division of about six bulbs from a friend. This should not be too hard, as chives need dividing at least every 3 years to rejuvenate the clump. You can also divide chives in autumn.

Care—Stimulate tender fresh new growth by trimming chives back to 2 inches after flowering. To have chives indoors in the winter, start seeds in late summer or dig a small clump in autumn, place it in a container, and leave it outside until the soil freezes; then bring it indoors.

Herb Glossary

Cilantro

DESCRIPTION

Cilantro looks a lot like parsley, but it has a decidedly different fragrance and taste. Cilantro, the bright green leaves and stems of the coriander plant, has a pungent yet lively citrus flavor. Not everyone is a fan of cilantro; some complain it tastes soapy. It is also known as Chinese parsley. Cilantro, an annual, is native to the Mediterranean region and southern Europe, but its popularity has spread around the world. The seeds, which are generally known as coriander, also have culinary value. They have a mellow, complex spicy flavor, and are included in pickling spice mixes and curry blends.

TRADITIONAL USES

Cilantro (the leafy part of the plant) is an important seasoning in the cuisines of North Africa, the Middle East, Southeast Asia, India and Latin America. It provides a refreshing contrast to the highly spiced foods typical of these cuisines.

PREPARATION AND COOKING TIPS

Cilantro can be gritty, so wash and dry thoroughly (page 8). Coarsely slivered, cilantro has a fluffy quality and is more attractive than when finely chopped. Since cilantro stems are quite tender, you can be casual about stripping leaves from stems; just trim the thick part of the stems below the point where leaves branch out. Whole cilantro leaves make an appealing garnish for Asian soups and curries. Use cilantro in uncooked preparations or add it to cooked dishes at the very end of cooking. Enhance prepared tomato salsa or canned black bean soup with some fresh cilantro.

STORAGE

Wrap bunch of fresh cilantro in paper towel, enclose in a plastic food-storage bag and refrigerate up to 4 days. Alternatively, use the *bouquet of flowers* method outlined on page 8. If you have a large quantity of cilantro to put up for future use, freeze it (page 10) or use in sauces, such as *Cilantro Pesto* (page 164) or *Moroccan Charmoula Sauce* (page 166).

COMPLEMENTS

Cilantro works well with hot chiles, ginger, cumin, avocados, tomatoes, cheese and rice.

GROWING CILANTRO

Coriandrum sativum

Plant type—Annual.

Size—12 to 18 inches tall, 1 foot wide.

Light—Full sun to light shade.

Soil—Humus-rich, moist, well-drained.

Propagation—Sow seeds directly into the garden in the spring after the last frost. Plant seeds 1/2-inch deep, thinning to 6 inches apart. Make successive sowings at 2-week intervals until early summer. Seeds may also be sown in autumn in the South. You can also grow cilantro in containers filled with a fast-draining potting mix. Feed monthly with a balanced fertilizer.

Care—Cilantro grows best in the cool months of spring and autumn. Mulch during the growing season to keep the soil cool and prolong growth. Another way to prolong growth is to remove the flower stalk as soon as it appears.

DILL

DESCRIPTION

Perhaps because of its association with old-fashioned dill pickles, dill is a familiar herb to most North Americans. It is a member of the parsley family, but it bears a close resemblance to fennel. The feathery leaves have a refreshing piquant flavor and perk up a wide variety of dishes. The seeds have a stronger flavor and, in addition to flavoring pickles, are used in breads and long-cooked soups and stews. Dill is an annual that is believed to have originated around the Mediterranean and southern Russia.

TRADITIONAL USES

An important seasoning in the cuisine of Scandinavia, dill is an essential flavoring in the Swedish specialty *gravlax* (cured salmon). It is also widely used in Germany, Eastern Europe and Russia, where it turns up in a variety of dishes such as potato salad, borscht and mushroom-barley soup. French and Italian cooks seem to ignore dill, but it is popular in Greek and Turkish cooking. It complements tangy feta cheese in savory pastry fillings and, allied with lemon and egg in avgolemono, provides a beautiful finish to a Greek soup or stew.

PREPARATION AND COOKING TIPS

Trim thick stems from dill sprigs. Wash and dry feathery leaves, then chop with a chef's knife. To maximize dill's fresh flavor, add at the end of cooking. Dried dill weed does not compare to fresh.

STORAGE

Store a bunch of fresh dill like a bouquet of flowers (page 8) in the refrigerator. Alternatively, wrap in paper towel, enclose in a plastic food-storage bag and refrigerate up to 4 days.

COMPLEMENTS

Salmon and delicate fish (such as halibut), eggs, cucumbers, beets, mushrooms, cottage and feta cheese all pair well with dill.

GROWING DILL
Anethum graveolens

Plant type—Annual.

Size—18 inches to 4 feet tall, 1 foot wide.

Light—Full sun.

Soil—Humus-rich, moist, well-drained.

Propagation—Sow seed directly into the garden in the spring after the last frost, thinning to 1 foot apart. For a continuous supply of foliage, sow every 3 weeks until midsummer. Dill adapts readily to containers, with 'Fernleaf' being most recommended. Use a fast-draining potting mix and fertilize monthly with a balanced fertilizer according to the manufacturer's directions.

Care—Protect taller types from wind or stake the stems. If desired, allow at least one plant to self-sow for an early crop next year.

Herb Glossary

EPAZOTE

DESCRIPTION

Mexican food aficionados may know of this herb as an ingredient in authentic *frijoles* (bean) recipes. Epazote is also known as Mexican tea and by the unappetizing names of pigweed and wormseed. It is native to Latin America, but it grows wild in many parts of the United States. Weedlike in appearance, epazote has pointed, serrated leaves. It has a pungent aroma and a slightly bitter taste that mellows during cooking. Unless you live in an area where there is a large Hispanic population, epazote can be difficult to purchase. However, it is easy to grow from seed.

TRADITIONAL USES

Mexican cooks routinely flavor bean-cooking water with a sprig of epazote. It is considered a carminative, a substance that reduces flatulence. Epazote is also used in a variety of Mexican dishes, such as stuffed chiles, cheese quesadillas, moles (pronounced moh-lay) and soups.

PREPARATION AND COOKING TIPS

Add a whole sprig of epazote when you begin cooking beans, and then remove before serving, just as you would a bay leaf. Strip leaves from stems and chop before adding to quesadilla fillings. Fresh epazote is preferable, but dried can be substituted in bean dishes and soups.

STORAGE

To store fresh epazote sprigs, wrap in paper towel and enclose in a plastic food-storage bag and refrigerate up to 4 days. You can dry epazote by hanging it or using a food dehydrator (page 11).

COMPLEMENTS

Black beans and Mexican *queso fresco* (fresh cheese) can be enhanced with epazote.

GROWING EPAZOTE

Chenopodium ambrosioides

Plant type—Annual.

Size—1 to 3 feet tall, although it can reach up to 4 feet.

Light—Full sun.

Soil—Moist, well-drained soil.

Propagation—Epazote plants are inexpensive and readily available from spring through midsummer at nurseries that specialize in herbs. Sow seed in early summer. Space plants 2 feet apart. Takes high temperatures to germinate. Epazote grows easily from seed and doesn't necessarily need good soil, but the richer the soil, the larger and faster the plant tends to grow. Most epazote plants will grow with morning sun and afternoon shade.

Care—Pinch off the flowers regularly to encourage new growth.

 LAVENDER

DESCRIPTION

Although best known for its sweet scent used to perfume potpourris and aroma-therapy products, lavender is an interesting herb to incorporate into your cooking repertoire. This perennial is native to the Mediterranean, but it has been introduced to North America successfully. It is an attractive plant with silvery gray leaves and fragrant purple blossoms. The flowers are the most useful in cooking, and their flavor is best described as perfumed. In season, you can find lavender plants at most nurseries. You can find dried lavender flowers in specialty stores.

Fern leaf lavender

VARIETIES

There are a number of varieties to choose from, including fern leaf, French and lady lavender, but English lavender is the most useful in cooking. This common variety is also the hardiest and most suitable for growing if you live in a cool climate.

TRADITIONAL USES

Lavender flowers may be included in the French *herbes de Provence* mixture (page 14). In Provence, lavender is sometimes used to impart a delicate fragrance to sweet custards and ice creams.

French lavender

PREPARATION AND COOKING TIPS

Easy does it. Lavender is most successful when used subtly. Infuse the milk destined for custard with lavender flowers to impart a delicate flavor. Dried flowers make an interesting crust for roast lamb or lamb chops; grind them in a spice grinder before using. Dried lavender is a good stand-in for fresh; substitute one third of the quantity of dried for fresh.

STORAGE

You can hold a bouquet of fresh lavender in a container of water in the refrigerator for a few days. Alternatively, enclose lavender flowers in a plastic food-storage bag and refrigerate up to 4 days.

COMPLEMENTS

Use lavender with lamb, honey, vanilla and summer fruits such as plums and raspberries.

Lady lavender

GROWING LAVENDER

Lavandula species and cultivars

Plant type—The most common types are evergreen, woody perennials. There are also tender species often grown as annuals.

Size—8 inches to 3 feet tall, 1 to 4 feet wide.

Light—Full sun.

Soil—Humus-rich, well-drained.

Propagation—Lavender is seldom started from seed. Plant lavenders into the garden after all frost danger is past, spacing 1 to 3 feet apart depending on mature height. Take cuttings in summer from the side shoots, place in a cold frame and grow there for a year before transplanting to the garden.

Care—Lavenders need good air circulation around them, which helps prevent fungal diseases. Trim plants the first year after planting to prevent flowering and to encourage branching. Thereafter, prune after flowering and again in the spring to remove any dead wood; never cut into old wood, as it will not sprout new growth. Lavenders grow very well in containers.

Herb Glossary 31

LEMON BALM

DESCRIPTION

Also known as melissa, bee balm or simply "balm," lemon balm has a delightful citrus fragrance with a hint of mint. The name *melissa* is derived from the Greek word for honeybees. (The plant's exceptional fragrance is attractive to bees.) It is a member of the mint family and its ragged-edged leaves closely resemble mint. This hardy perennial thrives with minimal care, so it is a practical choice for casual gardeners.

TRADITIONAL USES

Dried leaves are used in herbal tea blends.

PREPARATION AND COOKING TIPS

Instead of mint, use shredded lemon balm leaves to add a fresh finish to vegetable and fruit salads. Sweeten fruit salads and sorbets with a lemon-balm infused sugar syrup. When making roast chicken, tuck lemon balm leaves under the skin and in the cavity to subtly flavor the meat during roasting. Use a few fresh sprigs to garnish lemonade or iced tea or to enhance a pot of brewed black tea.

STORAGE

Enclose lemon balm sprigs inside a plastic food-storage bag and refrigerate up to 4 days. If you have an abundant supply of lemon balm in your garden at the end of summer, it is worth drying it in a dehydrator (page 11) for use in potpourris and teas.

COMPLEMENTS

Lemon balm works well with citrus fruits, melon and peaches.

GROWING LEMON BALM
Melissa Officinalis

Plant type—Perennial.

Size—2 feet tall, 2 feet wide.

Light—Full sun to light shade.

Soil—Humus-rich, moist, well-drained.

Propagation—Sow seeds outdoors after all danger of frost is past in spring. Barely cover the seeds and keep moist until they germinate. Thin to 2 feet apart. Take cuttings or layer in spring or summer or divide in spring or autumn. Lemon balm brings a fresh, bright green color to the garden. Lemon balm easily grows in containers filled with a fast-draining potting mix and a monthly feeding with a balanced fertilizer according to the manufacturer's directions. Bring the plants inside during the winter or overwinter them outdoors in a protected place with a mulch around the pots.

Care—It may take a year for plants to reach their stride. Trim back faded flowers before seed sets to keep the plants from self-sowing.

LEMONGRASS

DESCRIPTION

This tropical grass is a key flavoring in Thai and Vietnamese cooking. A lemongrass stalk looks a bit like a brittle scallion. Its flavor is reminiscent of lemon oil with a whisper of ginger. Although it is native to tropical regions, it can be grown in North America. You can find lemongrass in Asian markets and large supermarkets.

TRADITIONAL USES

Southeast Asian broths, soups and curries are frequently infused with lemongrass. Minced lemongrass is used to flavor marinades and stir-fries.

PREPARATION AND COOKING TIPS

Lemongrass tends to be somewhat fibrous. Remove the tough outer leaves of lemongrass stalks. Trim the upper fibrous part of the stalk at the point where the leaves branch out. If using lemongrass in an infusion that will be strained, cut the bulb into 2-inch lengths and smash with the side of a chef's knife to release maximum flavor. If using lemongrass in a marinade or stir-fry, mince as finely as possible, then mix with other seasonings in the recipe and mash into a paste with a mortar and pestle or in a mini food processor. For an interesting presentation, use lemongrass stalks as skewers for Asian-flavored grilled foods (page 19). Dried lemongrass might be more readily available than fresh. If using dried lemongrass, soak in hot water for 30 minutes before using.

STORAGE

You can enclose lemongrass stalks in a plastic food-storage bag and refrigerate for several days. Since it can be difficult to find lemongrass, you might want to buy a few extra stalks when you come across them. Trim, then enclose in a plastic food-storage bag and store in the freezer.

COMPLEMENTS

Garlic, ginger, chiles, cilantro, fish sauce, coconut milk, chicken and seafood work well with lemongrass.

GROWING LEMONGRASS

Aloysia triphylla

Plant type—Perennial.

Size—3 to 5 feet tall, 4 feet wide.

Light—Full sun.

Soil—Humus-rich, moist, well-drained soil.

Propagation—Sow seeds indoors 6 weeks before the last frost in spring. Plant outdoors after the last frost, spacing 2 to 4 feet apart or plant in containers. Divide in spring or early summer, trimming the leaves to 4 inches long.

Care—Lemon grass is very easy to grow, although cats may nibble on the leaves or dig the plant up. If you don't want to overwinter lemon grass indoors, simply treat it as an annual. Because lemon grass does not withstand freezing temperatures, most gardeners grow it in containers filled with a fast-draining potting mix and a monthly fertilizing with a balanced fertilizer. Overwinter indoors in bright light.

Herb Glossary

Lemon Verbena

DESCRIPTION

I have always been fascinated by this herb's lyrical name. When I finally found lemon verbena at a local nursery and started to experiment with it in cooking, I became completely enchanted. The long pointed leaves have a pronounced lemon-oil scent and flavor. Lemon verbena is a tropical shrub originally from South America.

TRADITIONAL USES

Lemon verbena is used in small quantities to impart an exquisite flavor to desserts and drinks.

PREPARATION AND COOKING TIPS

Lemon verbena has a strong flavor; use sparingly. Rinse sprigs and pat dry, then strip leaves from stems. Since the leaves are somewhat tough, it is important to mince them finely. Use a small amount of minced lemon verbena to flavor whipped cream, custards and fruit salads. Alternatively, infuse milk for custards or sugar syrup for fruit salads and sorbets with lemon verbena sprigs, and then remove before serving. Lemon verbena sprigs make especially attractive garnishes for desserts.

STORAGE

Enclose lemon verbena sprigs in a plastic food-storage bag and refrigerate up to 2 days. At the end of the growing season, lemon verbena is a good candidate for the dehydrator. Dried lemon verbena is a pleasant addition to herb tea.

COMPLEMENTS

Lemon verbena works well with strawberries, peaches, apricots and custards.

GROWING LEMON VERBENA

Cymbopogon citratus

Plant type—Perennial.

Size—Where hardy, 10 feet tall and 8 feet wide. In containers, 2 to 3 feet tall and 18 inches wide.

Light—Full sun.

Soil—Humus-rich, moist, well drained.

Propagation—Seeds are difficult to germinate, so it's best to buy a plant. Take cuttings in late spring or early summer. Place lemon verbena where it can easily be brushed against, releasing the fresh, lemony scent. Try placing a pot on the outdoor dining table or near a garden bench.

Care—Pinch the growing tips out or cut the entire plant back by half in midsummer to encourage branching. Spray spider mites or whiteflies with horticultural soap. In the autumn, cut the plant back by half and bring indoors before the first frost. Place in bright light and keep the soil barely moist. Increase watering in the spring and mist the stems with water.

Lovage

DESCRIPTION

Lovage looks a lot like a large parsley plant, but its strong, lively flavor is reminiscent of celery. It offers the intense flavor of celery stalks but without the bulk. Since you are unlikely to find lovage in a supermarket or green grocer, it is an important addition to an herb garden. This tough perennial is easy to grow. (In hot climates it is treated as an annual.)

TRADITIONAL USES

Lovage is one of the flavorings in the popular European seasoning called *maggi*. The leaves give a special nip to a green salad and are used to season soups and stews. The stems can be cooked and eaten as a celery-like vegetable, while the seeds are used in pickling brine.

PREPARATION AND COOKING TIPS

Use the leaves as you would parsley. However, lovage has assertive tendencies, so proceed with caution. Because of its intense flavor, lovage is a useful seasoning in salt-reduced recipes. Lovage is a good complement to tomatoes; use it to flavor a robust tomato sauce or to perk up a Bloody Mary (see *Bloody Mary Mix*, page 142). Here are some additional ideas for lovage: Toss a handful of torn leaves into a green salad; use chopped lovage to season a poultry stuffing; use leaves to garnish a potato salad; add a sprig to a *bouquet garni* used to flavor a stock or broth.

STORAGE

Enclose lovage sprigs in a plastic food-storage bag and refrigerate up to 4 days. If you wish to freeze lovage for use over the winter months, it is best to blanch it first (page 10).

COMPLEMENTS

Lovage enhances tomatoes, potatoes, greens, lettuce, cream soups and poultry.

GROWING LOVAGE
Levisticum officinale

Plant type—Perennial.

Size—6 feet tall, 2 to 3 feet wide.

Light—Full sun to light shade.

Soil—Humus-rich, moist, well-drained.

Propagation—Sow fresh seed outdoors in late summer or early autumn. Space plants 2 feet apart in the garden, although one plant is all you usually need. Divide in spring or early summer. Lovage grows big and makes a bold statement in the garden, so plant it near the center of beds or the backs of borders.

Care—Clip off the flower stems; they appear to encourage bushy growth.

Herb Glossary

Marjoram

DESCRIPTION

Marjoram is often called *sweet marjoram* and *knotted marjoram*. The plant has small oval, fuzzy leaves and tiny flowers that have a knotty appearance. It is closely related to oregano and is sometimes used interchangeably. But its flavor is distinct: Marjoram tastes sweet and spicy with a pungent balsam-like accent. It has long been cultivated in the region around the Mediterranean. Marjoram is a perennial in warmer climates, but in colder regions it is treated as an annual.

VARIETIES

Pot marjoram, which is used in the Eastern Mediterranean region, is not as sweet as the more common sweet marjoram. "Wild" marjoram is actually another name for oregano.

TRADITIONAL USES

Marjoram is often associated with Italian and Greek cooking. However, according to food historian Waverley Root, Greeks and Italians often prefer oregano, while cooks in the more northern regions of France, England and Germany favor marjoram. Both typically use it to season tomato sauces and sausages.

PREPARATION AND COOKING TIPS

Rinse sprigs and pat dry. Strip leaves from stems and chop. It is best to add marjoram toward the end of cooking, but if cooking time is short, it can be added at the beginning. Dried marjoram is available in supermarkets and is a reasonable alternative to fresh; add it at the beginning of cooking. Marjoram tends to take over and works best with more assertive flavors. Marjoram contributes an almost meaty taste to a simple tomato sauce and lends an interesting herbal note to sausage patties and meat loaf. For a flavorful grilling combination, try marinating portobello mushroom slices in lemon juice, olive oil, garlic and marjoram.

STORAGE

Enclose in a plastic food-storage bag and refrigerate up to 4 days. Marjoram is suitable for home drying (page 11).

COMPLEMENTS

Marjoram pairs well with tomatoes, meat, mushrooms and corn.

GROWING MARJORAM
Origanum majorana

Plant type—Perennial.

Size—1 foot tall, 6 inches wide.

Light—Full sun.

Soil—Well-drained.

Propagation—Start seeds indoors 8 weeks before the last spring frost. Transplant outdoors after all danger of frost is past. Space 6 to 8 inches apart. Divide in spring or autumn. Take cuttings in summer. Sweet marjoram is a good companion to some of the other Mediterranean herbs such as winter savory, sage, thyme and oregano. Grow sweet marjoram in a container filled with fast-draining potting mix and a monthly feeding with a balanced fertilizer according to the manufacturer's directions. Bring plants indoors in the autumn.

Care—Pinch off the growing tips to encourage branching.

Mint

DESCRIPTION

Appreciated for its sweet, refreshing taste, mint is one of the most flexible and valuable herbs in cooking. It is distinguished by its square stems and fragrant leaves. The characteristic aroma and flavor come from menthol. You don't have to be an experienced gardener to have an abundant crop of mint. This very hardy perennial has a reputation for spreading and taking over gardens. Fresh mint is available in supermarkets.

VARIETIES

The two most important kinds of mint are spearmint and peppermint. Spearmint, which is suitable for sweet and savory dishes, is most practical for cooking. Peppermint contains more menthol and is used primarily as a flavoring for candies, teas and sweet dishes. Apple mint has a milder, more delicate flavor than spearmint. Orange mint has a seductive citrus fragrance. Pineapple mint has a fruity, tropical aroma. Chocolate mint is a no-cal way to get an olfactory chocolate fix. These flavored mints often have more fragrance than real flavor, so they are more valuable as garnishes than flavorings.

TRADITIONAL USES

Mint is an important seasoning in Greek, Turkish, North African, Middle Eastern and Southeast Asian cuisines. To many North American and British diners, mint jelly is indispensable with roast lamb. Mint gives a lift to the popular Middle Eastern grain salad, *tabbouleh*, and provides a fresh finish to Vietnamese spring rolls. Mint is frequently paired with tea and is the key flavoring in the mint julep cocktail. It is one of the few herbs that is widely used in desserts.

PREPARATION AND COOKING TIPS

Wash and dry mint sprigs. Strip leaves from stems and cut into slivers or chop finely. Use mint as a garnish or add to a dish at the end of cooking. For a change of pace, try mint instead of basil in a summer tomato sauce. Pair it with ginger and chiles to make a bracing chutney (see *Mint & Ginger Chutney* page 161) to accompany salmon or lamb chops. Fresh mint is preferred to dry.

STORAGE

You can place stems in a container of water, cover tops with a plastic wrap and store in the refrigerator for up to 4 days. Alternatively, wrap sprigs in a paper towel and enclose in a plastic food-storage bag before refrigerating. At the end of the growing season, you can freeze mint (page 10) or dry in a dehydrator (page 11).

COMPLEMENTS

Try mint with lamb, peas, cucumbers, tomatoes, yogurt, chocolate and summer fruits such as melon and strawberries, as well as with citrus fruits and tea.

GROWING MINT

Mentha species and cultivars

Plant type—Perennial.

Size—Most culinary types grow to 2 feet tall, but there are some low-growing ornamentals.

Light—Light shade, but full sun is tolerated.

Soil—Humus-rich, moist, well-drained.

Propagation—Few mints come true from seed. It's better to buy plants. Space plants 18 to 24 inches apart. Divide or take cuttings in spring or autumn.

Care—To contain a plant, cut the bottom out of a 5-gallon bucket and bury it to within an inch of the rim; plant the mint inside. Spray aphids, spider mites or flea beetles with horticultural soap. Try to choose an area that gets some shade. Only if you have a wild corner of the yard or an area that can easily be mowed around should you plant without any boundaries. One of the best ways to confine mint is to grow it in containers filled with a fast-draining potting mix and feed monthly.

Herb Glossary

Oregano

DESCRIPTION

Pungent, peppery oregano is typically associated with robust pizza and pasta sauces. Oregano is similar to marjoram, but the flavor is milder. A member of the mint family, this perennial has small, dark green leaves. Defining oregano is tricky because the term covers a group of plants whose distinguishing characteristic is the flavor imparted by the essential oil carvacrol. The strength of oregano flavor may vary considerably. When purchasing oregano, either as a garden plant or a packet of cut herbs, always check that it has a distinctive pungent aroma.

VARIETIES

Greek oregano (*origanum vulgare* subspecies *hirtum*) is preferred by cooks in the know because of its strong flavor. Be wary of wild "common" oregano (*o. vulgare* subspecies *vulgare*) because it lacks the distinctive oregano pungency. Although unrelated to true oregano, Mexican oregano (actually a member of the verbena family) has a strong oregano-like flavor.

TRADITIONAL USES

Oregano is a key flavoring in hearty Italian tomato sauces, tangy Greek souvlaki marinades and spicy Mexican stews.

PREPARATION AND COOKING TIPS

Rinse sprigs and pat dry. Strip leaves from stems and chop. Oregano stands up well to heat, so add it at the beginning of cooking. Dried oregano has excellent flavor; feel free to substitute at a ratio of 1 part dried for 3 parts fresh. In addition to simmered tomato sauces and chilies, use oregano in marinades for lamb, fish or vegetables. Oregano works best with strong flavors like lemon juice, garlic and olives. Try marinating black olives in a mixture of oregano, lemon juice and olive oil. Serve Greek salad the way they often do in Greece: Instead of crumbling feta cheese into the salad, top salad with a slab of feta that has been generously sprinkled with fresh or dried oregano.

STORAGE

Enclose fresh oregano sprigs in a plastic food-storage bag and refrigerate up to 4 days. To preserve the harvest, hang to dry or use a dehydrator.

COMPLEMENTS

Use oregano with tomatoes, garlic, chiles, cumin, lemon, olives, feta cheese, lamb, fish and seafood, and summer vegetables such as eggplant and zucchini.

GROWING OREGANO

Origanum species and cultivars

Plant type—Perennial.

Size—18 inches to 2 feet tall, 18 inches wide.

Light—Full sun, except for golden forms, which do best in light shade.

Soil—Well-drained.

Propagation—Because the flavor varies greatly from seed-started plants, it's better to purchase plants that are propagated by cuttings or division from plants known to have good flavor. Take cuttings in summer or divide in spring or autumn. Space plants 18 inches apart.

Care—Spray spider mites with horticultural soap. Protect plants with a winter mulch. The true oreganos (*Origanum*) generally form rounded, bushy, spreading plants that make good groundcover or filler plants in the garden. You can also grow oreganos in containers filled with fast-draining potting mix. Feed monthly with a good fertilizer.

Parsley

DESCRIPTION

Parsley may be dismissed as an unimaginative garnish, but this ubiquitous herb enhances the flavor and appearance of an unparalleled variety of foods. Parsley has a gentle flavor, which is often characterized as fresh tasting. It usually plays a supporting role in dishes, bringing out the best in the main ingredients without dominating. Parsley is highly compatible with other herbs and works well in herb blends. Native to the eastern Mediterranean, parsley is a biennial but is generally treated as an annual.

VARIETIES

The three main types are curly leaf, flat-leaf (Italian) and parsnip-rooted (also called turnip-rooted or Hamburg parsley). Most cooks favor flat-leaf parsley for its somewhat stronger flavor. Parsnip-rooted parsley is grown for its roots rather than leaves. The roots are cooked like any root vegetable (they make a good addition to mashed potatoes) and have a flavor similar to celeriac.

TRADITIONAL USES

Parsley is essential in the *bouquet garni* (page 13) used to flavor French stocks and braised dishes, and in delicate *fines herbes* (page 13). Italians take advantage of its fresh flavor in the gremolada (page 15). Parsley is also a good alternative to basil in pesto (see *Parsley-Walnut Pesto*, page 162). It is a key ingredient in the Middle Eastern salad (and now popular American deli item) *tabbouleh*.

PREPARATION AND COOKING TIPS

Leafy parsley can harbor grit. Strip leaves from stems, then wash carefully as you would salad greens (page 8). Dry thoroughly using a salad spinner or with paper towels before chopping with a chef's knife or in a food processor. When you are making a stew or stock, use parsley stems in the *bouquet garni* or aromatics; reserve leaves to finish the dish or for garnish. With the exception of *bouquet garni*, add parsley at the end of cooking or as garnish.

STORAGE

Store parsley in the refrigerator like a bouquet of flowers (page 8). Alternatively, wrap sprigs in paper towels, enclose in a plastic food-storage bag and refrigerate up to 4 days. For long-term storage, you can freeze parsley (page 10). Put extra parsley to good use by making up a batch of parsley-flavored compound butter (page 163) to keep in the freezer.

COMPLEMENTS

Parsley offers an interesting, refreshing contrast to biting garlic. Otherwise, it is good in almost any savory dish.

GROWING PARSLEY

Petroselinum crispum

Plant type—Biennial, often grown as an annual.

Size—8 to 18 inches tall.

Light—Full sun to light shade.

Soil—Humus-rich, moist, well-drained.

Propagation—To speed up seed germination process, soak overnight in warm water, then rinse thoroughly before planting. Sow indoors 8 weeks before the last spring frost. Transplant outdoors one week before the last frost. Space plants 8 to 12 inches apart.

Care—To prolong the life of parsley for at least a couple of weeks, cut out the flower stalks as they appear. Parsley grows well in containers with a fast-draining potting mix. Feed monthly during the growing season with balanced fertilizer. Start seeds or buy young plants in the fall to pot up for growing indoors with bright light in winter.

Herb Glossary

ROSEMARY

DESCRIPTION

Highly aromatic rosemary is not a shy herb. The narrow leaves, which resemble needles, have the woodsy aroma of pine with a hint of lemon. This perennial evergreen shrub comes from the coastal regions of the Mediterranean.

VARIETIES

Gardeners can choose from a number of varieties. These are distinguished by their shape (upright or trailing), color of flowers and hardiness.

TRADITIONAL USES

Rosemary is highly appreciated in Italian cooking. It figures prominently in roasts and grills, and is also used to flavor hearty meat sauces and soups.

PREPARATION AND COOKING TIPS

Rinse and dry sprigs. Strip needles from stems and chop finely. Add chopped rosemary at the beginning of cooking or use it in marinades. Smear lamb, pork and chicken roast with a rosemary-garlic paste. Toss potatoes and root vegetables with olive oil and a little chopped rosemary before roasting. You can also infuse whole sprigs in broths and sauces. Secure sprigs in a cheesecloth bag or tea infuser (the needles tend to fall off during cooking) and then remove the cheesecloth bag before serving. When you are grilling, drop a few rosemary sprigs directly onto the fire to create aromatic smoke. Rosemary is great in yeast breads and quick breads. Try it in unexpected ways, such as lemon-flavored desserts or in a compote of orange sections.

STORAGE

Enclose sprigs in a plastic food-storage bag and refrigerate up to 4 days. Although fresh rosemary is preferred to dried, you can preserve rosemary by drying, either by hanging or in a dehydrator (page 11).

COMPLEMENTS

Rosemary enhances garlic, lemon, mustard, potatoes, beans, lamb, pork and chicken.

GROWING ROSEMARY

Rosmarinus officinalis

Plant type—Evergreen, woody perennial.

Size—2 to 6 feet tall, 1 to 4 feet wide.

Light—Full sun.

Soil—Well-drained.

Propagation—Seed is difficult to germinate. It is better to take cuttings. Space plants 1 to 3 feet apart, planting outdoors when night temperatures are consistently 55°F or warmer.

Care—Pinch out the growing tips on rosemary to encourage bushy growth. Control aphids, mealybugs, spider mites or whiteflies with horticultural soap. Rosemary readily grows in containers filled with fast-draining potting mix and a monthly feeding with a balanced fertilizer. In colder climates, bring the pots indoors in winter.

Sage

DESCRIPTION

The flavor of sage is unmistakable. It is pungent and slightly bitter with a somewhat musty aroma. This hearty perennial has large, velvety grayish-green leaves.

VARIETIES

In addition to common garden sage, there are a large number of cultivars. Some notable varieties include decorative sages (such as golden and tricolor) and fruity pineapple sage. Pineapple sage makes an interesting garnish for fruit desserts and drinks. It should not, however, be substituted for common sage in savory dishes.

TRADITIONAL USES

Most North Americans recognize sage as the distinctive herbal seasoning in turkey stuffing, but it is also used in a variety of interesting ways. It is traditionally paired with rich meats because it is believed to make them more digestible. Italian cooks use pungent sage to the best advantage. In the Roman dish *saltimbocca*, whole sage leaves are tucked inside veal and prosciutto rolls. Another Italian specialty is sage fritters. These are made by dipping sage leaves into batter and deep-frying. You can cook chopped sage in butter and use it to flavor pasta sauces.

PREPARATION AND COOKING TIPS

Rinse sprigs and pat dry. Strip leaves from stems; leave whole or chop finely, depending on use. Sage is powerful, so pair with hearty foods and use with discretion. It is best suited to cooked dishes; add at the beginning of cooking. When roasting turkey or chicken, slip several sage leaves under the skin. Press a sage leaf onto a lightly oiled chicken breast, pork or veal chop before grilling. Thread leaves between pieces of meat or poultry when making kabobs. Sage makes a very attractive garnish. Arrange bouquets of fresh sage around a roast turkey. Try decorating bread loaves with sage leaves (see *Herbed Potato Bread*, page 68). Dried whole or rubbed sage is an acceptable substitute for fresh. The flavor becomes intense when dried, so substitute at a ratio of 4 parts fresh to 1 part dried. Avoid ground, dried sage because it is too strong.

STORAGE

Enclose sage sprigs in a plastic food-storage bag and refrigerate up to 4 days. Sage retains its flavor well when dried. However, since the leaves are thick, sage dries slowly. It is best to use a dehydrator (page 11).

COMPLEMENTS

Sage works especially well with onions, pork, veal, poultry, game and winter squash.

GROWING SAGE
Salvia officinalis

Plant type—Woody, evergreen perennial.

Size—2 to 3 feet tall, 2 to 3 feet wide.

Light—Full sun.

Soil—Humus-rich, well-drained.

Propagation—Sow seed indoors eight weeks before the last spring frost. Germination is erratic, but may be helped by freezing the seeds for three days prior to planting. Transplant outdoors one week before the last spring frost. Space 18 inches to 2 feet apart. Take cuttings or divide in early summer after flowering.

Care—Prune plants back after flowering to encourage fresh new growth. Control spider mites with horticultural soap and slugs with traps or barriers. The sages readily adapt to containers filled with a fast-draining potting mix and a monthly feeding with a balanced fertilizer. Overwinter outdoors in a protected location and surrounded by mulch.

Herb Glossary

Savory

DESCRIPTION

With a flavor reminiscent of peppery thyme, savory is a highly useful and versatile herb. It has been valued as a seasoning since ancient times, and it deserves more prominence in contemporary North American cooking. Savory is a member of the mint family and is native to the Mediterranean.

VARIETIES

The important distinction is between summer savory, an annual, and winter savory, a shrubby perennial. Summer savory is generally preferred for cooking because the flavor is more delicate. Winter savory has a stronger, more pine-like flavor. It has a bushy appearance, and its leaves are more needlelike and dense than summer savory.

TRADITIONAL USES

The German name for savory is *bohnenkraut*, which translates as "bean herb." It enhances bean and legume dishes and is believed to have carminative (antiflatulent) properties. In northern Europe, savory is used in sausages. The French seasoning mixture, *herbes de Provence* (page 14), generally includes savory.

PREPARATION AND COOKING TIPS

Both winter and summer savory have a strong peppery flavor; use in small quantities. Rinse sprigs and pat dry. Chop and add to salads or sprinkle over cooked vegetable dishes. When simmering beans or lentils, tie several sprigs together with kitchen twine and add cooking liquid; retrieve the bundle before serving. If you are cutting back on salt, try compensating by adding a pinch of savory to soups, salads, vegetables and meat dishes. Dried savory can be used in long-simmered dishes.

STORAGE

Enclose sprigs in a plastic food-storage bag and refrigerate up to 4 days. Savory is suitable for drying.

COMPLEMENTS

Savory enhances green beans, dried beans, lentils, split peas, meat, poultry and strongly flavored vegetables such as Brussels sprouts and cabbage.

GROWING SAVORY

Satureja species

Plant type—Summer savory is an annual. Winter savory is a woody, semi-evergreen perennial.

Size—Winter savory grows to 1 foot tall and as wide. Summer savory grows to 18 inches tall and 1 foot wide.

Light—Full sun.

Soil—Well-drained soil. Summer savory needs soil that is more moist.

Propagation—Start seeds of summer savory six weeks before the last frost and transplant outdoors after all danger of frost is past. Or sow directly into the garden about a week before the last frost. Space 6 inches apart. Savory seeds germinate more quickly if soaked overnight in hot water before planting.

Care—Summer savory needs good air circulation around it to prevent fungal diseases. To limit its sprawling tendencies, mound soil around the base of the stems. Both summer and winter savory adapt well to containers filled with fast-draining potting soil and a monthly feeding. Both kinds may be brought indoors during the winter.

Shiso

DESCRIPTION

Sushi fans may be familiar with the aromatic herb, shiso, which is used primarily in Japanese cooking. The English name is perilla. Shiso, an annual, belongs to the same family as mint and basil. It is native to Asia, but is also cultivated in Europe and North America. Graceful in appearance, shiso leaves are large (2 to 3 inches wide) and have attractive jagged edges. The flavor of shiso is fresh and delicate with a hint of cumin. You can find fresh shiso leaves in Japanese markets. Since shiso can be difficult to find, it may be worth growing your own.

Green Shiso

VARIETIES

Green shiso is the most common, but you can also find red (or purple) shiso. The red variety is sometimes called beefsteak plant. It provides color for the Japanese pickled plums known as *umeboshi*.

TRADITIONAL USES

Chopped shiso is used in sushi, salads, rice and noodle dishes. Leaves are dipped in batter and deep-fried as tempura.

PREPARATION AND COOKING TIPS

Rinse leaves and pat dry. Stack, then cut into thin slivers or chop. Stir chopped shiso into rice or sprinkle slivered shiso over salads with Japanese flavors. Use the pretty whole leaves as a garnish or as an attractive bed for a salad.

STORAGE

Enclose shiso in a plastic food-storage bag and refrigerate up to 4 days.

COMPLEMENTS

Use shiso in dishes with fish and seafood, soba noodles and rice.

GROWING SHISO
Perilla frutescens

Plant type—Annual.

Size—3 feet tall, 1 foot wide.

Light—Full sun.

Soil—Moist but well-drained soil. Extra organic matter in the soil is beneficial.

Propagation—Propagate by seed. Direct seed in good soil in midspring. Shiso germinates in about 11 days and grows rapidly. It has many medicinal uses such as treating fever, headache, nasal congestion and cough. It has antiseptic properties and also helps alleviate seafood poisoning. Shiso is extensively cultivated in Asia.

Care—Shiso self-seeds in most gardens, and some gardeners consider it a bit pesky.

Red Shiso

Herb Glossary

Sorrel

DESCRIPTION

Sorrel is considered both an herb and a vegetable. It is distinguished by its tangy, sour flavor, a characteristic highly appreciated by the French. The tartness is due to the presence of oxalic acid (also found in spinach and rhubarb). Sorrel is a hardy perennial with green leaves that resemble small spinach leaves. It is also known as dock and sour grass. You can sometimes find sorrel in specialty produce markets. But if you are a fan of this puckery plant, you will probably want to ensure a supply by growing it in your garden.

VARIETIES

Garden sorrel and true French sorrel are the varieties most commonly used in cooking. The two types are differentiated by the shape of their leaves. Garden sorrel has long and narrow leaves; true French sorrel has smaller, rounded leaves. True French sorrel is slightly less acidic and favored by some cooks.

TRADITIONAL USES

The best-known sorrel preparation is the French *potage Germiny*, a rich soup made from sorrel, broth, cream and egg yolks. Also in French cooking, a sauce of pureed sorrel, fish stock and butter is a classic pairing with fish.

PREPARATION AND COOKING TIPS

Trim stems and wash sorrel leaves as you would spinach. You can use a few torn *young* leaves to enliven a green salad. To make a chiffonade of sorrel, stack leaves and roll up. Use a chef's knife to cut the roll crosswise into thin strips. Sorrel cooks quickly, so add it toward the end of cooking. Sorrel also melts down into a puree easily. Just cook shredded sorrel in a little butter until it forms a puree. Finish the puree with cream or butter and use a sauce for fish. You can give sautéed spinach or Swiss chard an interesting tang with the addition of some shredded sorrel. Try sorrel in an omelet filling; sprinkle shredded sorrel over the egg mixture before folding the omelet.

STORAGE

Wrap in paper towel and enclose in a plastic food-storage bag. Store in the refrigerator up to 4 days. For long-term storage, make sorrel puree and freeze up to 6 months.

COMPLEMENTS

Fish, eggs, potatoes and tender greens, such as spinach and Swiss chard, are enhanced by sorrel.

GROWING SORREL
Rumex species

Plant type—Perennial.

Size—*R. acetosa* grows 6 inches tall, forming a ground-hugging mat, then reaches 18 inches when in bloom. Spreads rapidly.

Light—Full sun to light shade.

Soil—Humus-rich, moist, well-drained.

Propagation—Sow seed in spring directly into the garden several weeks before the last spring frost. Germination takes about a week. Space plants 1 foot apart. Divide in autumn at least every three years to help maintain vigorous plantings.

Care—Protect sorrel from slugs with traps or barriers. Choose a site carefully so that sorrel's invasive tendencies are not a problem. Growing sorrel in containers is a good way to limit its spreading ways. Use a fast-draining potting mix and a monthly feeding during the growing season with a balanced fertilizer. Overwinter in a protected place with mulch around the pot.

Tarragon

DESCRIPTION

One of the most prized culinary herbs, tarragon plays a prominent role in some of the best-known classical French dishes. The delicate, bittersweet flavor has a suggestion of anise. This hardy perennial has slender, dark green leaves. It is believed that tarragon originated in Siberia and southern Russia, but it is now widely cultivated in Europe and North America.

VARIETIES

Of the two types of tarragon, French and Russian, French is the kind you want for cooking. It has the best flavor but cannot be reliably grown from seed. Russian tarragon, which is easier to grow, has little flavor. When purchasing a plant, check the label to be sure it is indeed French tarragon and make sure it has a distinctive tarragon aroma. Sweet marigold (also known as Mexican tarragon) has a flavor similar to tarragon but is actually a member of the marigold family. It is a good option for gardeners who live in hot climates where French tarragon does not thrive.

TRADITIONAL USES

Tarragon is one of the herbs used in the French herb mixture *fines herbes* (page 13). It is an essential seasoning in béarnaise sauce and is featured in the classic French dish, chicken with tarragon. In addition, it is commonly used to infuse a subtle flavor in vinegar.

PREPARATION AND COOKING TIPS

Rinse sprigs and pat dry. Strip leaves from stems and chop. The flavor of tarragon does not withstand heat, so add chopped tarragon at the end of cooking, or use in uncooked dishes. The charm of tarragon lies in its delicacy; use sparingly. Dried tarragon is not as flavorful as fresh but is a reasonable substitute in a pinch. Some ideas for using tarragon in your cooking: Sprinkle it over soft-boiled eggs or stir it into scrambled eggs. Flavor dressings for chicken salad or egg salad with tarragon. Add torn tarragon leaves to green salads.

STORAGE

Enclose tarragon sprigs in a plastic food-storage bag and refrigerate up to 2 days. To preserve the summery taste of tarragon for winter, make tarragon vinegar (page 12). Alternatively, make a batch of tarragon butter (see NOTES, page 163) for the freezer.

COMPLEMENTS

Tarragon pairs well with mustard, lemon, eggs, chicken and mild white fish such as sole or halibut.

GROWING TARRAGON
Artemisia dracunculus

Plant type—Perennial.

Size—2 feet tall, 2 feet wide.

Light—Full sun to light shade.

Soil—Humus-rich, well-drained.

Propagation—French tarragon cannot be started from seed. Divide in early spring. Take cuttings in midsummer. Space plants 2 feet apart.

Care—Pinch out the growing tips several times during the growing season. French tarragon needs well-drained soil. To maintain vigor, divide plants every 2 or 3 years. Provide a winter mulch or grow tarragon as an annual. French tarragon grows well in a container filled with a fast-draining potting mix and a monthly feeding with a balanced fertilizer. If brought indoors during the winter, it needs very bright light. To overwinter outdoors, put in a protected spot and surround the plant and pot with mulch.

Herb Glossary

Thyme

DESCRIPTION

Thyme seems to work its magic behind the scenes. It doesn't make a splash like some of the livelier herbs, such as cilantro and dill. Yet it is one of the most useful and versatile herbs in the kitchen. Thyme has a warm, rich aroma with subtle pine undertones. It is a low-growing perennial shrub native to the western Mediterranean, and is a member of the mint family.

VARIETIES

There are numerous species of thyme. The type most widely used in cooking is common thyme. Within this group there is a popular variety called English thyme and also a variety called French thyme. Both varieties of common thyme are suitable for most recipes calling for thyme. In addition to the common variety, there are a number of flavored thymes that are of special interest to the cook. Lemon thyme has a delightful aroma, which complements light fish dishes, vegetables and fruits. Caraway thyme has a spicy fragrance that pairs well with red meats.

TRADITIONAL USES

Thyme is a component of *bouquet garni* (page 13), an essential flavoring in a large variety of French braised dishes, casseroles, soups, sauces and stocks. It is also typical in *herbes de Provence* (page 14). The Middle Eastern herb-spice blend called zatar (page 15) features thyme.

PREPARATION AND COOKING TIPS

Rinse sprigs and pat dry. Tie sprigs into a *bouquet garni* and add to long-simmered dishes; retrieve bouquet before serving. For chopped thyme, strip leaves from stems and chop. Thyme retains flavor well and is generally added at the beginning of cooking. Dried thyme is a reasonable alternative to fresh. Use 3 parts fresh thyme to 1 part dried thyme. Add several sprigs of fresh thyme or a generous pinch of dried whenever you are making a hearty soup, meat stew or bean dish. Toss root vegetables with chopped fresh or dried thyme before roasting. For a simple appetizer, marinate olives in thyme and lemon juice.

STORAGE

Enclose fresh thyme sprigs in a plastic food-storage bag and refrigerate up to 1 week. To preserve thyme, either hang to dry or use a dehydrator (page 11).

COMPLEMENTS

Red meat, pork, chicken, turkey, winter vegetables (such as squash, parsnips and celeriac), lentils, beans, apples and pears work well with thyme.

GROWING THYME

Thymus species

Plant type—Evergreen to semi-evergreen woody perennial. Hardiness varies, depending on the species and cultivar.

Size—Common thyme and lemon thyme grow to 12 inches tall. Broad-leaved thyme grows to 8 inches tall. Creeping thyme, caraway thyme and mother-of-thyme grow 2 to 3 inches tall.

Light—Full sun to light shade.

Soil—Well-drained.

Propagation—Start seed indoors 6 to 8 weeks before the last frost in spring. Germination is best at 70°F and takes about a week. Space plants 1 foot apart. Divide or take cuttings in spring. Thymes fill a container and cascade over the edges beautifully. Use a fast-draining potting mix and feed monthly with a balanced fertilizer.

Care—Trim plants in early spring to remove any dead growth and to encourage new branches. Trim again after flowering.

ABOUT GARLIC

Although it's not a true herb, one cannot underestimate the importance of garlic in cooking. Here are some ins and outs of using garlic. Distinguished by its notorious pungency, garlic is one of the key seasonings in Mediterranean and Asian cuisines. It is the most strongly flavored member of the onion (*allium*) family. Its potency varies depending on age and variety. The flavor is most delicate at the beginning of the season in late spring and early summer. The color of garlic ranges from white to burgundy. The giant elephant garlic has a much milder flavor than standard-sized bulbs. To help you get the most out of garlic, here are some tips for using it:

To Peel and Crush Garlic: Separate a clove from the bulb and place it on a cutting board. Set the flat side of a chef's knife over the garlic and pound knife gently with your fist. The skin should separate from the flesh; discard skin. If you are peeling a lot of garlic, before peeling, soak cloves in water for 15 to 30 minutes to loosen skin and reduce stickiness.

To Mince Garlic: Hold the side of chef's knife over a garlic clove, pound knife again to crush the clove further. If using garlic raw, remove the dark green germ if there is any. (The germ can be bitter.) Holding the knife at an angle, use an up-and-down motion to mince garlic finely. Minced garlic can be used in cooked dishes, marinades, and sparingly in salads.

To Mash Garlic with Salt: Place crushed, peeled garlic in a mortar and pestle, and sprinkle with salt. Mash into a paste with the pestle. (If you do not have a mortar and pestle, leave garlic on cutting board, sprinkle with salt and use side of chef's knife to mash.) Mashed garlic is preferred in salads and sauces that will not be cooked because it has a mellower flavor than coarsely chopped garlic or garlic that has been crushed in a garlic press.

To Roast Garlic: Peel away the papery outer layer and slice the tip off a garlic bulb to expose cloves. Place on a square of aluminum foil, sprinkle with 1 tablespoon olive oil or water. Pinch edges of foil together to seal packet. Bake at 400°F for about 45 minutes or until garlic flesh is soft. Let cool slightly and then squeeze the soft garlic into a bowl. Use roasted garlic to enrich mashed potatoes and salad dressings or to spread over country bread.

For a Delicate Touch with Garlic: Just rub the cut side of a garlic clove over a salad bowl or baking dish.

When Cooking Minced Garlic: Take care not to let it burn because it will become bitter.

GROWING GARLIC
Allium Sativum

Plant type—Perennial bulb.

Size—2 feet tall, 8 inches wide.

Light—Full sun.

Soil—Humus-rich, moist, well-drained.

Propagation—Although you can start garlic from seed, it is much easier to plant individual cloves. Plant the cloves 2 inches deep and 4 inches apart, 4 to 6 weeks before the first frost in autumn. Use only the larger cloves. The smaller ones can be eaten or planted in a separate area, spacing 2 inches apart for spring baby garlic (which is eaten like scallions). Plant in rows or plant groups of six or eight bulbs. Garlic is a good companion plant for roses, cabbage, eggplant, tomatoes and fruit trees.

Care—Apply several inches of mulch in late autumn. Remove the flower stalks in spring or early summer so that all the plant's energy goes into the developing bulb.

Herb Glossary

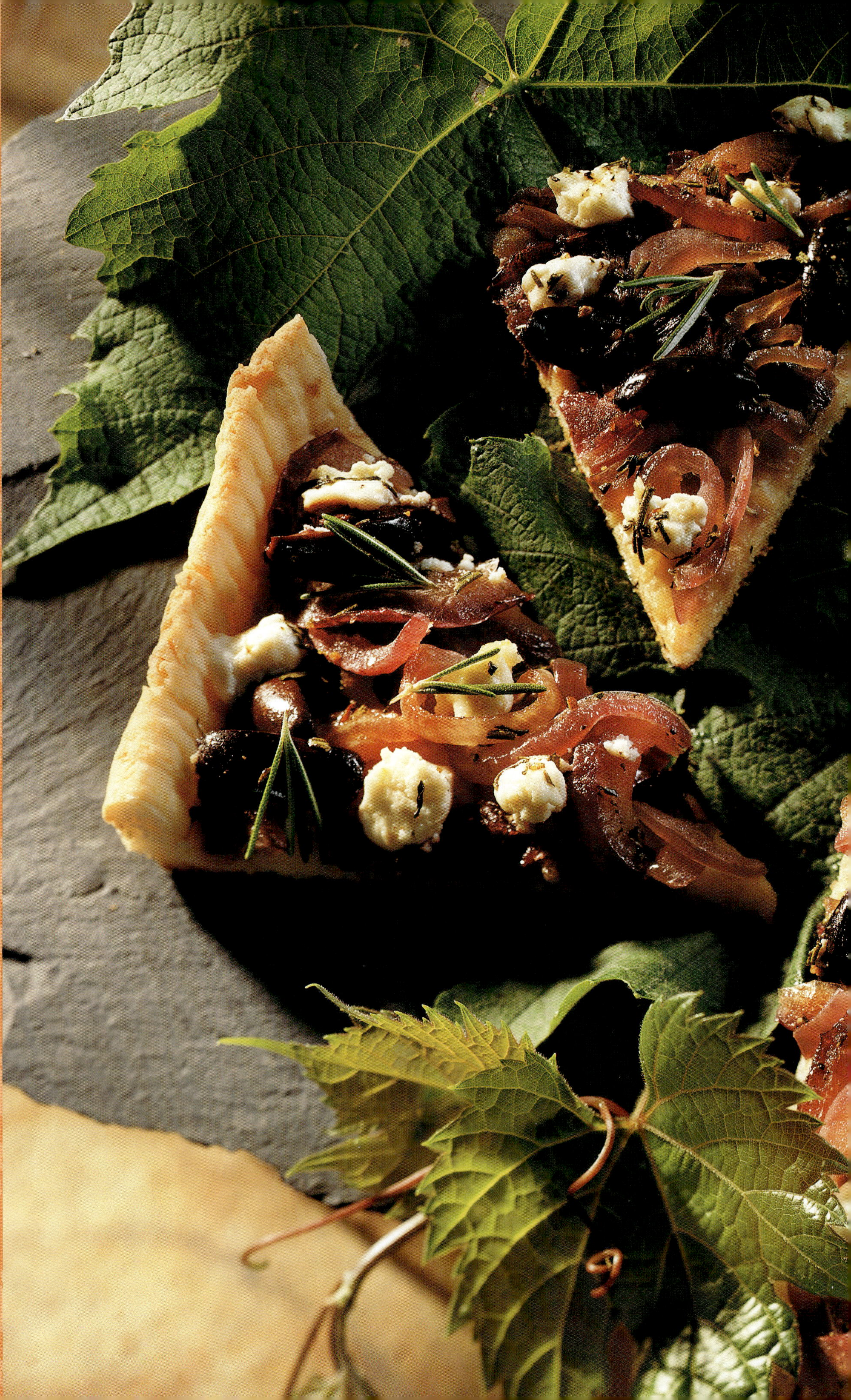

Recipe Potpourri

What better way to start a meal than with an herb-flecked appetizer or a fragrant herb bread? A veritable potpourri of little meals, this chapter features an eclectic selection of breakfast and brunch dishes, snacks, appetizers, breads and pizzas.

Carmelized Red Onion, Olive
and Goat Cheese Galette, page 64

Baked Eggs with Tarragon

Celebrate the return of tarragon in your garden by making this simple French egg dish for a spring breakfast. To make the cream topping, I like to thin low-fat sour cream with milk because the mixture has a light tang that is reminiscent of crème fraiche (and I appreciate the lower fat content), but if you have whipping cream on hand, substitute 4 tablespoons for the sour cream and milk.

- 4 eggs
- Dash of salt
- Dash of freshly ground pepper
- 4 teaspoons chopped fresh tarragon
- 2 tablespoons reduced-fat sour cream
- 2 tablespoons reduced-fat milk

❶ Heat oven to 325°F. Heat tea kettle of water to a boil. Spray 4 (6-oz. or 1/3-cup) custard cups or ramekins with cooking spray.

❷ Carefully crack 1 egg into each custard cup; season lightly with salt and pepper. Sprinkle each egg with 1 teaspoon tarragon.

❸ Place sour cream in small bowl; gradually add milk, whisking until smooth. Top each egg with 1 tablespoon sour cream mixture.

❹ Place custard cups in small baking dish with sides. Add enough boiling water to come one-fourth of the way up sides of custard cups. Place baking dish in oven; cover loosely with sheet of parchment paper or aluminum foil.

❺ Bake 10 to 14 minutes or just until eggs are set. Serve immediately.

4 servings.

Preparation time: 15 minutes. Ready to serve: 30 minutes.

Per serving: 90 calories, 5.5 g total fat (2 g saturated fat), 215 mg cholesterol, 145 mg sodium, 0 g fiber.

CHEF'S NOTES:
- Use any delicate fresh-flavored herb, such as chervil, chives, basil or dill, alone or in a combination, such as *fines herbes* (page 13).
- Timing baked eggs can be tricky — they turn from nicely set to hard in a flash — so monitor them carefully. To test, touch eggs lightly with your finger; whites should be firm around the edges and yolks should not be runny, but not too firm.

Mexican Potato Omelet

Omelets are always a treat for breakfast or brunch, and an easy solution for a light supper. This potato omelet is seasoned with chiles and cilantro. Smoked mozzarella contributes a wonderful complex flavor, but you can substitute Monterey Jack or just about any cheese you have on hand. Serve with your favorite salsa.

- 4 teaspoons olive oil
- 3/4 cup diced cooked potatoes or frozen hash brown potatoes
- 1/4 teaspoon salt
- 1/8 teaspoon freshly ground pepper
- 1/2 cup chopped onion
- 1 (4.5-oz.) can chopped mild green chiles
- 4 large eggs
- 1/2 cup (2 oz.) grated smoked mozzarella cheese
- 1/3 cup coarsely chopped fresh cilantro

❶ In medium nonstick ovenproof skillet*, heat 2 teaspoons oil over medium-high heat until hot. Add potatoes; cook 3 to 5 minutes or until golden brown, shaking pan and tossing potatoes from time to time. Add salt, pepper, onion and chiles; cook 1 to 2 minutes or until onion is tender, stirring frequently. Transfer to plate; let cool. Rinse and dry skillet.

❷ In medium bowl, stir eggs briskly with fork. Stir in cooled potato mixture, cheese and cilantro.

❸ Set rack about 4 inches from broiler element. Heat broiler.

❹ In same skillet, heat remaining 2 teaspoons oil over medium heat until hot. Pour in egg mixture, tilting pan to distribute evenly. Reduce heat to medium-low; cook 2 to 3 minutes or until bottom is light golden, lifting edges to allow uncooked egg to flow underneath. Place skillet under broiler; broil 1 1/2 to 2 minutes or until top is set. Slide omelet onto platter and cut into wedges.

TIP *If the handle of your skillet is not ovenproof, wrap it in aluminum foil to protect it from the direct heat of the broiler.

4 servings.

Preparation time: 15 minutes. Ready to serve: 25 minutes.

Per serving: 200 calories, 13 g total fat (4.5 g saturated fat), 225 mg cholesterol, 550 mg sodium, 1.5 g fiber.

Smoked Salmon Canapes

These simple, crowd-pleasing appetizers feature the time-honored combination of salmon and dill. Vodka provides an appetite-teasing kick, but if you prefer to avoid alcohol, substitute brewed black tea.

- 2 tablespoons fresh lemon juice
- 2 tablespoons vodka, if desired
- 1 tablespoon extra-virgin olive oil
- 2 teaspoons Dijon mustard
- 1/4 teaspoon freshly ground pepper
- 8 oz. sliced smoked salmon, finely chopped
- 1/4 cup finely diced red onion
- 3 tablespoons chopped fresh dill
- 2 tablespoons drained capers, coarsely chopped
- 24 slices baguette (1/4 inch)
- 24 fresh dill sprigs

1. In medium bowl, combine lemon juice, vodka, oil, mustard and pepper; blend with wire whisk. Add salmon, onion, chopped dill and capers; toss to mix well. *(Topping can be prepared up to 8 hours ahead. Cover and refrigerate.)*

2. Heat oven to 325°F. Spray baking sheet with nonstick cooking spray. Arrange baguette slices in single layer on baking sheet. Spray tops of slices lightly with nonstick cooking spray.

3. Bake baguette slices 15 to 20 minutes or just until crisp and very light golden. *(Toasts can be prepared up to 8 hours ahead. Store in airtight container at room temperature.)*

4. Just before serving, mound about 1 tablespoon topping on each slice of toast. Garnish each with 1 dill sprig.

24 appetizers.

Preparation time: 15 minutes. Ready to serve: 30 minutes.

Per appetizer: 30 calories, 1.5 g total fat (0.5 g saturated fat), 0 mg cholesterol, 120 mg sodium, 0 g fiber.

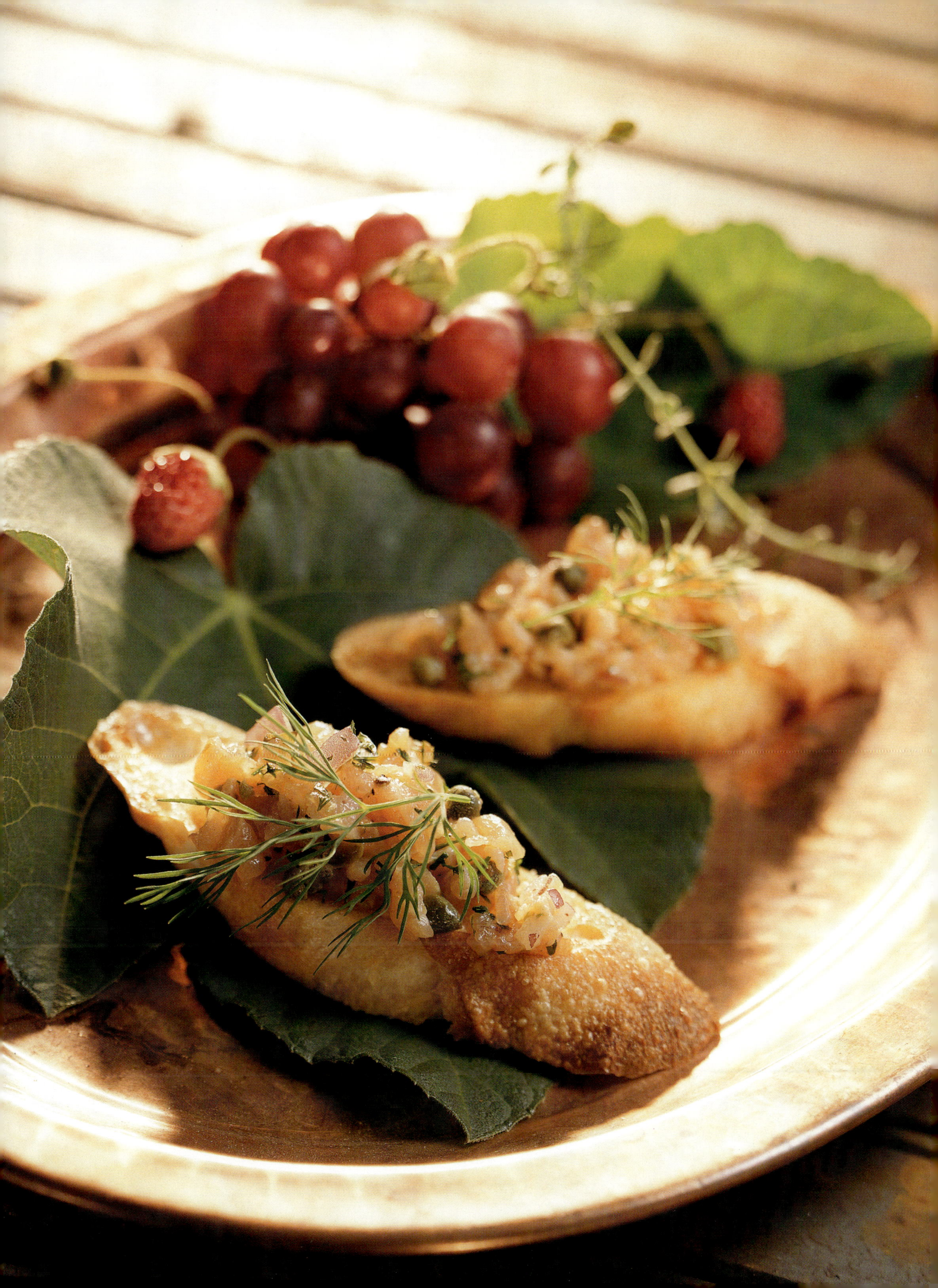

Cherry Tomatoes Filled with Pesto Cream Cheese

This is a perfect appetizer to serve in summer when addictive cherry tomatoes and fresh basil are at their peak. But with the featured ingredients now available year-round in supermarkets, these festive-looking hors d'oeuvres make perfect holiday fare.

- 2 medium garlic cloves, crushed
- 1 teaspoon kosher (coarse) salt
- 3 cups fresh basil leaves
- 1/3 cup pine nuts plus 2 tablespoons, toasted*
- 1/4 teaspoon freshly ground pepper
- 1 tablespoon extra-virgin olive oil
- 1 (8-oz.) pkg. reduced-fat cream cheese, cut into chunks
- 2 pints cherry tomatoes
- 48 fresh basil leaves (2 cups)

❶ Using mortar and pestle or side of chef's knife, mash garlic and salt into paste. In food processor, combine 3 cups basil, 1/3 cup pine nuts, pepper and mashed garlic mixture; process until pine nuts are ground. With motor running, drizzle in olive oil. Add cream cheese; pulse until smooth and creamy. *(Filling can be prepared up to 2 days ahead. Cover and refrigerate.)*

❷ Shortly before serving,** with serrated or sharp paring knife, cut an X on rounded side (opposite stem) of each tomato. Using grapefruit spoon or your fingertips, scoop out seeds, taking care to keep tomatoes intact.

❸ Place filling in pastry bag fitted with star tip or small plastic food bag with 1/2-inch hole cut in corner. Pipe rosette of filling into each tomato cavity. Set each filled tomato on basil leaf; arrange on serving platter. Garnish each with pine nut.

TIP *To toast pine nuts, heat small, heavy skillet over medium-low heat. Add pine nuts and stir constantly 2 to 3 minutes or until light golden and fragrant. Transfer to a small bowl and let cool.

TIP **Wait until shortly before serving to stuff the tomatoes. Cherry tomatoes lose their charm once they have been refrigerated.

About 48 appetizers.

Preparation time: 35 minutes. Ready to serve: 35 minutes.

Per serving: 25 calories, 2 g total fat (0.5 g saturated fat), 0 mg cholesterol, 60 mg sodium, 0.5 g fiber.

CHEF'S NOTE:
- Try cherry tomatoes stuffed with *Herbed Goat Cheese Spread* (page 61).

WHITE BEAN SPREAD WITH ROSEMARY

When unexpected guests arrive, pluck a sprig from your rosemary plant, open a can of beans and whip up this easy appetizer. You can also use the spread as a sandwich filling — it is great with sourdough bread and assorted vegetables.

- 2 medium garlic cloves, crushed
- 1/2 teaspoon kosher (coarse) salt
- 1/8 teaspoon crushed red pepper
- 1 (19-oz.) can cannelini beans, drained, well-rinsed
- 2 tablespoons plus 1 teaspoon extra-virgin olive oil
- 2 tablespoons fresh lemon juice
- 1/8 teaspoon freshly ground pepper
- 1 1/2 teaspoons chopped fresh rosemary
- Dash of cayenne pepper
- 1 fresh rosemary sprig

❶ Using mortar and pestle or side of chef's knife, mash garlic, salt and red pepper into a paste. In food processor, combine beans and garlic mixture; pulse into a chunky puree. Add 2 tablespoons olive oil, lemon juice and ground pepper; pulse just until mixed. Transfer puree to medium bowl. Stir in chopped rosemary. *(Spread can be prepared up to 2 days ahead. Cover and refrigerate.)*

❷ Spoon mixture into serving bowl. Drizzle with 1 teaspoon olive oil and sprinkle with cayenne. Garnish with rosemary sprig.

12 (1-tablespoon) servings.

Preparation time. 15 minutes. Ready to serve: 15 minutes.

Per serving: 65 calories, 3 g total fat (0.5 g saturated fat), 0 mg cholesterol, 140 mg sodium, 2 g fiber.

CHEF'S NOTE:
- Even though the garlic is destined for the food processor, resist the temptation to dump in whole cloves. Mashing garlic into a paste with salt is the key to bringing out its mellow and rich flavor.

Recipe Potpourri

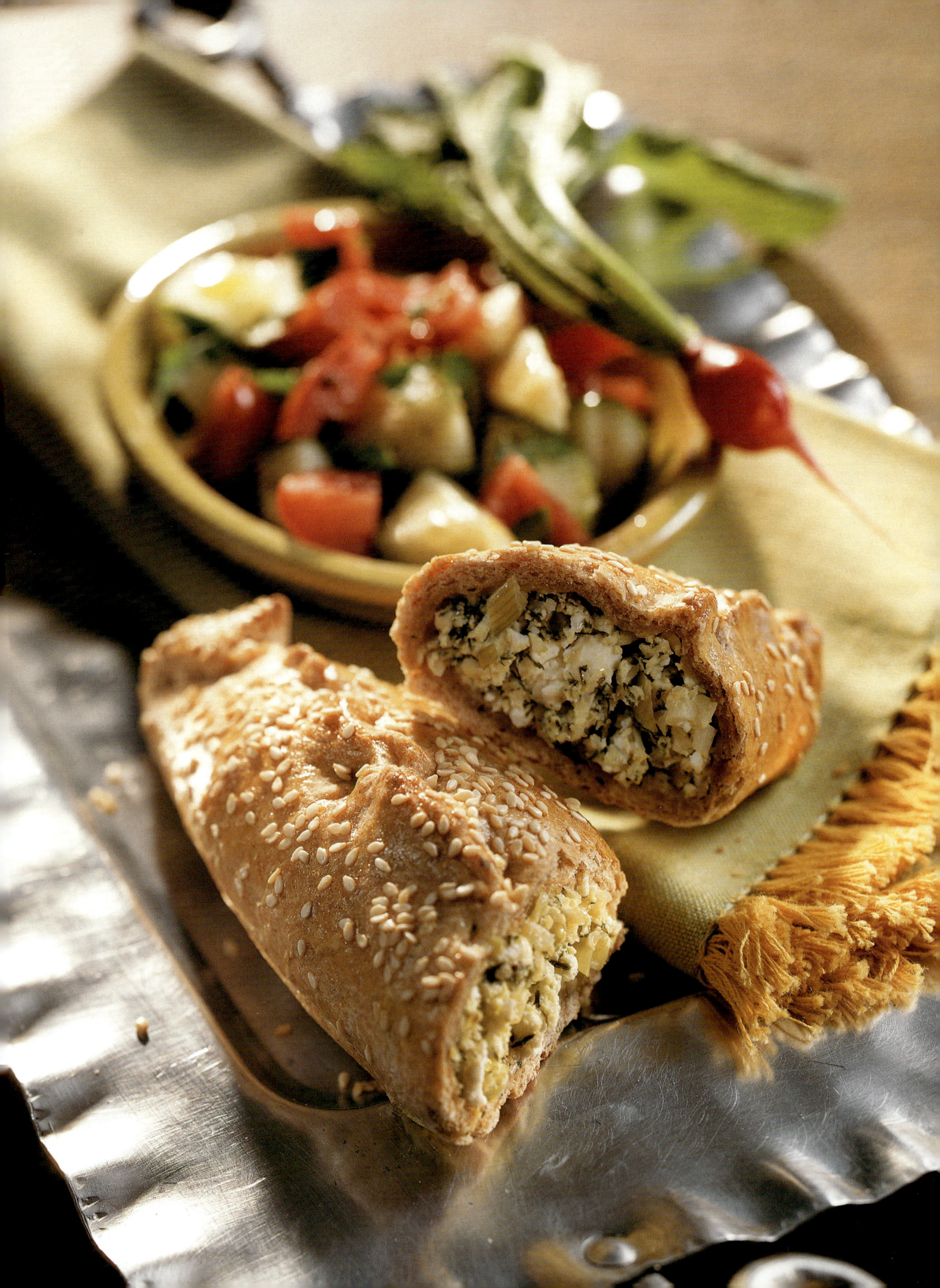

Turkish Pide with Feta and Dill Filling

While traveling in Turkey, I enjoyed incredible flatbreads and very special Turkish pizzas called pide. *These pizzas come in two basic forms: flat, oval breads with toppings; and filled breads that resemble calzone. Here is my adaptation of a pide featuring a feta and dill filling. To reduce saltiness, the feta is lightened with some cottage cheese. These flatbreads are often eaten as snacks in Turkey, but they are substantial enough for a light meal. Accompany with a Turkish-style shepherd's salad of chopped tomato, onion, cucumber and bell pepper dressed with parsley, olive oil and lemon juice.*

Quick Whole Wheat Pizza Dough for 4 (8-inch) crusts (page 59)
2 large eggs
1/2 cup reduced-fat (1 percent) cottage cheese
1/2 cup (2 oz.) crumbled feta cheese
1/2 cup trimmed chopped scallions
1/3 cup chopped fresh dill
1/4 teaspoon freshly ground pepper
1 tablespoon water
1 tablespoon sesame seeds

❶ Prepare Whole Wheat Pizza Dough.

❷ Meanwhile, place baking stone or inverted baking sheet on bottom rack of oven to heat. Heat oven to 450°F. (Let baking stone heat 25 minutes before baking.)

❸ In medium bowl, whisk 1 of the eggs. Add cottage cheese, feta cheese, scallions, dill and pepper; mix with rubber spatula.

❹ Spray baking sheet with cooking spray. In small bowl, combine remaining 1 egg and water; stir briskly with fork. Set aside to use for glaze.

❺ Divide dough into 4 pieces. On lightly floured surface, use rolling pin to roll 1 piece of dough into 8 1/2 x 6 1/2-inch oval, slightly less than 1/4-inch thick. (Keep remaining pieces of dough covered while you work.) Brush a little egg glaze around border of oval. Place about 1/3 cup feta filling in center of oval, leaving a 1 1/2-inch border. Bring edges of long sides of oval together; pinch to seal from end to end. Fold tips at narrow ends over; pinch to seal. Using wide metal spatula, transfer pide to baking sheet. Repeat with remaining dough and filling.

❻ Brush tops of pide with egg glaze; sprinkle with sesame seeds. Place baking sheet on heated baking stone. Bake 15 to 20 minutes or until golden. Transfer to wire rack; cool at least 10 minutes before serving hot or warm.

4 servings.

Preparation time: 40 minutes. Ready to serve: 1 hour, 10 minutes.

Per serving: 365 calories, 11.5 g total fat (4 g saturated fat), 120 mg cholesterol, 890 mg sodium, 5.5 g fiber.

Recipe Potpourri

Semolina Focaccia with Olives and Rosemary

This savory focaccia features an olive-rosemary topping sandwiched between layers of dough so that just a few olives peek through the surface.

SEMOLINA DOUGH
- 1 1/2 cups all-purpose flour
- 1/2 cup semolina, plus more for dusting
- 1 (1/4-oz.) pkg. quick-rising yeast
- 1 teaspoon salt
- 1/2 teaspoon sugar
- 2/3 cup hot water (120°F to 130°F)
- 1 tablespoon olive oil

TOPPING
- 2/3 cup kalamata olives, pitted, coarsely chopped
- 4 teaspoons chopped fresh rosemary
- 1 tablespoon olive oil
- 1 tablespoon water

1. In food processor, combine flour, semolina, yeast, salt and sugar; pulse to mix. In measuring cup, combine hot water and 1 tablespoon oil. With motor running, gradually pour hot liquid through food processor feed tube. Process until dough forms a ball, then process an additional 1 minute to knead. The dough should be quite soft. Transfer dough to lightly floured surface and knead a few times. Spray sheet of plastic wrap with cooking spray and place, sprayed side down, over dough. Let dough rest 30 minutes.

2. Place baking stone or inverted baking sheet on bottom rack of oven to heat. Heat oven to 450°F. (Let baking stone heat for 25 minutes before baking.)

3. Coat another baking sheet with cooking spray and dust with semolina. On lightly floured surface, use rolling pin to roll dough into 16x12-inch rectangle. Sprinkle olives and 2 teaspoons of the rosemary over half of the rectangle, leaving a 1/4-inch border along outside edges. Fold dough in half to enclose olives and form a 12x8-inch rectangle. Press edges together to seal. Continue to roll until 15x11-inch rectangle about 1/4-inch thick is formed. Roll dough back over rolling pin; set rolling pin over baking sheet and unroll, letting dough ease onto baking sheet. Cover with plastic wrap; let rise 20 minutes.

4. In small bowl, combine 1 tablespoon oil and 1 tablespoon water. Brush oil mixture over top of foccacia. Sprinkle with remaining 2 teaspoons rosemary. Dip fingertips in any remaining oil mixture; press top at intervals to form dimples. Pinch and pleat rim to finish edges. Place baking sheet on heated baking stone. Bake 15 to 20 minutes or until bottom of crust is golden and crisp. Transfer to cutting board; use pizza cutter to cut into 8 rectangles. Serve warm or at room temperature.

8 servings.

Preparation time: 1 hour. Ready to serve: 1 hour, 20 minutes.

Per serving: 165 calories, 5 g total fat (0.5 g saturated fat), 0 mg cholesterol, 400 mg sodium, 1.5 g fiber.

Quick Whole Wheat Pizza Dough

Quick-rising yeast allows you to make great pizza crust in just minutes, and a food processor takes the muscle out of the mixing and kneading process. I like to include whole wheat flour because, in addition to the nutritional benefits, it contributes a pleasant nutty flavor. If you prefer, you can make the dough entirely with all-purpose flour.

TO MAKE FOUR (8-INCH) CRUSTS (1 LB. DOUGH)
- 1 cup all-purpose flour
- 1 cup whole wheat flour
- 1 (1/4-oz.) package quick-rising yeast
- 1 teaspoon salt
- 1/2 teaspoon sugar
- 3/4 cup hot water (120°F to 130°F)
- 1 tablespoon olive oil

TO MAKE ONE (12-INCH) CRUST (3/4 LB. DOUGH)
- 3/4 cup all-purpose flour
- 3/4 cup whole wheat flour
- 2 teaspoons quick-rising yeast
- 3/4 teaspoon salt
- 1/4 teaspoon sugar
- 2/3 cup hot water (120°F -130°F)
- 2 teaspoons olive oil

1 In food processor, combine all-purpose flour, whole wheat flour, yeast, salt and sugar; pulse to mix. In measuring cup, combine hot water and oil. With motor running, gradually pour hot liquid through food processor feed tube. Process until dough forms a ball, then process an additional 1 minute to knead. The dough should be quite soft. If it seems dry, add 1 to 2 tablespoons warm water; if too sticky, add 1 to 2 tablespoons flour. Transfer dough to lightly floured surface. Spray sheet of plastic wrap with cooking spray and place, sprayed-side down, over dough. Let dough rest 20 minutes. *(Dough can be prepared ahead. Place in plastic food storage bag and refrigerate overnight. Bring to room temperature before using.)*

4 to 6 servings.

Preparation time: 10 minutes.

Per 1 serving: 250 calories, 4 g total fat (.5 g saturated fat), 0 mg cholesterol, 585 mg sodium, 5 g fiber.

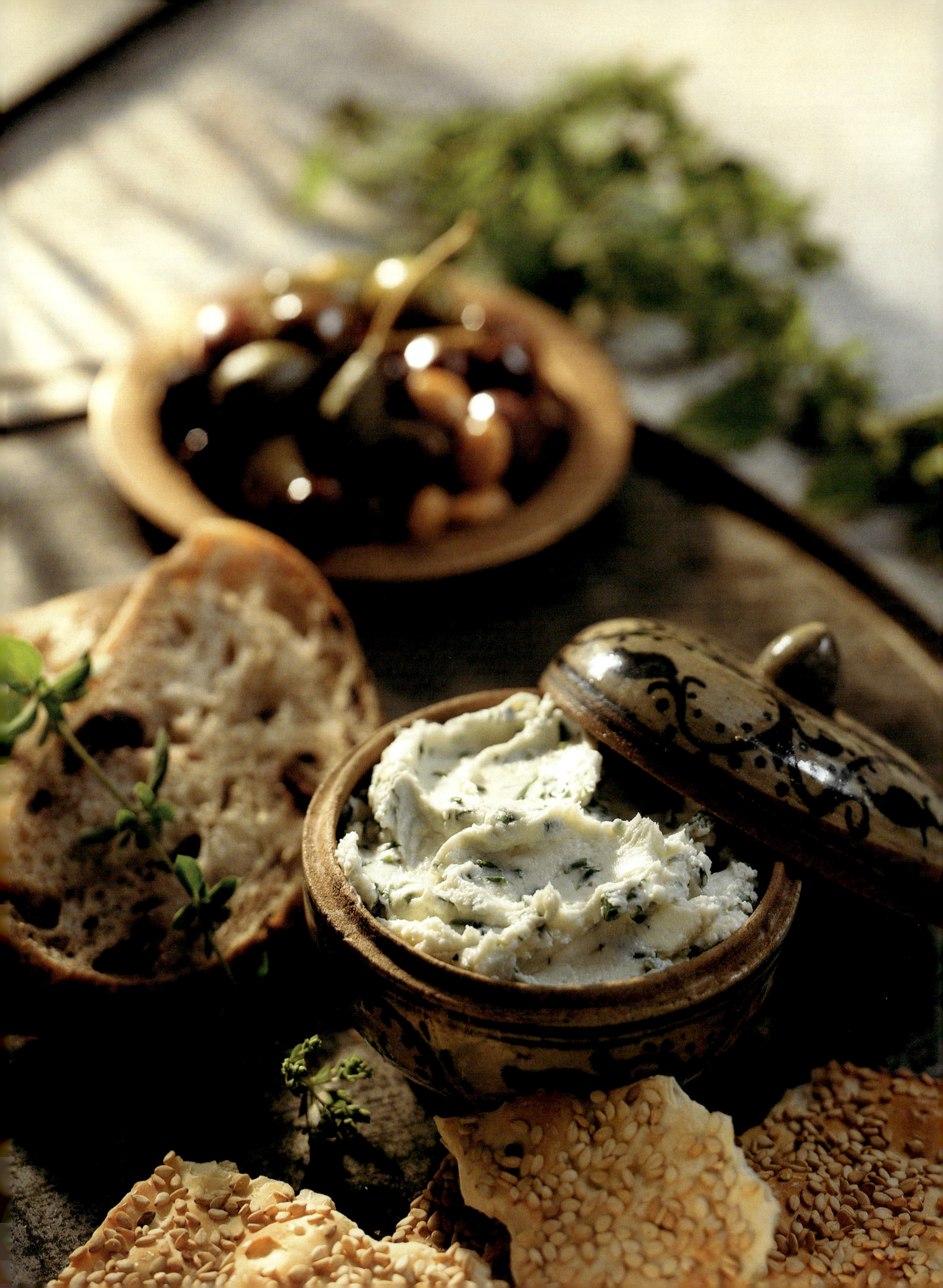

Herbed Goat Cheese Spread

Goat cheese seasoned with dried herbs is widely available in cheese stores and supermarkets these days. Herbed goat cheese, however, is so much better when you make your own with fresh herbs. Accompany with toasted French bread.

- 6 oz. creamy goat cheese
- 1 tablespoon extra-virgin olive oil
- ¼ cup chopped fresh chives
- 3 tablespoons chopped fresh parsley
- 1 tablespoon chopped fresh savory, if desired
- 1 small garlic clove, minced

1 In medium bowl, beat goat cheese at medium speed until smooth and creamy. Add oil; beat until smooth. Add chives, parsley, savory and garlic; mix with rubber spatula. *(Spread can be prepared up to 2 days ahead. Cover and refrigerate.)*

6 (1 tablespoon) servings.

Preparation time: 20 minutes. Ready to serve: 20 minutes.

Per serving: 60 calories, 5 g total fat (2.5 g saturated fat), 15 mg cholesterol, 60 mg sodium, 0 g fiber.

CHEF'S NOTE:

- To make attractive bite-sized goat cheese "truffles," use a melon baller to scoop out small balls of herbed goat cheese about 1 inch in diameter. With lightly oiled hands, form balls into smooth truffles. Roll and coat half the balls in chopped parsley; the other half in chopped pitted black olives.

EDAMAME WITH SHISO-SESAME SALT

Edamame is a special variety of soy bean that is harvested when not fully ripe. It is a popular snack in Japan and generally served in the pod and shelled before being popped into the diner's mouth. Consider it the ultimate healthy snack food. It is truly addictive, yet low in fat and a good source of soy protein. You can find frozen edamame in health food stores.

- 2 tablespoons sesame seeds, toasted*
- 4 teaspoons finely chopped fresh shiso
- 1/2 teaspoon kosher (coarse) salt or sea salt
- 1 (10- or 12-oz.) pkg. frozen edamame beans in pods
- 6 to 8 fresh red shiso leaves

❶ In small bowl, mix sesame seeds, chopped shiso and salt.

❷ In large saucepan of boiling salted water, cook edamame 3 minutes or until tender. Drain thoroughly under cold running water. Line small serving plate with shiso leaves. Mound edamame in center. Place 1 1/2 teaspoons shiso-sesame salt in each of 4 small saucers or bowls for dipping.

TIP *To toast sesame seeds, heat small skillet over medium-low heat. Add sesame seeds; stir constantly 3 to 4 minutes or until seeds are lightly browned. Transfer to small bowl and let cool.

4 servings.

Preparation time: 15 minutes. Ready to serve: 18 minutes.

Per serving: 110 calories, 6 g total fat (1 g saturated fat), 0 mg cholesterol, 210 mg sodium, 4 g fiber.

CHEF'S NOTES:
- The shiso-sesame salt is also delicious sprinkled over rice, stir-fries and Asian noodle salads.
- Substitute mint for shiso, if you wish.

Middle Eastern Bean Spread

In Egypt, a spread like this would be made with fava beans. Frozen limas, however, are much easier to find in North America and, when pureed, have an appealing pale green hue, which is highlighted by attractive flecks of green herbs. The trio of mint, cilantro and dill contributes a lively and fresh flavor to the spread. Serve with pita crisps or sesame lavash crackers.

- 1 (10-oz.) pkg. frozen lima beans
- 4 garlic cloves, crushed
- 3 tablespoons extra-virgin olive oil
- 4 teaspoons fresh lemon juice
- 1 teaspoon ground cumin
- 1/2 teaspoon salt
- 1/4 teaspoon crushed red pepper
- 1/8 teaspoon freshly ground pepper
- 1 tablespoon chopped fresh mint
- 1 tablespoon chopped fresh cilantro
- 1 tablespoon chopped fresh dill

1 In medium saucepan of lightly salted boiling water, cook lima beans and garlic about 10 minutes or until tender. Remove from heat; let beans and garlic cool in liquid.

2 Reserve about 1/4 cup cooking liquid. Drain beans and garlic; transfer to food processor. Add oil, lemon juice, cumin, salt, red pepper and ground pepper; puree until smooth. Place in medium bowl. Stir in mint, cilantro and dill. If spread seems thick, thin with a little of the reserved cooking liquid. *(Spread can be prepared up to 2 days ahead. Cover and refrigerate.)*

24 (1-tablespoon) servings.

Preparation time: 10 minutes. Ready to serve: 1 hour.

Per serving: 30 calories, 2 g total fat (0 g saturated fat), 0 mg cholesterol, 80 mg sodium, 1 g fiber.

Recipe Potpourri

Caramelized Red Onion, Olive and Goat Cheese Galette

This savory tart is great for parties and potlucks. It is based on the Provençal specialty, pissaladière, which plays the sweetness of caramelized onions against savory ripe olives and fragrant herbs.

CRUST
- 2 cups all-purpose flour
- 1/4 cup (1 oz.) freshly grated Parmesan cheese
- 2 teaspoons baking powder
- 1/2 teaspoon salt
- 3/4 cup reduced-fat cottage cheese
- 1/3 cup reduced-fat milk
- 1/4 cup olive oil
- 1 1/2 teaspoons sugar

TOPPING
- 3 teaspoons olive oil
- 6 cups thinly sliced red onions
- 1 teaspoon salt
- 1 tablespoon balsamic vinegar
- 2 garlic cloves, minced
- 1 cup (4 oz.) creamy goat cheese, crumbled
- 1/2 cup pitted kalamata olives, quartered
- 2 teaspoons each chopped fresh thyme, rosemary
- 1/2 teaspoon freshly ground pepper

❶ In medium bowl, combine flour, Parmesan cheese, baking powder and 1/2 teaspoon salt; mix well. In food processor, puree cottage cheese until smooth. Add milk, oil and sugar; process until smooth. Add flour mixture; pulse 4 to 5 times or just until dough begins to form.

❷ On lightly floured surface, knead dough several times; do not overwork. Press dough into flattened round; dust with flour. Wrap in plastic wrap; refrigerate while preparing filling. *(Dough can be prepared up to 2 days ahead. Cover and refrigerate.)* In large skillet, heat 1 teaspoon of the oil over medium heat until hot. Add onions and salt; cook 10 to 15 minutes or until very tender and lightly caramelized, stirring frequently. (If onions start to scorch, add a few tablespoons of water.) Add vinegar and garlic; cook and stir 1 minute. Remove from heat; cool. *(Onions can be prepared up to 2 days ahead. Cover and refrigerate.)*

❸ Heat oven to 400°F. Spray 15x10x1-inch pan with nonstick cooking spray. On lightly floured surface, roll dough to form 15 1/2x10 1/2-inch rectangle. Place dough in pan, folding in edges as necessary. Press edges with fork to flute. Spread onion filling over dough. Scatter goat cheese and olives over filling. Sprinkle with thyme, rosemary and pepper. Drizzle with remaining 2 teaspoons oil.

❹ Bake 20 to 30 minutes or until crust is golden brown and firm. Cool in pan on wire rack 5 minutes. (Galette can be made up to 1 day ahead; cool completely. Cover and refrigerate. To reheat, cover loosely with foil; bake at 325°F 10 to 15 minutes.) Slide galette onto cutting board. With pizza cutter or knife, cut into 24 pieces. Serve warm or at room temperature.

24 (appetizer) servings.

Preparation time: 45 minutes. Ready to serve: 1 hour 20 minutes.

Per serving: 105 calories, 5 g total fat (1.5 g saturated fat), 5 mg cholesterol, 280 mg sodium, 1 g fiber.

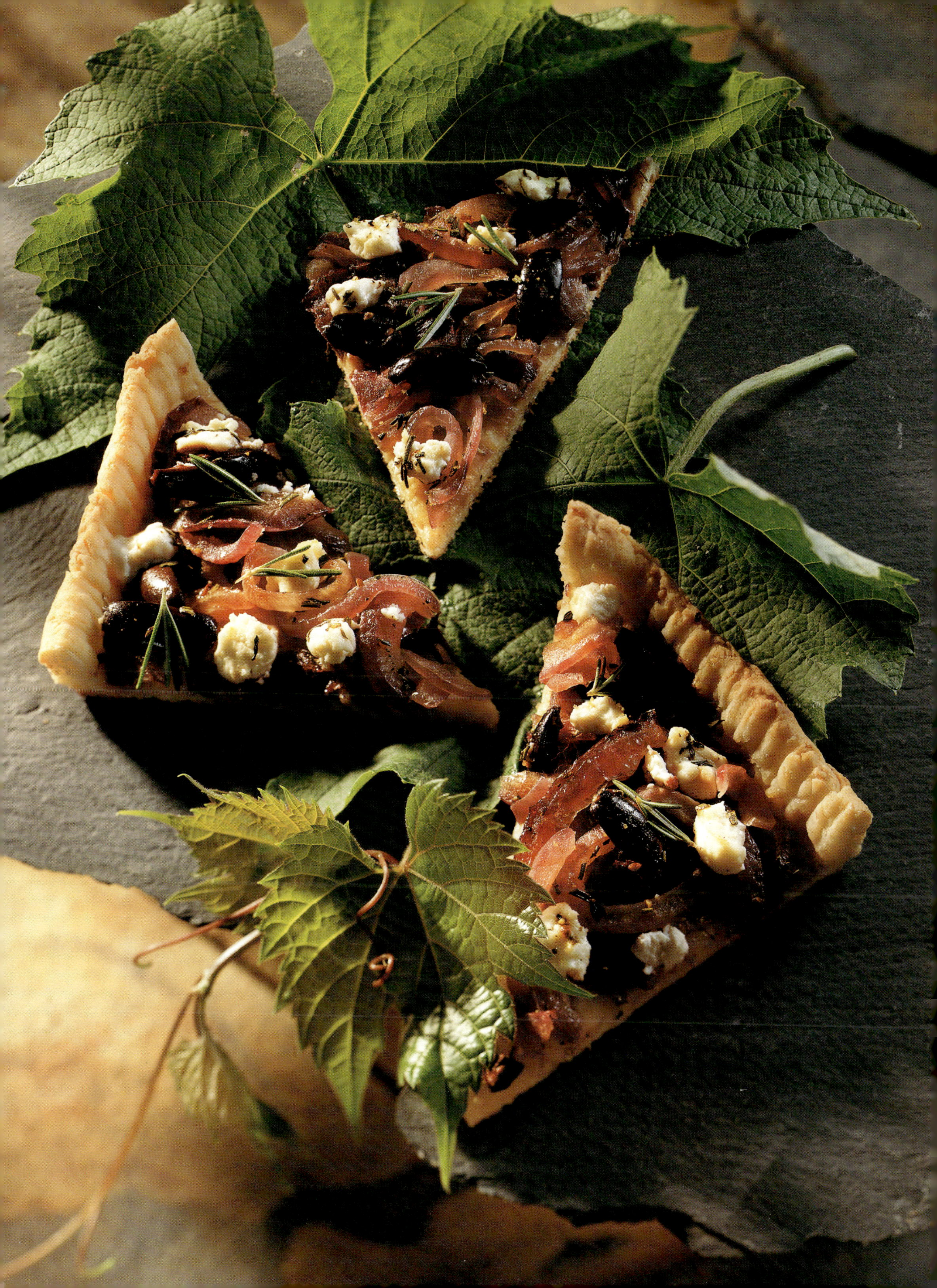

Herbed Pinwheel Biscuits

Like their sweet cousins, cinnamon rolls, these tender, savory biscuits are addictive. A basket of these warm fragrant herb rolls is a welcome accompaniment to any meal.

BISCUIT DOUGH
- 1½ cups all-purpose flour
- ½ cup whole wheat flour
- 1 tablespoon baking powder
- ½ teaspoon baking soda
- ¾ teaspoon salt
- 6 tablespoons butter, cut into small pieces
- 1 cup buttermilk

HERB FILLING
- ⅓ cup chopped fresh parsley
- ⅓ cup chopped fresh dill
- ¼ cup chopped scallions
- 2 garlic cloves, minced
- 2 tablespoons butter, melted

❶ Heat oven to 400°F. Spray baking sheet with cooking spray.

❷ In large bowl, combine all-purpose flour, whole wheat flour, baking powder, baking soda and salt; whisk to blend. Using pastry blender, cut in butter until mixture crumbles. Make a well in center of flour mixture; add buttermilk, stirring with fork just until dough holds together. Turn out onto lightly floured surface and knead several times. Wrap in plastic wrap; refrigerate while preparing filling.

❸ In small bowl, combine parsley, dill, scallions and garlic; toss with fork to blend.

❹ On lightly floured surface, roll out dough into rough 15x10-inch rectangle. Brush with about 1 tablespoon butter leaving ½-inch margin. Sprinkle parsley mixture evenly over buttered area; press lightly into dough. Starting at long edge, roll up dough, jellyroll style. Pinch edges together along seam. With sharp knife, cut roll into 12 pieces. Set rolls, cut side up, on baking sheet. Brush with remaining butter. Bake rolls 20 to 25 minutes or until dark golden and firm. Serve warm.

12 biscuits.

Preparation time: 20 minutes. Ready to serve: 45 minutes.

Per biscuit: 155 calories, 8.5 g total fat (5 g saturated fat), 20 mg cholesterol, 390 mg sodium, 1 g fiber.

Pizza with Potato-Rosemary Topping

Not your standard pizza delivery fare. This unusual potato-topped pizza is well worth making at home. You will need uniformly thin potato slices for the topping. A food processor fitted with a thin (2 mm) slicing disk works well, as does a mandolin-style vegetable slicer.

	1	cup *Quick Tomato Sauce*, without optional herbs (page 158)
	1	recipe *Quick Whole Wheat Pizza Dough* for 12-inch pizza (page 59)
		Cornmeal for sprinkling
3 to 4		Yukon Gold potatoes
	1	tablespoon extra-virgin olive oil
	2	cups (8 oz.) grated whole-milk mozzarella cheese
	¼	teaspoon salt
	⅛	teaspoon freshly ground pepper
	1	tablespoon chopped fresh rosemary

❶ Prepare Quick Tomato Sauce; let cool.

❷ Meanwhile, prepare Quick Whole Wheat Pizza Dough.

❸ Set rack in middle of oven. Place baking stone or inverted baking sheet on rack. Heat oven to 500°F or highest setting. Spray 12-inch pizza pan with cooking spray; sprinkle with cornmeal.

❹ Slice potatoes ⅛-inch thick. Place in steamer basket over boiling water. Cover and steam potatoes 5 to 6 minutes or just until tender. Rinse with cold water to stop cooking. Pat dry.

❺ On lightly floured surface, roll pizza dough into 12½-inch circle. Transfer to pizza pan. Turn edges under to make slight rim around perimeter. With pastry brush, brush rim of crust with a little of the olive oil. Spread cooled tomato sauce over crust. Sprinkle with cheese. Arrange potato slices, slightly overlapping, in concentric circles over cheese layer. Dab potatoes with remaining olive oil and season with salt and pepper. Sprinkle with rosemary.

❻ Place pizza pan on heated baking stone. Bake 8 to 10 minutes or until bottom of crust is crisp and lightly browned. (If desired, during the last few minutes of baking, slide pizza directly onto baking stone to ensure a crisp bottom crust.)

2 to 3 servings.

Preparation time: 50 minutes. Ready to serve: 1 hour.

Per serving: 990 calories, 44.5 g total fat (20 g saturated fat), 100 mg cholesterol, 2000 mg sodium, 12.5 g fiber.

Herbed Potato Bread

Adding a mashed potato to the dough is an easy way to produce a crusty bread that resembles a more complicated sourdough loaf. This yeast bread is flavored with chopped herbs and decorated with an arrangement of whole herb sprigs. In addition to making an impressive presentation, the herb sprigs give a great flavor to the crust.

BREAD
- 1 (6-oz.) potato, peeled, halved
- 1 tablespoon olive oil
- 1/2 teaspoon sugar
- 2 tablespoons lukewarm water
- 1 1/4 teaspoons active dry yeast
- 1 1/2 cups whole wheat flour
- 1 tablespoon chopped fresh rosemary
- 1 tablespoon chopped fresh thyme
- 1 teaspoon chopped fresh sage
- 1 1/4 teaspoons salt
- 1 1/2 to 1 3/4 cups all-purpose flour
- Cornmeal for sprinkling

GLAZE AND DECORATION
- 6 fresh chive sprigs
- 4 fresh Italian parsley sprigs
- 2 fresh sage sprigs
- 1 egg white
- 1 tablespoon water

❶ In small saucepan, cover potato with water. Bring to a boil over medium-high heat. Reduce heat to medium-low; cook, covered, 15 to 20 minutes or until tender. Drain potato, reserving 1 cup cooking liquid. Place potato in bowl; mash with fork or potato masher. Drizzle with oil. Cool mashed potato and reserved cooking liquid to lukewarm.

❷ In large bowl, dissolve sugar in 2 tablespoons lukewarm water. Sprinkle in yeast; let stand about 5 minutes or until foamy. Add reserved mashed potato and cooking liquid. Gradually beat in whole wheat flour. Beat 1 minute. Stir in rosemary, thyme, sage and salt. Gradually beat in just enough of the all-purpose flour to make dough too stiff to beat. Turn dough out onto lightly floured surface. Knead about 10 minutes or until smooth and elastic, adding just enough flour to prevent sticking. Place dough in lightly oiled bowl. Turn to coat; cover with plastic wrap. Let rise about 1 1/2 hours or until doubled in bulk.

❸ Coat baking sheet with cooking spray. Sprinkle with cornmeal. Punch dough down. Turn out onto work surface and knead several times. Divide dough in half; shape each piece into ball. Arrange loaves 3 inches apart on baking sheet. Cover with plastic wrap; let rise 1 hour. About 30 minutes before baking, place baking stone or inverted baking sheet on middle rack of oven. Place small baking pan on rack below stone. Heat oven to 450°F.

❹ Meanwhile, place large bowl of cold water beside stove. Drop chive, parsley and sage sprigs into large saucepan of boiling water 3 seconds. Retrieve sprigs with tongs or slotted spoon and drop into cold water. Pat herb sprigs dry with paper towels.

❺ When loaves have risen, in small bowl, blend egg white and 1 tablespoon water with fork. Brush over loaves. Arrange herb sprigs decoratively over loaves. Brush again with egg-white glaze. Pour 1 cup water into baking pan in oven. Place baking sheet on baking stone. Bake loaves 20 minutes. Reduce oven temperature to 400°F. Bake an additional 10 to 15 minutes or until loaves are golden and sound hollow when tapped. Transfer loaves to wire rack and cool.

2 small loaves (about sixteen 1/2-inch slices).

Preparation time: 45 minutes. Ready to serve: 3 hours, 30 minutes.

Per slice: 100 calories, 1 g total fat (0 g saturated fat), 0 mg cholesterol, 185 mg sodium, 2 g fiber.

CHEF'S NOTES:
- The trick to making a beautiful decoration of herb leaves on a loaf of bread is to blanch the herbs.
- You can use a stand-up mixer fitted with dough hook to mix and knead the dough.

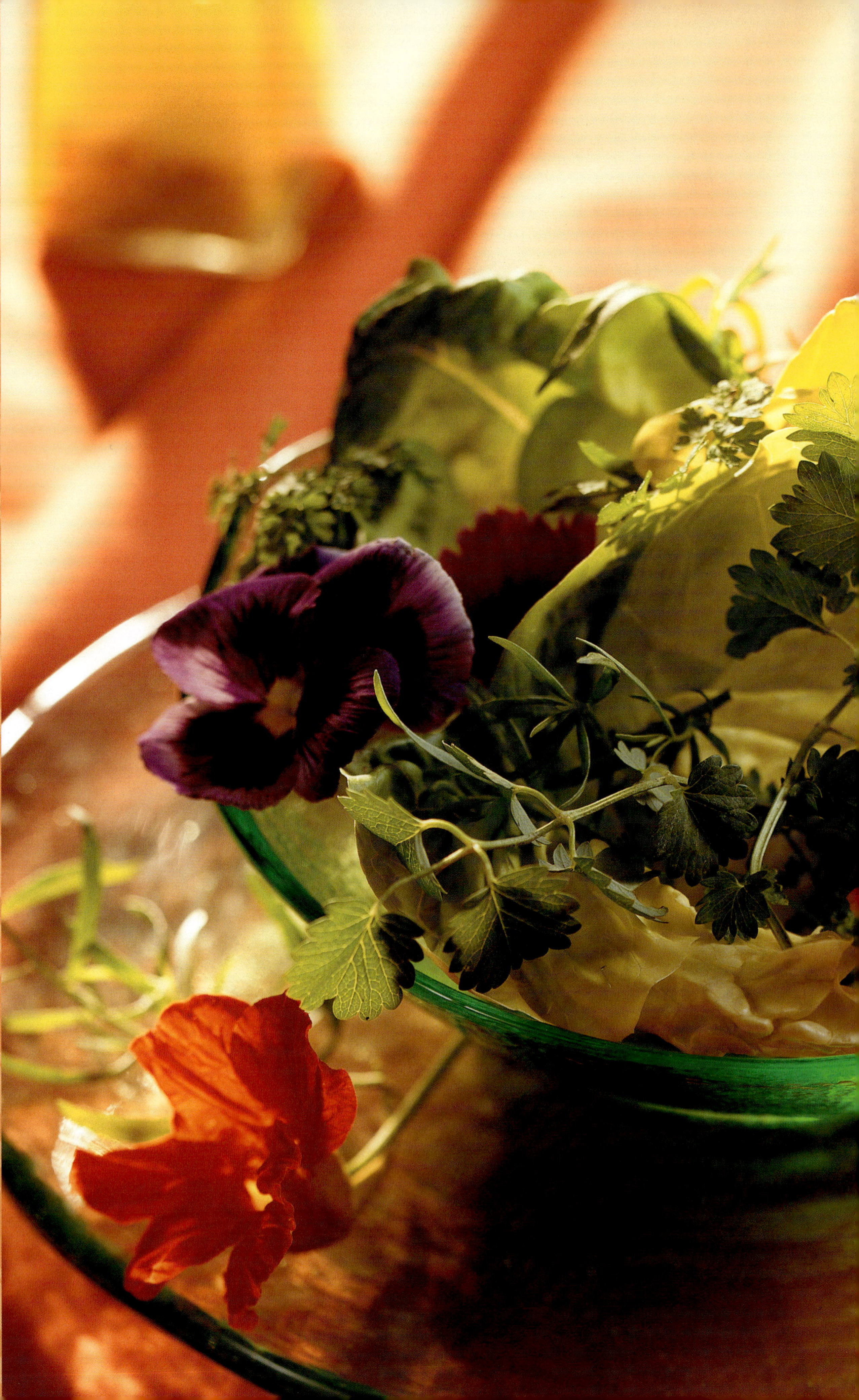

Soups, Salads & Sides

Herbs can be used to infuse the broth or provide a flavorful finish to a soup; either way, they play a key role in making beautiful soup. Herbs are also integral in salads, and make a natural pairing with vegetables for superb side dishes. This chapter presents a selection of herbal possibilities on all these culinary fronts.

Herb Garden Salad, page 87

Herbed Tomato Gratin

This rustic gratin with a Provençal accent is a lovely accompaniment to grilled or roasted lamb or beef. Coating the gratin dish with a sprinkling of herbed bread crumbs is a flavorful way to absorb the tomato juices.

- 5 slices firm white sandwich bread, crusts trimmed, torn into pieces
- 1 tablespoon dried *herbes de Provence* (page 14)
- 1 garlic clove, minced
- 2 tablespoons extra-virgin olive oil
- 4 medium tomatoes, cut into 1/2-inch slices
- 1/8 teaspoon salt
- 1/8 teaspoon freshly ground pepper

❶ Heat oven to 425° F. Spray 2 1/2-quart gratin dish or shallow casserole with nonstick cooking spray.

❷ In food processor, process bread until it breaks down into coarse crumbs. Add *herbes de Provence* and garlic; process until blended. Add oil; pulse several times.

❸ Sprinkle 1/2 cup of the bread crumb mixture evenly over bottom of gratin dish. Bake crumbs 6 to 8 minutes or until light golden.

❹ Arrange tomato slices, slightly overlapping, over crumbs; season with salt and pepper. Sprinkle with remaining bread crumb mixture; return gratin to oven. Bake 20 to 30 minutes or until golden.

4 servings.

Preparation time: 15 minutes. Ready to serve: 45 minutes.

Per serving: 155 calories, 8 g total fat (1 g saturated fat), 0.5 mg cholesterol, 215 mg sodium, 2 g fiber.

Root Vegetable and Barley Soup

Nutty barley and root vegetables make a homey soup with an old-fashioned flavor. A splash of lemon juice and a generous sprinkling of dill give it a lively finish.

- 2 teaspoons olive oil
- 1 large onion, chopped
- 3 garlic cloves, minced
- ½ cup pearl barley
- 6 cups reduced-sodium chicken broth
- 2 medium carrots, diced
- 2 medium parsnips, diced
- 2 cups diced cooked chicken or turkey
- ⅓ cup chopped fresh dill
- 2 teaspoons fresh lemon juice
- ¼ teaspoon freshly ground pepper

❶ In 4- to 6-quart soup pot, heat oil over medium heat until hot. Add onion; cook 2 to 3 minutes or until tender, stirring constantly. Add garlic; cook 30 seconds, stirring constantly. Add barley; stir to coat. Add broth; bring to a simmer. Reduce heat to low; skim off any foam. Simmer, covered, 20 minutes.

❷ Add carrots and parsnips; simmer, covered, 15 to 20 minutes or until barley and vegetables are just tender. Add chicken, simmer an additional 3 to 4 minutes or until heated through. Stir in dill, lemon juice and pepper.

8 (1-cup) servings.

Preparation time: 20 minutes. Ready to serve: 1 hour.

Per serving: 185 calories, 4.5 g total fat (1 g saturated fat), 30 mg cholesterol, 400 mg sodium, 4 g fiber.

CHEF'S NOTE:
- To shorten cooking time, substitute quick-cooking barley for pearl barley; add carrots and parsnips with barley and simmer soup for a total of 20 minutes.

Thai Chicken Soup

The base of this first-course soup is an intense spicy chicken broth infused with lemongrass, ginger and garlic. Coconut milk gives it a creamy finish.

2	(14.5-oz.) cans reduced-sodium chicken broth
¾	cup unsweetened coconut milk
6	(¼-inch) slices peeled fresh ginger
2	stalks lemongrass, trimmed (page 9), cut into 2-inch lengths, crushed
4	garlic cloves, crushed
12	oz. boneless skinless chicken breast halves, trimmed
2	tablespoons cornstarch
2	tablespoons fresh lime juice
1	teaspoon fish sauce
2	teaspoons Thai red or green curry paste
4	thin lime slices
¼	cup chopped scallions
¼	cup chopped fresh cilantro

❶ In Dutch oven, combine broth, coconut milk, ginger, lemongrass and garlic; bring to a simmer. Add chicken; reduce heat to low. Simmer, covered, 15 to 20 minutes or until chicken juices run clear. With tongs, transfer chicken to cutting board.

❷ Increase heat under broth mixture to medium-high. Cook, uncovered, 5 minutes to intensify flavors. Strain broth into large saucepan, pressing on solids to extract juices. Bring broth to a simmer over medium heat.

❸ In small bowl, mix cornstarch and lime juice. Add to simmering broth; cook about 1 minute or until slightly thickened, whisking constantly. Reduce heat to low. Add fish sauce and curry paste; whisk to blend. Thinly slice cooked chicken; add to soup. Cook over low heat until heated through. Ladle soup into bowls; garnish each serving with lime slice and a sprinkling of scallions and cilantro.

4 (1-cup) servings.

Preparation time: 15 minutes. Ready to serve: 40 minutes.

Per serving: 255 calories, 13.5 g total fat (9.5 g saturated fat), 45 mg cholesterol, 535 mg sodium, 1 g fiber.

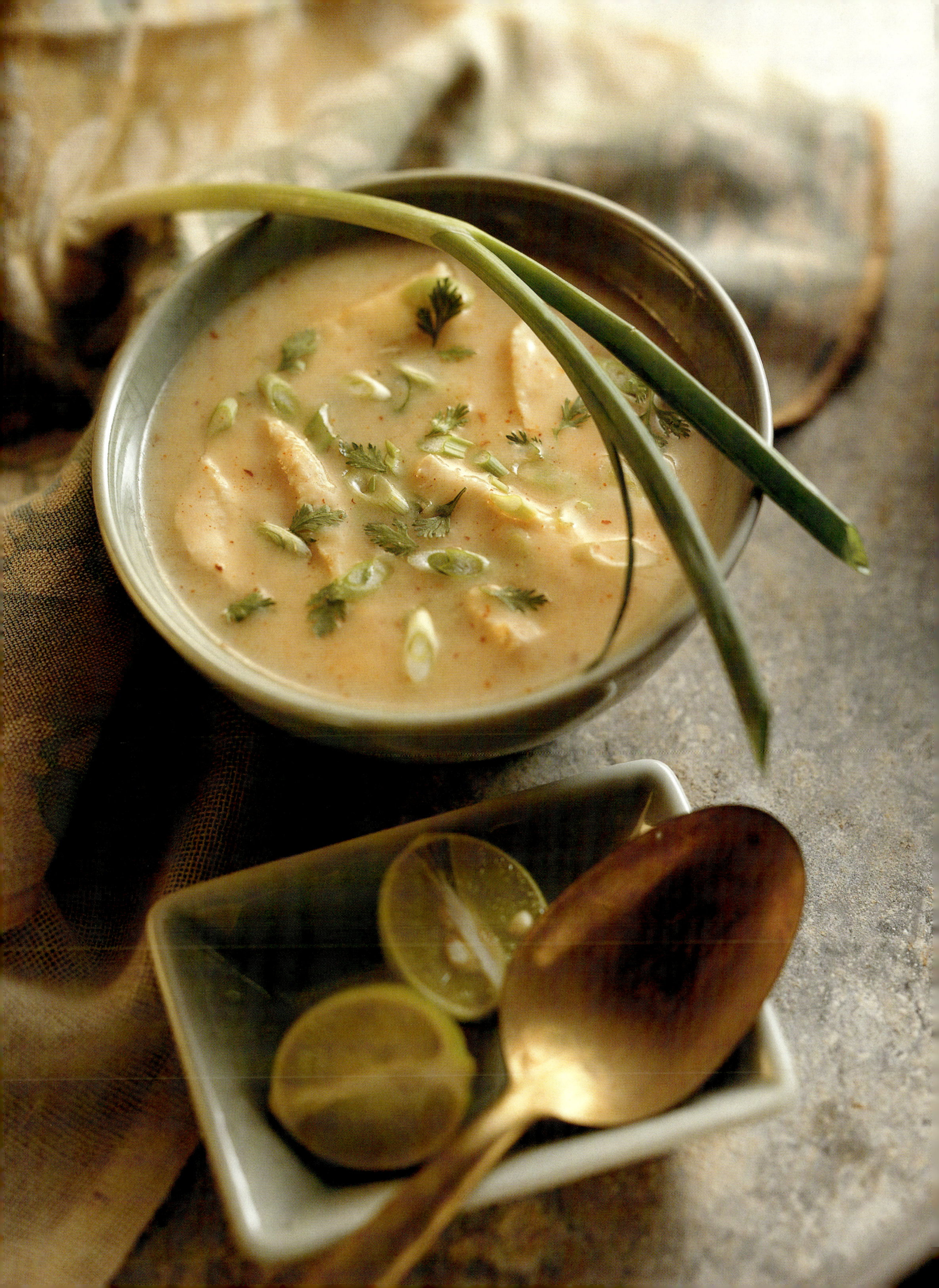

Southwestern Hominy Soup

This hearty chili-seasoned soup is a great way to transform leftover chicken or turkey into a distinctive and satisfying meal.

- 2 teaspoons olive oil or vegetable oil
- 1 large onion, chopped
- 1 small red bell pepper, seeded, diced
- 3 garlic cloves, minced
- 1 (4-oz.) can diced green chiles
- 1 tablespoon chili powder
- 1 teaspoon ground cumin
- 1 tablespoon chopped fresh oregano or 1 teaspoon dried
- 5 cups reduced-sodium chicken broth
- 2 (15-oz.) cans white hominy, drained, rinsed
- 1 (15-oz.) can diced tomatoes, undrained
- 2 cups diced cooked chicken or turkey
- 1/2 cup chopped fresh cilantro
- 1/4 teaspoon freshly ground pepper
- Lime wedges

❶ In 4- to 6-quart soup pot, heat oil over medium-high heat until hot. Add onion and bell pepper; cook 3 to 5 minutes or until tender, stirring frequently. Add garlic, green chiles, chili powder, cumin and oregano; cook 30 seconds, stirring constantly. Add broth, hominy and tomatoes; bring to a simmer. Reduce heat to low. Skim off any foam. Simmer, covered, about 20 minutes or until vegetables are tender and flavors have blended.

❷ Add chicken and 1/4 cup of the cilantro; simmer 3 to 4 minutes or until heated through. Stir in pepper. Ladle soup into bowls. Garnish with a sprinkling of remaining cilantro. Serve with lime wedges.

10 (1-cup) servings.

Preparation time: 20 minutes. Ready to serve: 1 hour, 10 minutes.

Per serving: 155 calories, 4 g total fat (1 g saturated fat), 20 mg cholesterol, 575 mg sodium, 3.5 g fiber.

CHEF'S NOTE:

- Hominy, which is made from dried, degermed and hulled corn kernels, contributes an appealing corn flavor to this southwestern-flavored soup. You can find convenient canned hominy in the Latin sections of many supermarkets, Latin markets and specialty stores.

TORTELLINI IN ROSEMARY-SCENTED BROTH

This soup is a statement in simplicity and elegance. A flavorful broth and good Parmesan cheese are all you need to turn prepared tortellini into a satisfying soup.

- 3 (14.5-oz.) cans reduced-sodium chicken broth
- 4 garlic cloves, crushed
- 2 sprigs fresh rosemary
- ¼ teaspoon crushed red pepper
- 1 (8-oz.) pkg. fresh or frozen cheese tortellini
- ¼ cup (1 oz.) freshly grated Parmesan cheese

❶ In large saucepan, bring broth to a boil over medium-high heat. Place garlic, rosemary and red pepper in tea infuser; place infuser in broth, or add these seasonings directly to broth. Reduce heat to medium-low. Simmer, partially covered, 15 minutes to intensify flavors. Remove tea infuser from broth, or pass broth through strainer and return to saucepan.

❷ Meanwhile, in large pot of boiling lightly salted water, cook tortellini according to package directions. Drain tortellini; add to infused broth. Ladle into wide soup bowls; sprinkle with Parmesan cheese.

4 (1¼-cup) servings.

Preparation time: 10 minutes. Ready to serve: 30 minutes.

Per serving: 180 calories, 8 g total fat (3.5 g saturated fat), 55 mg cholesterol, 800 mg sodium, 0.5 g fiber.

CHEF'S NOTE:

- When you don't have time to make broth from scratch, you can quickly doctor canned broth by infusing it with fresh herbs and garlic. If you use a tea infuser to enclose the herbs and flavorings, you won't have to bother with straining the broth. Rosemary-scented broth works particularly well in Italian soups and tastes great with Parmesan cheese.

Soups, Salads & Sides

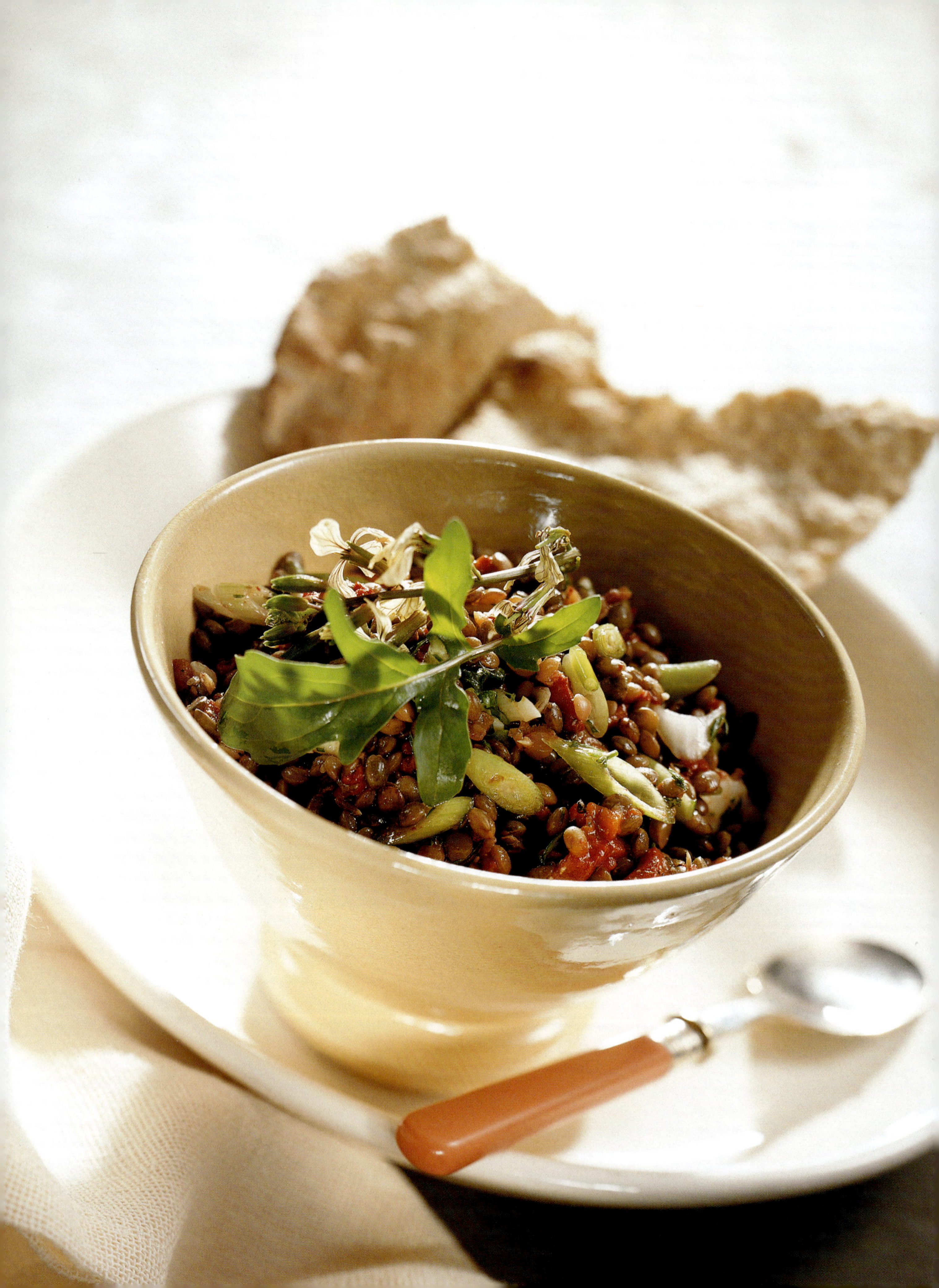

Greek Lentil Salad

Small green lentils (often known as Le Puy lentils) are preferred for salads because they retain their shape and have an appealing chewy texture, but common brown lentils are a reasonable substitute. This salad makes a satisfying lunch or the perfect filling for a pita sandwich.

LEMON VINAIGRETTE
- 1 garlic clove, crushed
- 1/2 teaspoon salt
- 3 tablespoons fresh lemon juice
- 2 tablespoons extra-virgin olive oil
- 1/4 teaspoon freshly ground pepper

SALAD
- 1 cup green or brown lentils, rinsed
- 1/2 teaspoon salt
- 1 cup trimmed chopped scallions
- 1 (12-oz.) jar roasted red bell peppers, rinsed, diced
- 1/2 cup (2 oz.) crumbled feta cheese
- 1/3 cup chopped fresh dill
- 6 cups torn arugula

❶ In mortar and pestle or with side of chef's knife, mash garlic and 1/2 teaspoon salt into a paste; transfer to small bowl. Whisk in lemon juice, oil and pepper.

❷ In large saucepan, cover lentils with water. Bring to a simmer over medium-high heat. Reduce heat to medium-low. Simmer, partially covered, 15 minutes. Add 1/2 teaspoon salt; cook an additional 5 to 10 minutes or just until lentils are tender but not broken down. Drain and cool slightly.

❸ In large bowl, combine warm lentils and dressing; toss gently to mix. Add scallions, roasted peppers, feta and dill to lentil mixture; toss again. *(Salad can be prepared up to 8 hours ahead. Cover and refrigerate. Bring to room temperature before serving.)* To serve, mound lentil mixture on a bed of arugula.

8 (1/2-cup) servings.

Preparation time: 20 minutes. Ready to serve: 45 minutes.

Per serving: 150 calories, 5.5 g total fat (1.5 g saturated fat), 5 mg cholesterol, 355 mg sodium, 6.5 g fiber.

Green Bean and Fresh Cranberry Bean Salad

Fresh cranberry beans often turn up in farmers' markets and Italian grocers in summer. When you see them, snap them up — they are a special summer treat. If you cannot find cranberry beans, substitute 1½ cups frozen lima beans; cook according to package directions.

DRESSING
- 3 tablespoons apple cider vinegar
- 4 teaspoons grainy mustard
- 1 tablespoon apple juice concentrate, thawed
- ½ teaspoon salt
- ⅛ teaspoon freshly ground pepper
- ¼ cup vegetable oil

SALAD
- 1 lb. fresh cranberry beans, shelled
- ¾ lb. fresh green beans, stem ends trimmed
- ½ cup finely diced red onion
- 3 tablespoons chopped fresh summer savory

❶ In small bowl, whisk vinegar, mustard, apple juice concentrate, salt and pepper. Gradually whisk in oil. *(Dressing can be prepared up to 2 days ahead. Cover and refrigerate.)*

❷ In large saucepan of lightly salted boiling water, cook cranberry beans over medium-high heat about 25 minutes or until tender. Drain and rinse under cold running water; drain thoroughly. Meanwhile, cook green beans in another large saucepan of lightly salted boiling water over medium-high heat 3 to 6 minutes or until just tender. Drain and rinse under cold water; drain again.

❸ Just before serving, in large bowl, combine cranberry beans and green beans, onion and 2 tablespoons of the savory. Add dressing; toss to coat. Sprinkle with remaining 1 tablespoon savory.

4 (1-cup) servings.

Preparation time: 20 minutes. Ready to serve: 30 minutes.

Per serving: 220 calories, 14 g total fat (2 g saturated fat), 0 mg cholesterol, 365 mg sodium, 6.5 g fiber.

CHEF'S NOTE:
- In Germany, summer savory is known as "bean herb." Not only does the mildly peppery taste of savory enhance bland bean dishes, the herb may help reduce the gas-producing properties of beans.

BUTTERNUT SQUASH GRATIN

A gratin is distinguished by its golden crisp crust. In this squash version, the Parmesan cheese topping is complemented by a lively parsley, lemon and garlic gremolada. This makes a fine accompaniment for roast chicken, turkey or pork. To make squash easier to peel and cut, see the tip on page 82.

- 1 garlic clove, halved
- 2 garlic cloves, minced
- 2/3 cup chopped fresh Italian parsley
- 1 tablespoon freshly grated lemon peel
- 3 lb. butternut squash (1 large), seeded, cut into 3/8-inch slices
- 1/2 teaspoon salt
- 1/4 teaspoon freshly ground pepper
- 1/2 cup vegetable or reduced-sodium chicken broth, heated
- 1/4 cup fine dry bread crumbs
- 1 teaspoon olive oil
- 3/4 cup (3 oz.) freshly grated Parmesan cheese

❶ Heat oven to 400°F. Rub surface of 2 1/2-quart gratin dish or shallow casserole with cut side of halved garlic clove. Spray gratin dish with nonstick cooking spray.

❷ In small bowl, mix minced garlic, parsley and lemon peel. Spread half of the squash slices in dish. Season with 1/4 teaspoon salt and 1/8 teaspoon pepper. Sprinkle half of the parsley mixture over squash layer; cover and refrigerate remaining parsley. Top with remaining squash. Gently pour broth over squash. Season with remaining 1/4 teaspoon salt and 1/8 teaspoon pepper. Cover dish with aluminum foil. Bake gratin 30 minutes or until squash is almost tender.

❸ Meanwhile, in small bowl, mix bread crumbs and oil. Sprinkle remaining parsley mixture evenly over top of gratin. Top with cheese, then bread crumb mixture. Bake, uncovered, 15 minutes or until squash is tender and top is golden.

8 (3/4-cup) servings.

Preparation time: 30 minutes. Ready to serve: 1 hour, 15 minutes.

Per serving: 145 calories, 4 g total fat (2 g saturated fat), 5 mg cholesterol, 390 mg sodium, 5 g fiber.

CHEF'S NOTES:
- Try replacing the Parmesan cheese in the topping with ground walnuts.

Soups, Salads & Sides

Harvest "Thyme" Squash Soup

Pears contribute an underlying sweetness to this luxurious squash soup. A thyme-infused cream swirl gives it a beautiful finish. Try infusing milk or cream with thyme when you are making mashed potatoes or cream sauce.

1	tablespoon olive oil	1	cup water
2	cups sliced leeks, white and light green parts only	¼	cup whipping cream
2	lb. butternut squash, seeded, cut into 2-inch cubes*	6	fresh thyme sprigs or 1 teaspoon dried
2	firm ripe pears, such as Bartlett or Anjou, cored, diced	¼	cup low-fat plain yogurt or reduced-fat sour cream
2	garlic cloves, crushed	1	tablespoon fresh lemon juice
1	tablespoon chopped fresh thyme or 1 teaspoon dried	¼	teaspoon salt
2	(14.5-oz.) cans reduced-sodium chicken broth	⅛	teaspoon freshly ground pepper Chopped fresh chives

❶ In 4- to 6-quart soup pot, heat oil over medium heat. Add leeks; cook 3 to 4 minutes or until tender, stirring frequently. Add squash, pears, garlic and chopped thyme; cook 1 minute, stirring constantly. Add broth and water; bring to a simmer. Reduce heat to low. Simmer, covered, 30 minutes or until squash is tender.

❷ Meanwhile, in small saucepan, heat cream until steaming. Remove from heat; add thyme sprigs. Cover and steep 20 minutes. Strain cream into small bowl, pressing on thyme to extract flavor. Add yogurt; whisk until smooth.

❸ Strain soup through colander into large bowl. Place solids in food processor; process until smooth. Return puree and broth to soup pot; heat through. Stir in lemon juice; season with salt and pepper. *(Soup can be prepared up to 2 days ahead. Cover and refrigerate.)*

❹ To serve, ladle soup into bowls; add large dollop (or several small dollops) of infused cream to each bowl. Draw tip of knife or toothpick through cream to make decorative swirls. Garnish with chives.

TIP *To make a squash easier to peel, try this trick: Pierce squash in several places with a fork or skewer and microwave on High for 2 minutes just to soften skin. Let stand for several minutes. Use a vegetable peeler or paring knife to remove skin.

8 (1-cup) servings.

Preparation time: 30 minutes. Ready to serve: 1 hour, 15 minutes.

Per serving: 145 calories, 5 g total fat (2 g saturated fat), 10 mg cholesterol, 525 mg sodium, 5 g fiber.

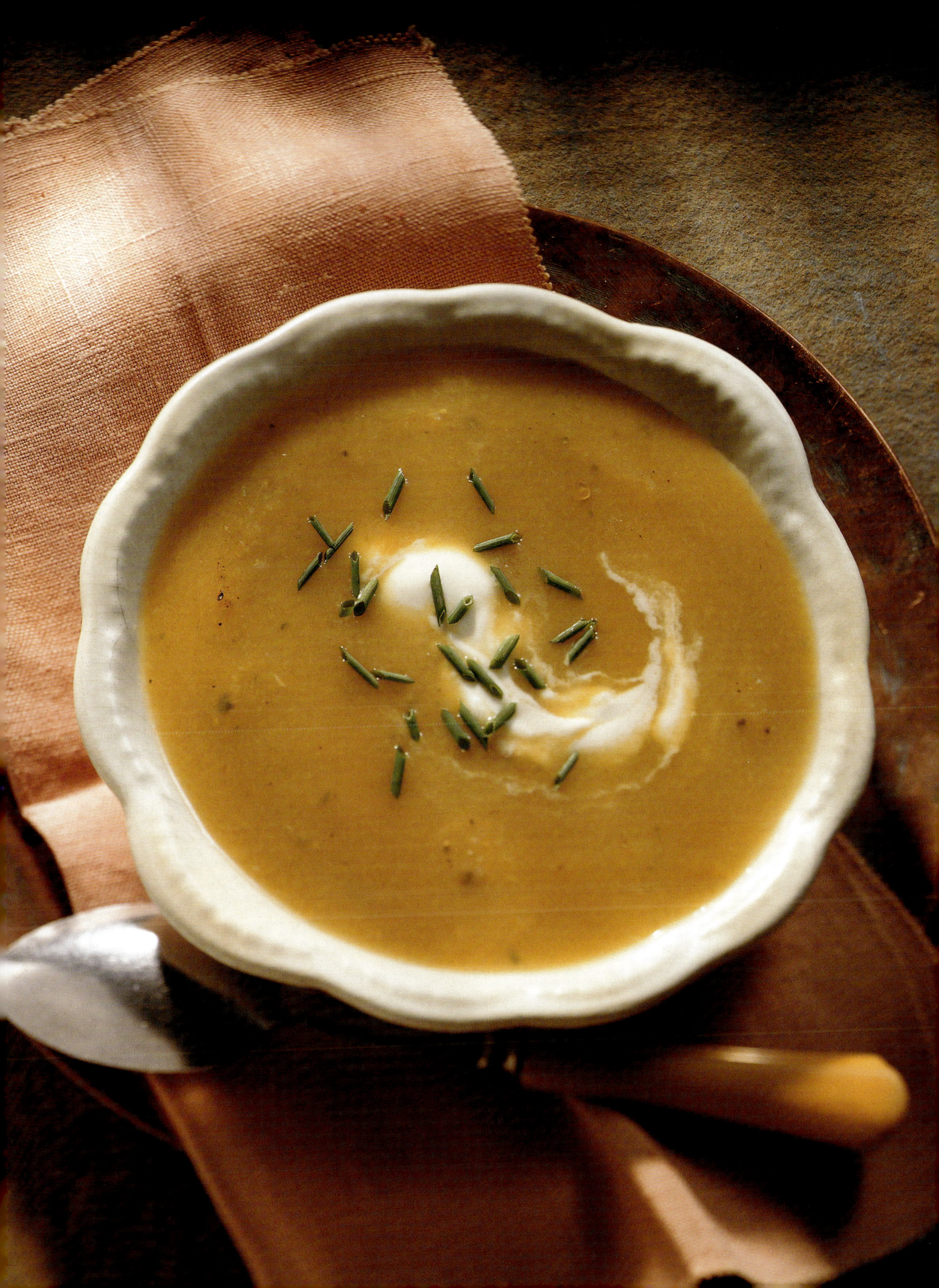

Spinach and Sorrel Soup

Sorrel and spinach make a good team in this French country soup. Sorrel contributes a refreshing tartness, while spinach ensures an appealing green color. (Sorrel turns yellowish green when cooked.) In classic French cooking, an extremely rich, luxurious sorrel soup is known as potage Germiny. *The rustic version that follows is much lighter.*

- 2 teaspoons butter
- 1 cup chopped scallions, white and light green parts only
- 2 medium potatoes, sliced
- 2 (14.5-oz.) cans reduced-sodium chicken broth
- 6 oz. baby spinach, stems trimmed
- 2 oz. sorrel, stems trimmed
- ½ cup reduced-fat sour cream
- ½ teaspoon salt
- ⅛ teaspoon freshly ground pepper
- ¼ cup chopped fresh chervil or parsley

❶ In 4- to 6-quart soup pot, heat butter over medium heat. Add scallions; cook 1½ to 2 minutes or until tender, stirring frequently. Add potatoes; stir to coat. Add broth; bring to a simmer. Reduce heat to low. Simmer, covered, 15 minutes.

❷ Stir in spinach and sorrel. Cook, covered, 5 to 10 minutes or until potatoes are tender and spinach and sorrel have wilted.

❸ Strain soup through colander into large bowl. Place solids in food processor; pulse several times until mixture breaks down into chunky puree. Return puree and broth to pot; heat through. Add sour cream; whisk to blend. Heat through, but do not boil. Season with salt and pepper. *(Soup can be prepared up to 2 days ahead. Cover and refrigerate.)* Ladle soup into bowls; garnish with chervil.

6 (1-cup) servings.

Preparation time: 20 minutes. Ready to serve: 45 minutes.

Per serving: 110 calories, 3.5 g total fat (2 g saturated fat), 10 mg cholesterol, 540 mg sodium, 2.5 g fiber.

CHEF'S NOTE:

- If sorrel is not available, leave it out. Compensate with additional spinach and season with a drop of lemon juice at the end.

CAULIFLOWER AND SPINACH CURRY

Light coconut milk enriches this basil-scented Southeast Asian curry, making it a satisfying vegetarian entrée. Serve over jasmine rice.

2	teaspoons vegetable oil
2	cups slivered onions
1 to 2	teaspoons Thai green curry paste
1	(14-oz.) can light unsweetened coconut milk
2	tablespoons low-sodium soy sauce
2	teaspoons packed brown sugar
1	(2-lb.) head cauliflower, cut into 1½-inch florets
2	tomatoes, seeded, coarsely chopped
1/3	cup slivered fresh Thai basil
6	oz. baby spinach
	Lime wedges

❶ In Dutch oven, heat oil over medium heat until hot. Add onions; cook 2 to 3 minutes or until tender, stirring frequently. Add curry paste; cook about 30 seconds or until fragrant, stirring constantly. Add coconut milk, soy sauce and brown sugar; bring to a simmer. Add cauliflower, tomatoes and basil; return to a simmer. Reduce heat to medium-low. Simmer, covered, 10 minutes or until cauliflower is tender.

❷ Add spinach to stew; cook 1 to 2 minutes or until spinach has wilted, stirring frequently. Serve with lime wedges.

6 (1-cup) servings.

Preparation time: 20 minutes. Ready to serve: 35 minutes.

Per serving: 105 calories, 5.5 g total fat (3 g saturated fat), 0 mg cholesterol, 260 mg sodium, 4.5 g fiber.

CHEF'S NOTES:

- Thai green curry paste is a convenient way to simplify the seasoning mix in this easy curry. You can find it (and light coconut milk) in the Asian section of most supermarkets, or in specialty stores. Curry paste is quite potent so be warned: a little goes a long way.
- Standard supermarket-variety sweet basil is fine for this recipe, but if available, use Thai basil.

Soups, Salads & Sides

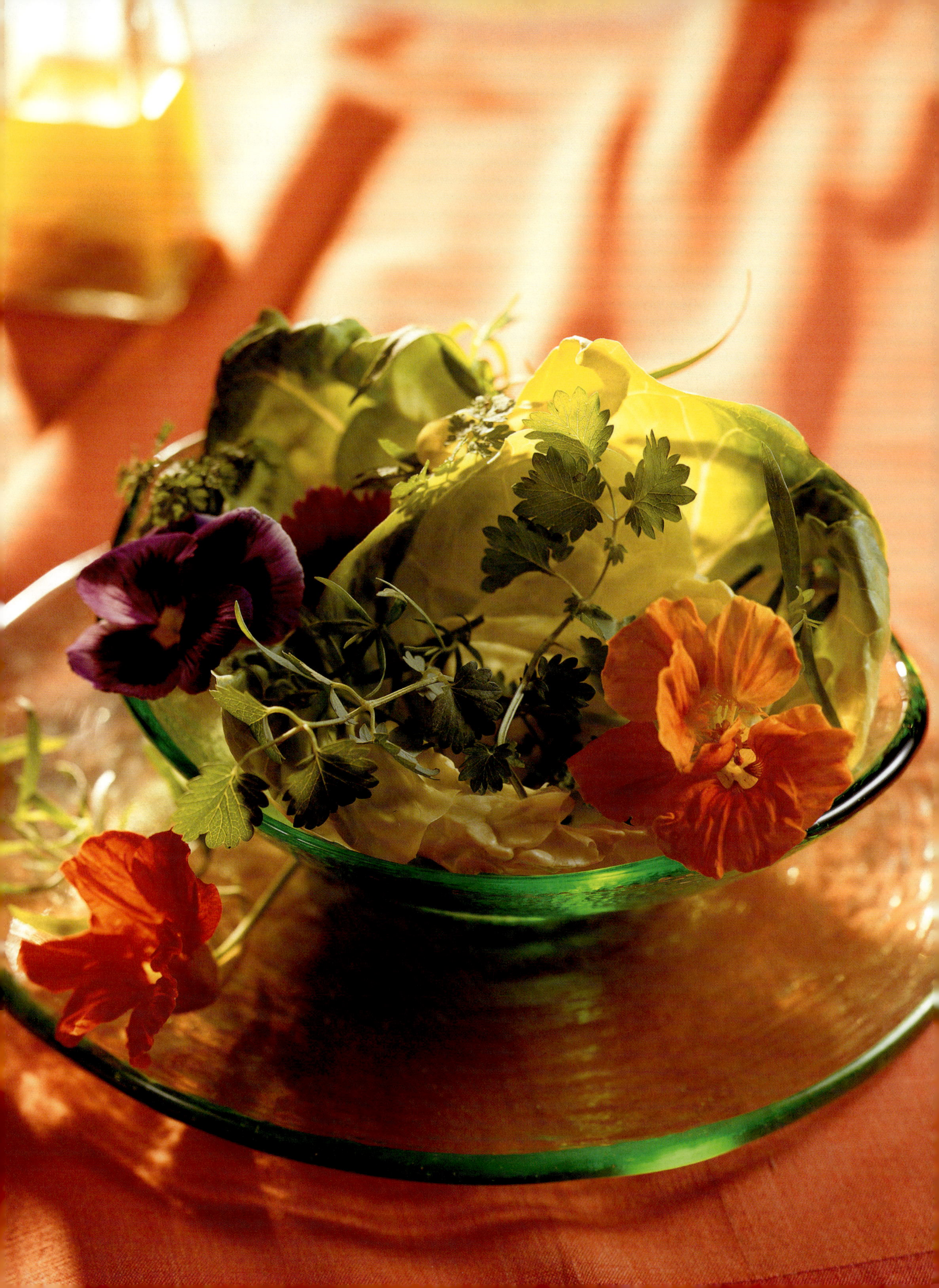

HERB GARDEN SALAD

Of course, fresh herbs make a great addition to any salad dressing, but supplementing salad greens with a lively and generous mixture of torn herb leaves is one of the best ways to give a salad a delightful herbal fragrance. To showcase the flavor of the herbs, use a delicate lettuce like Boston, rather than stronger-tasting mesclun greens.

VINAIGRETTE
- 4 teaspoons tarragon vinegar or white wine vinegar
- 2 tablespoons finely chopped shallots
- 1/2 teaspoon Dijon mustard
- 1/4 teaspoon salt
- 1/8 teaspoon freshly ground pepper
- Dash of sugar
- 1/4 cup extra-virgin olive oil

SALAD
- 1 garlic clove, halved
- 2 medium heads butterhead (Boston or Bibb) lettuce leaves, torn into bite-sized pieces (8 cups)
- 1 cup fresh Italian parsley leaves, torn into 1/2-inch pieces
- 1 cup assorted herb leaves, torn into 1/2-inch pieces (burnet, chervil, lovage, tarragon, etc.)
- 1/2 cup chopped chives
- 12 unsprayed edible flowers (chive blossoms, nasturtiums, etc.), if desired

❶ In small jar with tight-fitting lid, combine vinegar, shallots, mustard, salt, pepper and sugar. Cover jar; shake to blend. Add oil; shake to blend. *(Dressing can be prepared up to 2 days ahead. Cover and refrigerate.)*

❷ Rub large salad bowl with cut sides of garlic clove. Place lettuce, parsley, assorted herbs and chives in bowl. Just before serving, drizzle dressing over salad; toss well. Garnish with flowers.

6 (2-cup) servings.

Preparation time: 25 minutes. Ready to serve: 25 minutes.

Per serving: 95 calories, 9.5 g total fat (1.5 g saturated fat), 0 mg cholesterol, 115 mg sodium, 1.5 g fiber.

CHEF'S NOTE:
- To keep washed greens and herbs fresh for up to 1 hour, place a damp kitchen towel over the salad bowl. For longer storage, refrigerate salad for up to 8 hours. If there is not enough room in the refrigerator for a large salad bowl, keep salad cool for several hours by placing a nonwooden salad bowl in a larger pan of ice water.

Herbed Goat Cheese Mashed Potatoes

Goat cheese and fresh herbs dress up a comforting dish of mashed potatoes. This is a nice side dish with chicken or lamb.

2	lb. Yukon Gold potatoes, peeled, cut into 2-inch chunks
8	garlic cloves, peeled
¾	cup reduced-fat milk
2	tablespoons extra-virgin olive oil
4	oz. creamy goat cheese, cut into small pieces
¼	cup chopped scallions
3	tablespoons chopped fresh parsley
3	tablespoons chopped fresh chives
½	teaspoon salt
¼	teaspoon freshly ground pepper

❶ In large pot, combine potatoes and garlic. Cover with lightly salted water. Bring to a boil over medium-high heat. Reduce heat to medium-low. Simmer, covered, 15 to 20 minutes or until tender. Drain potatoes and return to pot. Shake pot over low heat 1 minute or until potatoes dry slightly. Remove pot from heat.

❷ Meanwhile, in 1-cup glass measure, combine milk and oil; microwave on High power 1 to 2 minutes or until steaming. (Or heat milk mixture in small saucepan.)

❸ Add cheese to potatoes; mash with potato masher. Gradually stir in hot milk mixture to make smooth puree. Gently fold in scallions, parsley, chives, salt and pepper.

6 (¾-cup) servings.

Preparation time: 20 minutes. Ready to serve: 40 minutes.

Per serving: 230 calories, 9.5 g total fat (4 g saturated fat), 20 mg cholesterol, 285 mg sodium, 3 g fiber.

CHEF'S NOTE:

- To keep mashed potatoes warm until serving time, set the pan in a larger pan of barely simmering water; place a piece of parchment or waxed paper on the surface of the potatoes. You can hold the potatoes like this for up to 1 hour.

ASPARAGUS SALAD WITH MINT AND ALMONDS

During asparagus season, serve this prized vegetable as a special course. A light lemon vinaigrette highlighted with mint and toasted almonds showcases asparagus beautifully.

LEMON DRESSING
- 1 small garlic clove, crushed
- 1/4 teaspoon salt
- 2 tablespoons fresh lemon juice
- 3 tablespoons extra-virgin olive oil
- 1/2 teaspoon honey
- 1/8 teaspoon freshly ground pepper

SALAD
- 1 1/2 lb. asparagus, stem ends snapped
- 3 tablespoons chopped scallions
- 3 tablespoons slivered fresh mint
- 3 tablespoons slivered almonds (1 oz.), toasted*

❶ Using mortar and pestle or with side of chef's knife, mash garlic and salt into a paste. Transfer to small bowl. Whisk in lemon juice, oil, honey and pepper.

❷ Place asparagus in steamer basket over boiling water. Steam, covered, 3 to 6 minutes or until tender-crisp. Rinse thoroughly under cold running water. Drain and pat dry.

❸ To serve, arrange asparagus on serving platter. Spoon dressing over top. Sprinkle with scallions, mint and almonds.

TIP *To toast slivered almonds, spread in small baking pan. Bake at 375°F for 5 to 10 minutes or until golden and fragrant. Transfer to small bowl and let cool.

4 servings.

Preparation time: 20 minutes. Ready to serve: 25 minutes.

Per serving: 155 calories, 13.5 g total fat (1.5 g saturated fat), 0 mg cholesterol, 150 mg sodium, 2.5 g fiber.

Couscous Salad with Apricots, Pine Nuts and Mint

When you are cooking outdoors, coordinating side dishes can be tricky. You can avoid running between the outdoor grill and kitchen stove if you opt for a light but substantial grain salad instead of a traditional hot side dish. This couscous salad, which features a distinctive apricot dressing, is good with grilled chicken or lamb.

APRICOT DRESSING
- ¼ cup apricot nectar
- 2 tablespoons extra-virgin olive oil
- 4 teaspoons white wine vinegar
- ½ teaspoon honey
- 2 (¼-inch) slices fresh ginger, crushed
- 1 medium garlic clove, crushed
- ¼ teaspoon salt
- ⅛ teaspoon freshly ground pepper

SALAD
- 1 cup couscous
- ¼ cup chopped dried apricots
- ¼ teaspoon salt
- 1¼ cups hot water
- ½ cup trimmed chopped scallions
- ⅓ cup slivered fresh mint
- ¼ cup pine nuts, toasted (see TIP, page 54)

❶ In blender, combine apricot nectar, oil, vinegar, honey, ginger, garlic, ¼ teaspoon salt and pepper; cover and process until blended. *(Dressing can be prepared up to 2 days ahead. Cover and refrigerate.)*

❷ In large bowl, combine couscous, dried apricots and ¼ teaspoon salt. Pour in hot water. Let stand 20 minutes or until couscous is tender and water has been absorbed.

❸ Add scallions, mint and dressing to couscous mixture; toss gently to mix. Transfer to serving bowl and sprinkle with pine nuts. *(Salad can be held at room temperature for up to 45 minutes.)*

6 (¾-cup) servings.

Preparation time: 30 minutes. Ready to serve: 40 minutes.

Per serving: 205 calories, 8 g total fat (1 g saturated fat), 0 mg cholesterol, 203 mg sodium, 3 g fiber.

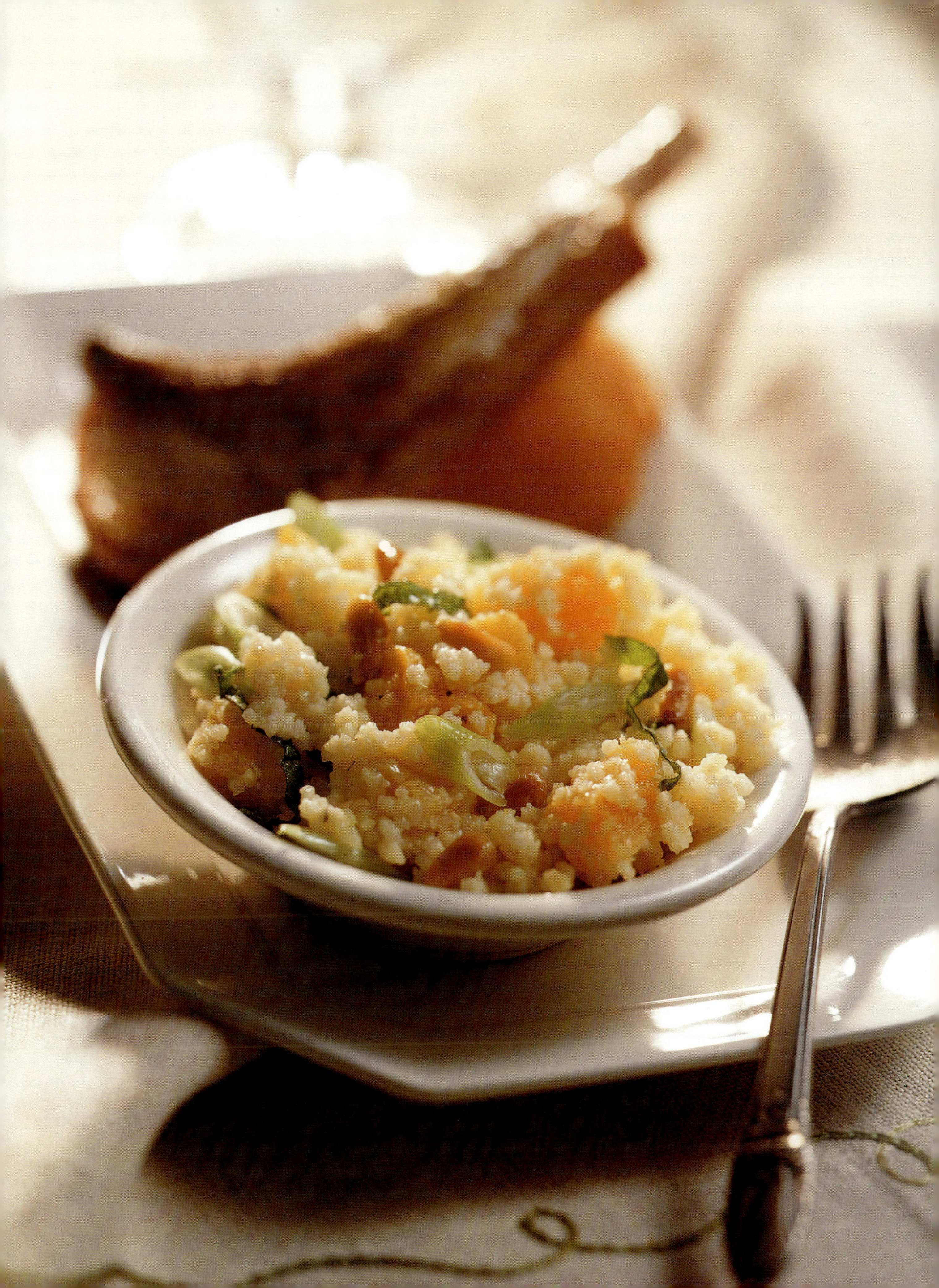

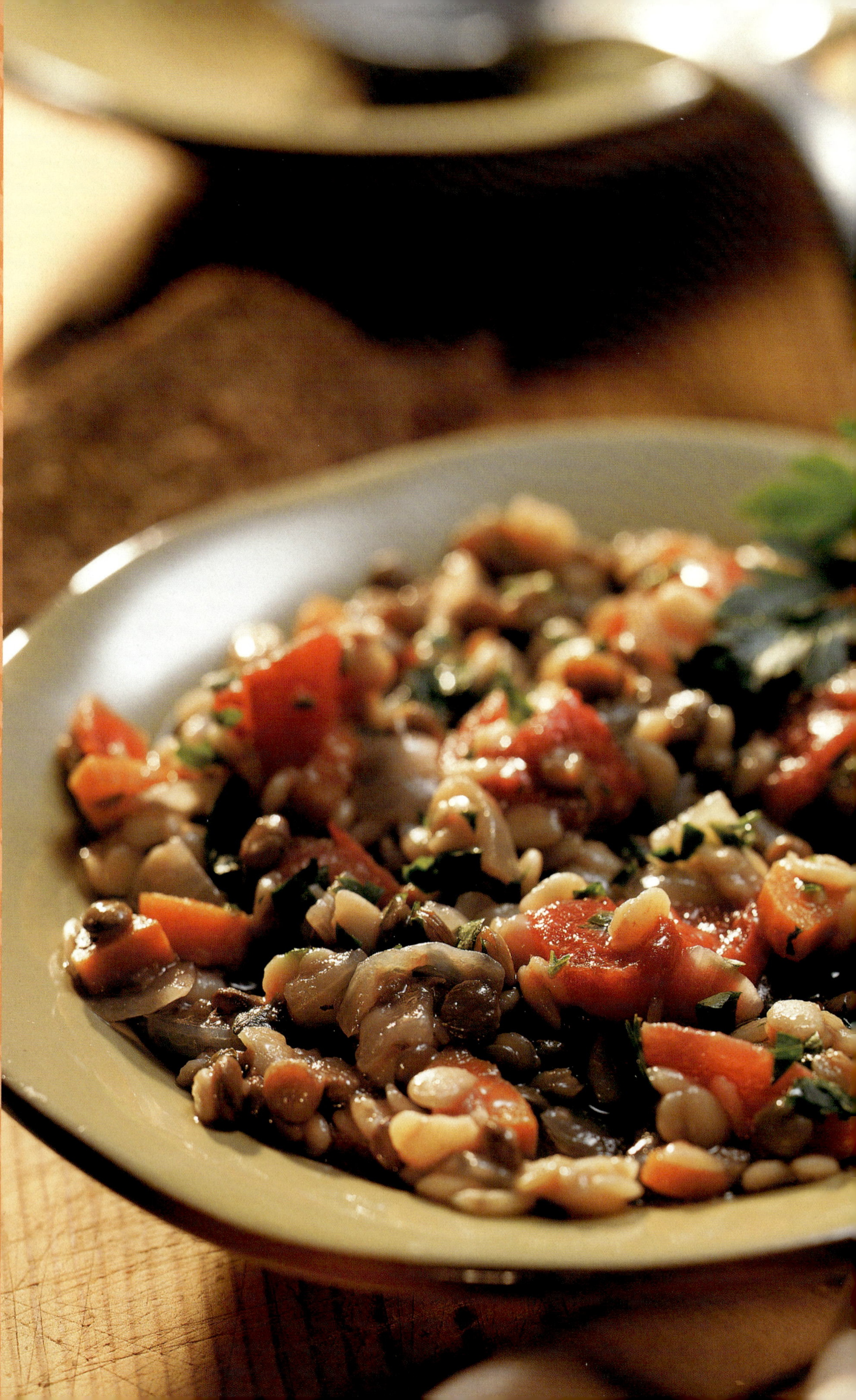

Pasta, Grains & Beans

Pasta with a heady basil pesto sauce is now a familiar and much-loved combination in America. But the possibilities for using herbs to enhance a variety of wholesome pasta, grain and bean dishes go much further. This chapter celebrates "pyramid" eating at its best.

Lenti-Orzo Stew, page 104

Penne with Pesto, Potatoes and Green Beans

To make this simple pasta dish more substantial and nutritious, I have taken a cue from Liguria in the northern Mediterranean region of Italy and added potatoes and green beans. As a bonus, the vegetable-steaming water produces a flavorful and vitamin-packed broth that is perfect for thinning and warming the pesto.

1	recipe *Health-Conscious Basil Pesto* (page 156)
4	small red potatoes, cut into ¾-inch chunks
1	cup green beans, tough ends trimmed, cut in half crosswise
¼	teaspoon salt
1	(12-oz.) pkg. penne

❶ Prepare Health-Conscious Basil Pesto; set aside.

❷ Place green beans in steamer basket over boiling water; season with salt. Cover; steam 8 to 10 minutes or until tender. Repeat for potatoes, steaming 10 to 12 minutes. (Be careful not to let the water run dry.) Transfer vegetables to large bowl; keep warm. Measure ⅓ cup of the water remaining in the bottom of the steamer; stir into Health-Conscious Pesto.

❸ Meanwhile, cook penne according to package directions. Drain and place in bowl with vegetables. Add pesto; toss well.

4 servings.

Preparation time: 25 minutes. Ready to serve: 35 minutes.

Per serving: 555 calories, 12.5 g total fat (3 g saturated fat), 5.5 mg cholesterol, 1,220 mg sodium, 7 g fiber.

Savory Noodle Kugel

This easy noodle pudding is pure comfort food. A sprinkling of grated lemon peel in the baking dish provides a subtle infusion of lemon that complements the fresh herbs.

- 2 teaspoons freshly grated lemon peel (yellow portion only)
- 2 slices whole wheat sandwich bread, crusts removed, torn into large pieces
- 2 teaspoons extra-virgin olive oil
- 1 (8-oz.) pkg. wide or medium egg noodles
- 2 large eggs
- 1½ cups reduced-fat (1 percent) cottage cheese
- 1 cup reduced-fat sour cream
- ¾ teaspoon salt
- ¼ teaspoon freshly ground pepper
- ½ cup trimmed chopped scallions
- 3 tablespoons chopped fresh parsley
- 3 tablespoons chopped fresh dill

❶ Heat oven to 325°F. Spray 2-quart glass casserole with cooking spray. Sprinkle with lemon peel; set aside.

❷ In food processor, grind bread into coarse crumbs. Add oil; pulse to blend.

❸ Cook noodles according to package directions. Drain thoroughly under cold running water.

❹ In large bowl, whisk eggs. Add cottage cheese, sour cream, salt and pepper; whisk until blended. Add scallions, parsley, dill and noodles; mix with rubber spatula. Scrape into casserole. Sprinkle evenly with reserved bread crumb mixture. (*Kugel can be made ahead to this point. Cover and refrigerate up to 8 hours.*)

❺ Bake kugel 35 to 45 minutes or until lightly browned and set. Let cool 5 minutes before serving.

4 servings.

Preparation time: 20 minutes. Ready to serve: 1 hour, 10 minutes.

Per serving: 435 calories, 12.5 g total fat (4.5 g saturated fat), 180 mg cholesterol, 1190 mg sodium, 3 g fiber.

CHEF'S NOTE:
- You can substitute ricotta for cottage cheese, and ½ cup chopped fresh basil for the dill and parsley.

PEANUT NOODLES

A spicy peanut butter dressing creates a satisfying Asian noodle salad. The vibrant garnish of herbs and cucumber brings this salad to life.

DRESSING
- ½ cup natural peanut butter*
- ⅓ cup reduced-fat firm silken tofu
- ¼ cup low-sodium soy sauce
- 3 tablespoons fresh lime juice
- 3 garlic cloves, minced
- 2 tablespoons packed brown sugar
- ¾ teaspoon crushed red pepper

SALAD
- 1 (12-oz.) pkg. spaghetti
- 2 teaspoons toasted peanut oil or toasted sesame oil
- 1 cup grated carrots
- 1 small red bell pepper, finely diced
- ¾ cup grated seedless (English) cucumber
- ¼ cup slivered fresh cilantro
- ¼ cup slivered fresh mint
- 4 scallions, chopped
- 3 tablespoons unsalted dry-roasted peanuts, chopped
- Lime wedges

❶ In food processor, combine peanut butter, tofu, soy sauce, lime juice, garlic, brown sugar and red pepper; process until smooth and creamy, stopping once or twice to scrape down sides of work bowl. Set aside. (*Dressing can be made ahead. Cover and refrigerate up to 2 days.*)

❷ Cook spaghetti according to package directions. Drain and rinse with cold running water. Drain again, shaking colander to release excess water. Transfer to large bowl. Drizzle with oil and toss to coat.

❸ Add carrot and bell pepper to spaghetti. Add dressing; toss to coat. Transfer to large shallow serving bowl. Sprinkle with cucumber, cilantro, mint, scallions and peanuts. Garnish with lime wedges.

TIP *Healthful silken tofu stretches the peanut butter and gives it a velvety consistency. Look for peanut butter labeled as natural; because it is not homogenized, it does not contain *trans* fatty acids.

6 (1-cup) servings.

Preparation time: 30 minutes. Ready to serve: 40 minutes.

Per serving: 445 calories, 16 g total fat (3 g saturated fat), 0 mg cholesterol, 750 mg sodium, 5.5 g fiber.

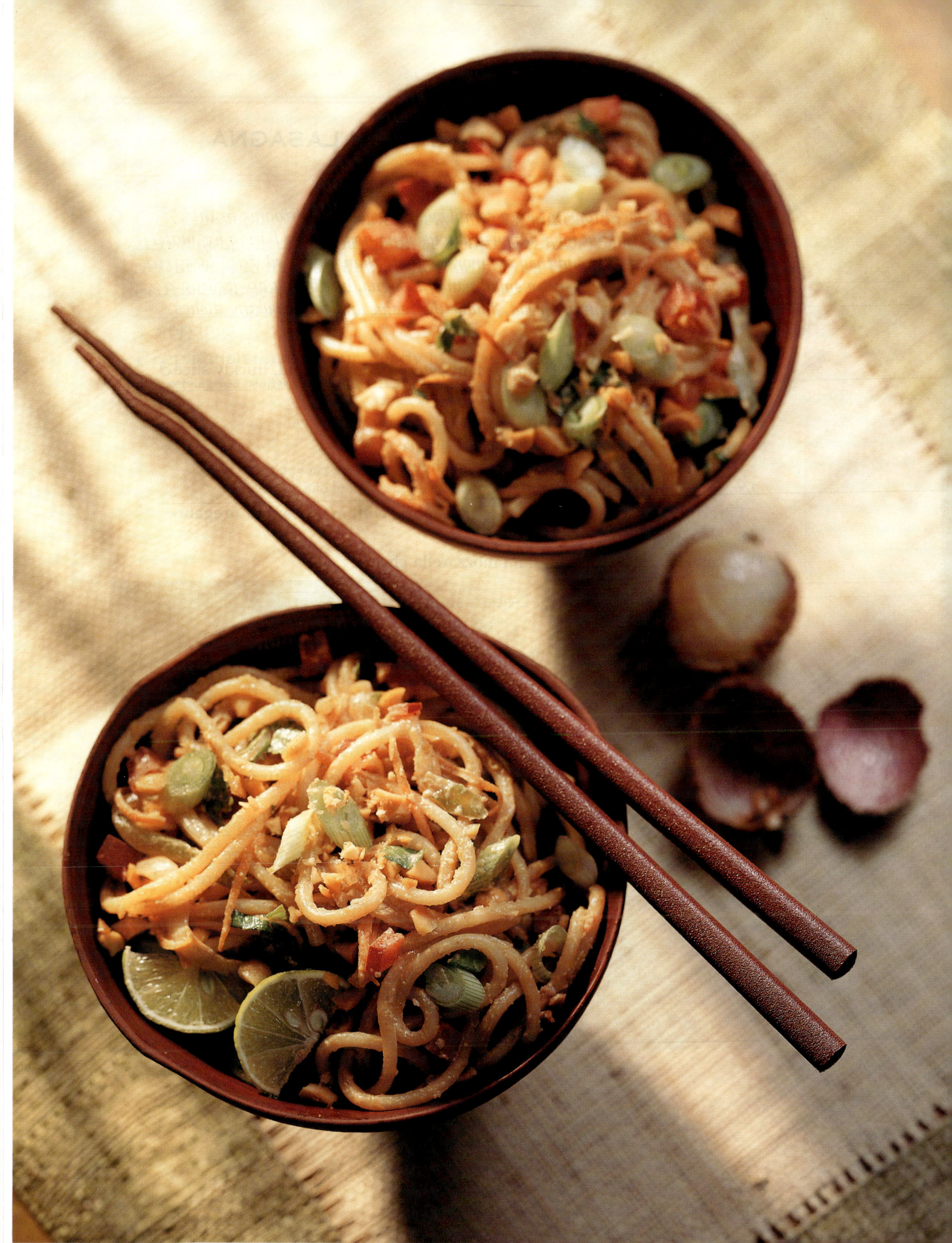

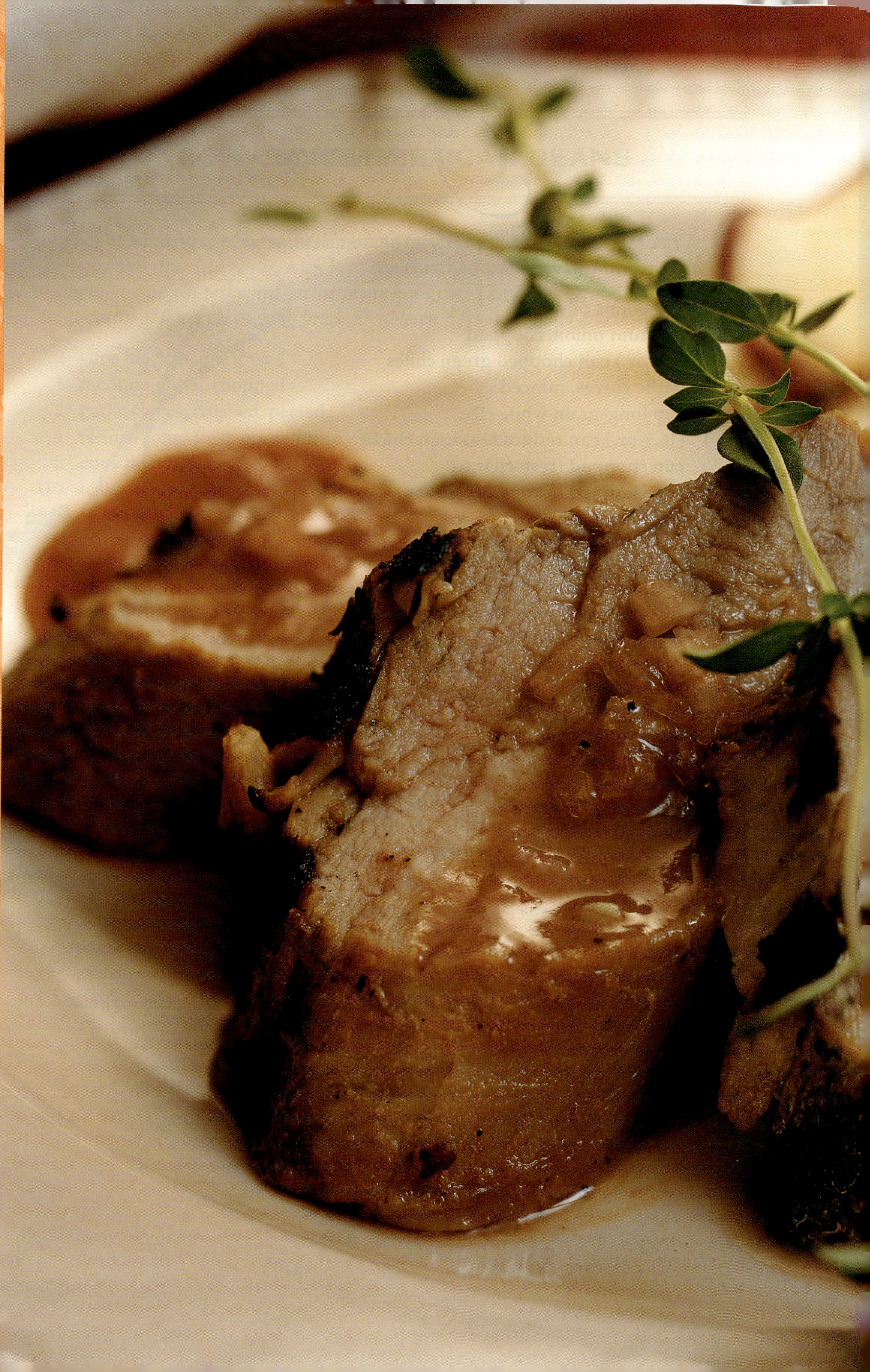

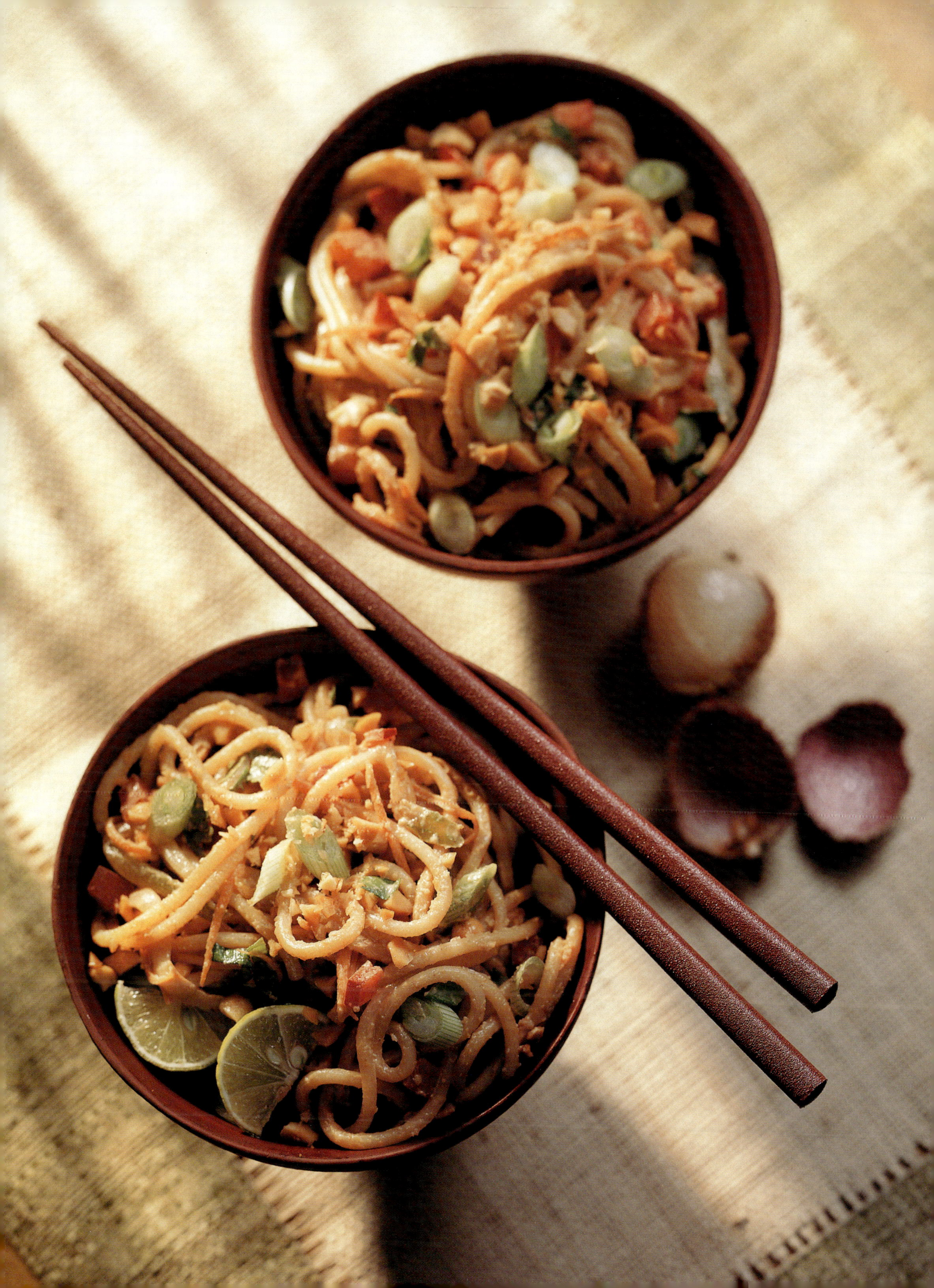

Mushroom-Marjoram Lasagna

A marjoram-laced tomato sauce complements meaty mushrooms in this simple vegetarian lasagna. Oven-ready lasagna noodles are handy for making a short-cut lasagna, and they are more delicate than standard dried lasagna noodles. This recipe makes a small pan of lasagna, but if you are feeding a large group or planning ahead, double the recipe and use 2 baking dishes.

- 2 teaspoons olive oil
- 1 lb. crimini or baby bella mushrooms, stem ends trimmed, thickly sliced
- 1/2 teaspoon salt
- 1 large egg
- 1 cup part-skim ricotta cheese
- 1 cup (4 oz.) freshly grated Parmesan cheese
- 1/4 teaspoon freshly ground pepper
- 1 recipe *Quick Tomato Sauce* (page 158), made with marjoram or oregano
- 8 oven-ready lasagna noodles (5 oz.)
- 1 1/2 cups (6 oz.) grated part-skim mozzarella cheese

❶ Heat oven to 400°F. Spray 2-quart shallow glass casserole with nonstick cooking spray.

❷ In large nonstick skillet, heat 1 teaspoon oil over medium-high heat until hot. Add half of the mushrooms and 1/4 teaspoon of the salt; cook 3 to 5 minutes or until browned and tender, stirring and shaking skillet occasionally. Transfer mushrooms to plate. Add remaining 1 teaspoon oil to skillet; repeat with remaining mushrooms and 1/4 teaspoon salt.

❸ In medium bowl, whisk egg and ricotta until smooth. Stir in 1/2 cup of the Parmesan cheese and pepper.

❹ Spread about 1/3 cup Quick Tomato Sauce in casserole. Place 2 lasagna noodles on tomato sauce. Spread about 1/2 cup ricotta mixture over noodles. Scatter one-third of the mushrooms over ricotta mixture and sprinkle with 1/3 cup mozzarella cheese. Top with 1/3 cup tomato sauce. Add another layer of noodles and repeat layering with ricotta mixture, mushrooms, mozzarella and tomato sauce 2 more times. Finish with layer of noodles; spread remaining tomato sauce evenly over top. (Lasagna can made ahead to this point. Refrigerate and cover up to 2 days. Alternatively, freeze up to 3 months. Thaw in refrigerator before continuing.)

❺ Cover lasagna with aluminum foil. Bake 30 minutes. Sprinkle with remaining 1/2 cup Parmesan and 1/2 cup mozzarella. Bake, uncovered, an additional 15 minutes or until hot and bubbly. Let stand 5 minutes before cutting and serving.

4 servings.

Preparation time: 1 hour. Ready to serve: 1 hour, 45 minutes.

Per serving: 630 calories, 29 g total fat (14.5 g saturated fat), 115 mg cholesterol, 1,535 mg sodium, 5 g fiber.

CHEF'S NOTE:
- If you prefer a meat lasagna, brown 8 oz. lean ground beef; drain and stir into tomato sauce before assembling lasagna.

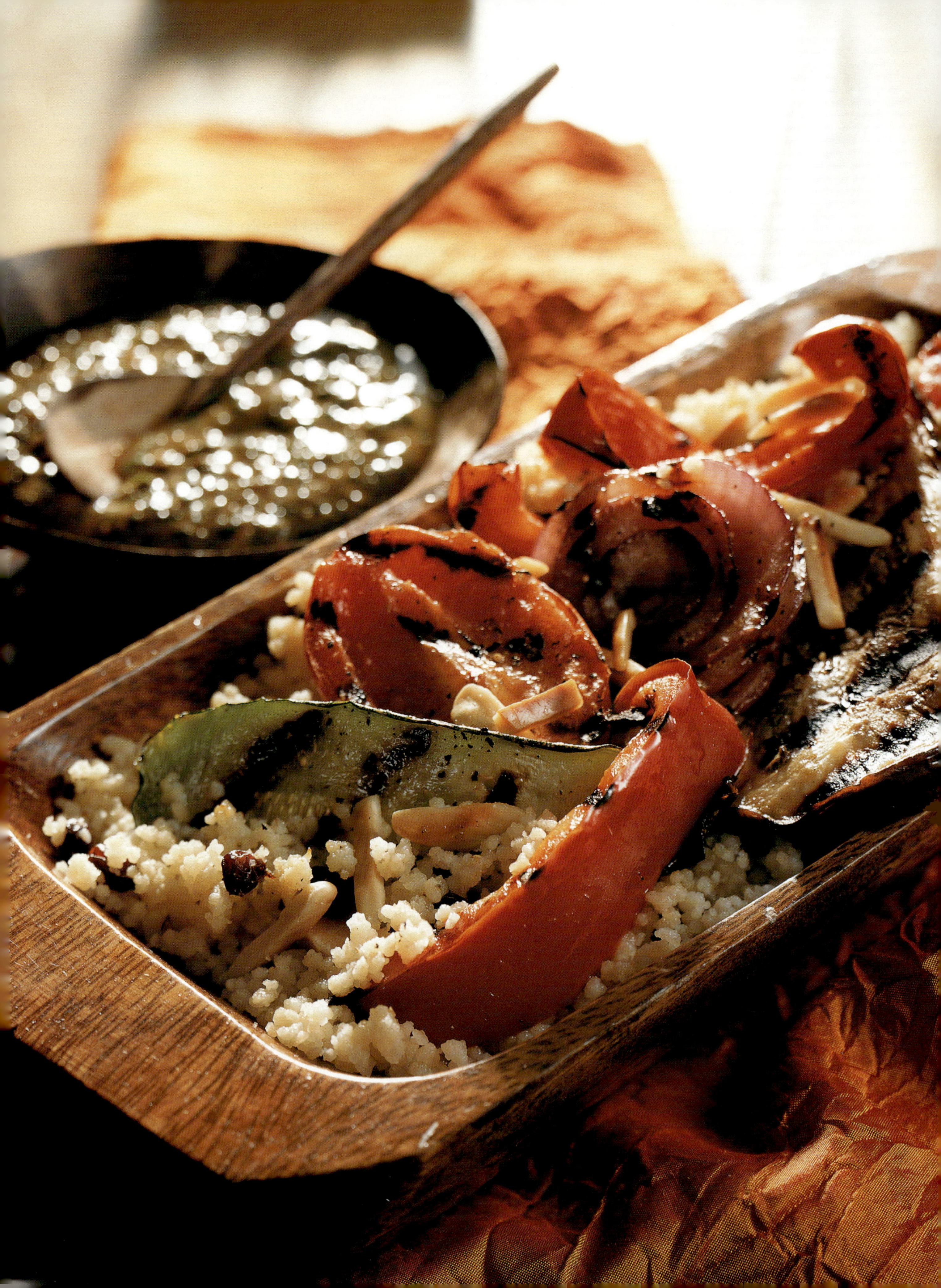

Couscous with Grilled Vegetables and Charmoula Sauce

Here is an elegant entrée for entertaining a group that includes both vegetarians and nonvegetarians — double the recipe, and supplement the vegetables with grilled chicken or tuna.

VEGETABLES
- 1 recipe *Moroccan Charmoula Sauce* (page 166)
- 1 (¾-lb.) eggplant, cut into ⅜-inch slices
- 1 medium red bell pepper, seeded, cut into 8 wedges
- 1 medium zucchini, cut into ⅜-inch slices
- 1 large red onion, cut into ⅜-inch slices
- 6 plum tomatoes, halved lengthwise
- Olive oil nonstick cooking spray
- ½ teaspoon salt
- ½ teaspoon freshly ground pepper

COUSCOUS
- 2 cups vegetable or reduced-sodium chicken broth
- 2 teaspoons extra-virgin olive oil
- ¼ teaspoon salt
- ¼ teaspoon freshly ground pepper
- 1 cup couscous
- ⅓ cup dried currants
- ⅓ cup slivered almonds, toasted (see TIP, page 164)

❶ Prepare Charmoula Sauce; set aside.

❷ Heat grill. Spray both sides of eggplant, bell pepper, zucchini, onion and tomatoes with olive oil nonstick cooking spray. Sprinkle with ½ teaspoon salt and ½ teaspoon pepper.

❸ Place vegetables on gas grill over medium-high heat or on charcoal grill 4 to 6 inches from medium-high coals. Cook 6 to 10 minutes, turning frequently and removing vegetables when they are browned and tender. (If desired, remove charred tomato skins.) Keep warm.

❹ In medium saucepan, combine 2 cups broth, 2 teaspoons oil, ¼ teaspoon salt and ¼ teaspoon pepper. Bring to a simmer. Remove from heat. Stir in couscous and currants; cover and let stand 5 minutes to plump. Fluff couscous with fork.

❺ Meanwhile, in small saucepan, heat sauce over medium heat until thoroughly heated, stirring occasionally.

❻ To serve, mound couscous in center of large platter. Surround with grilled vegetables. Drizzle sauce over vegetables and couscous. Sprinkle with almonds.

4 servings.

Preparation time: 30 minutes. Ready to serve: 50 minutes.

Per serving: 445 calories, 15 g total fat (2 g saturated fat), 0 mg cholesterol, 1,215 mg sodium, 9.5 g fiber.

Pasta, Grains & Beans

Butternut Squash Ravioli

This squash, prosciutto and leek filling is incredibly rich-tasting, yet surprisingly low in fat. Although there are several parts to this dish, it is simple to serve because most of the preparation can be done ahead.

RAVIOLI
- 2 teaspoons olive oil
- 1 medium leek, trimmed, diced
- 3 tablespoons thinly sliced prosciutto, finely diced
- 12 oz. butternut squash, seeded, cubed (3/4 inch)
- 1/3 cup vegetable or reduced-sodium chicken broth
- 1/4 cup part-skim ricotta cheese
- 1 egg yolk
- 1/8 teaspoon freshly ground pepper
- 1 (12-oz.) package wonton wrappers

ROSEMARY-INFUSED BROTH
- 3 cups reduced-sodium chicken broth
- 6 medium garlic cloves, crushed
- 4 (4 1/2-inch) fresh rosemary sprigs
- Dash of crushed red pepper
- 2 teaspoons butter
- 2 teaspoons chopped fresh rosemary
- 1/4 cup (1 oz.) freshly grated Parmesan cheese

❶ In medium saucepan, heat oil over medium heat until hot. Add leek and prosciutto; cook 1 1/2 to 2 minutes or until tender, stirring frequently. Add squash and 1/3 cup broth; bring to a simmer. Reduce heat to low; simmer, covered, 15 minutes or until squash is tender. (Check pan occasionally; add a little water if necessary.) Uncover; cook an additional 5 to 7 minutes or until liquid has evaporated, shaking pan occasionally. Remove from heat. Mash squash coarsely with potato masher or fork. Transfer to medium bowl and let cool completely. Stir in ricotta, egg yolk and pepper.

❷ Lay about 12 wonton wrappers on work surface. Using pastry brush, moisten edges with water. Place heaping teaspoonful squash filling in center of each wrapper. Top each with another wonton wrapper. With fingers, press wontons together around mounds of filling. Using a 2 1/2-inch serrated round cutter, cut out circles, discarding trimmings. Set ravioli on baking sheet. Repeat with remaining wontons and filling. (*Ravioli can be made ahead. Refrigerate and cover 8 hours.*)

❸ In medium saucepan, combine 3 cups broth, garlic, rosemary sprigs and red pepper; bring to a boil over medium-high heat. Reduce heat to medium; simmer, uncovered, 10 minutes or until reduced to 2 cups. Strain broth, pressing solids to extract flavor. (*Infused broth can be made ahead. Cover and refrigerate up to 2 days.*)

❹ To cook ravioli, bring large wide pot of lightly salted water to a boil over medium-high heat. In large skillet, bring infused broth to a simmer. Reduce heat to very low; stir butter into broth and keep warm. Drop about 8 ravioli into boiling water; cook about 2 minutes or until tender and ravioli float to top. With slotted spoon, retrieve ravioli; slip into broth in skillet. Repeat with remaining ravioli. Divide ravioli and broth among warm deep pasta plates. Sprinkle with chopped rosemary and Parmesan cheese.

4 servings (24 ravioli).

Preparation time: 50 minutes. Ready to serve: 1 hour, 10 minutes.

Per serving: 365 calories, 11.5 g total fat (5 g saturated fat), 100 mg cholesterol, 690 mg sodium, 4 g fiber.

CHEF'S NOTE:
- These ravioli freeze well. Place in freezer in a single layer on a baking sheet until frozen. Transfer ravioli to a plastic food bag and seal. Store in freezer up to 3 months.

Pasta, Grains & Beans

Lentil-Orzo Stew

I started making this hearty, one-pot meal when I was cooking in a bare-bones studio kitchen while vacationing in Crete. The mini-mart in the tranquil seaside village carried more suntan lotion and beach supplies than food, but I could always count on finding lentils, orzo, tomatoes, garlic and great olive oil. The hills where we enjoyed fabulous hikes were fragrant with wild thyme. Serve this stew in wide pasta bowls accompanied with toasted country bread and some good olive oil for dipping.

1 tablespoon olive oil	1¼ cups orzo
2 cups onions, chopped	1 (14.5-oz.) can diced tomatoes, undrained
1 cup finely chopped carrots	
6 garlic cloves, minced	¾ teaspoon salt
1¼ cups brown lentils, rinsed	¼ teaspoon freshly ground pepper
1 tablespoon chopped fresh thyme or 1 teaspoon dried	2 to 3 tablespoons fresh lemon juice
6 cups vegetable or reduced-sodium chicken broth	2 teaspoons butter
½ cup water	⅓ cup chopped fresh Italian parsley
1 bay leaf	

❶ Heat oil in large pot or Dutch oven over medium heat until hot. Add onions and carrots; cook 4 to 6 minutes or until tender, stirring frequently. Add garlic; cook and stir 1 minute. Stir in lentils and thyme. Add broth and water. Bring to a boil. Reduce heat to low; simmer, covered, 20 minutes.

❷ Add orzo; simmer, covered, 15 minutes or until lentils and orzo are almost tender, stirring occasionally.

❸ Add tomatoes; simmer, covered, 10 to 15 minutes or until lentils and orzo are tender, stirring occasionally. (Add about ½ cup water if stew begins to stick.) Remove and discard bay leaf.

❹ Stir in salt and pepper (*Stew can be made ahead. Cover and refrigerate up to 2 days. Reheat over medium-low heat, adding enough water to achieve stew-like consistency.*) Stir in lemon juice, butter and parsley.

8 (1⅓-cup) servings.

Preparation time: 20 minutes. Ready to serve: 1 hour, 15 minutes.

Per serving: 270 calories, 4.5 g total fat (1.5 g saturated fat), 5 mg cholesterol, 670 mg sodium, 10 g fiber.

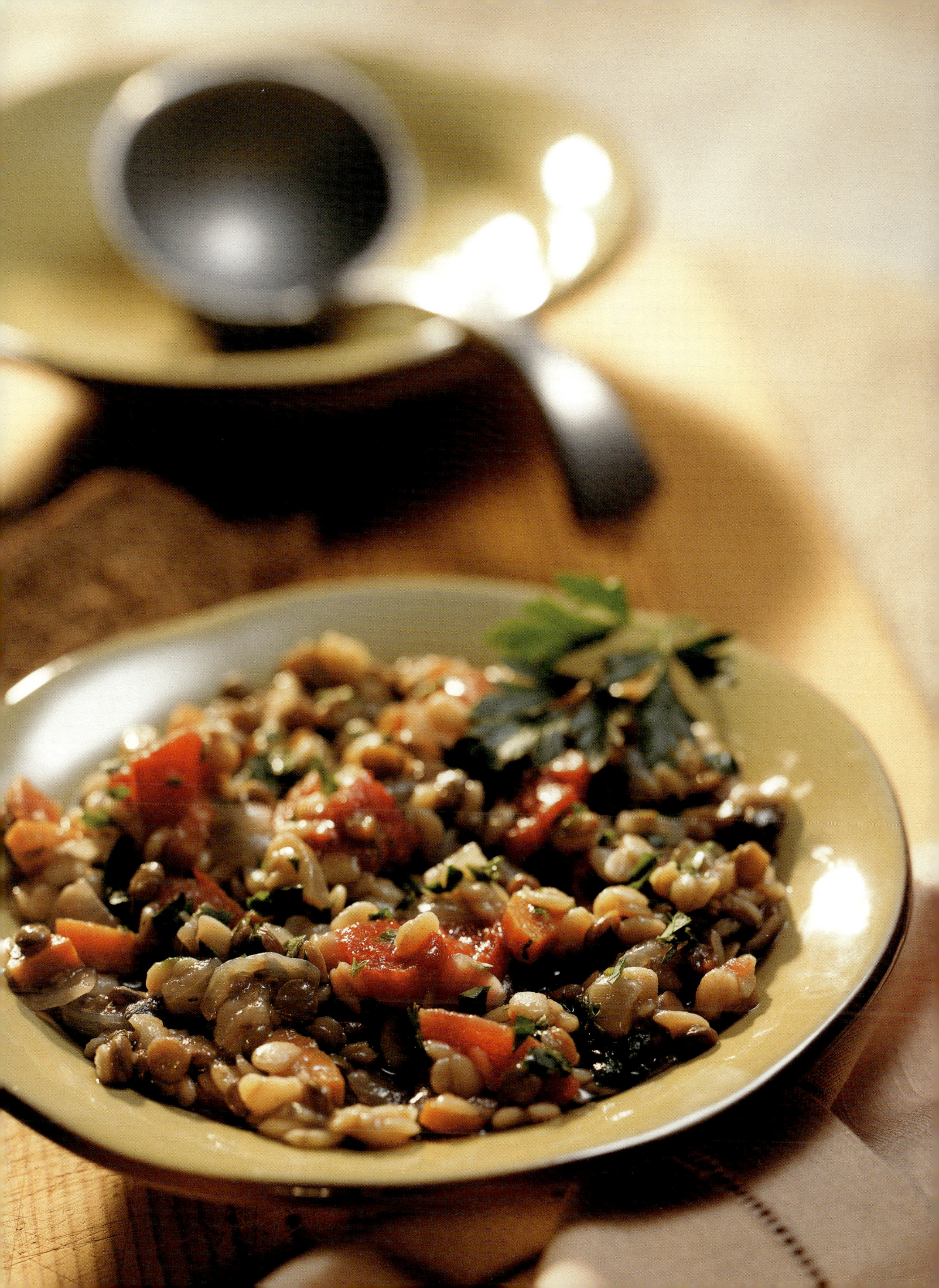

Penne with Eggplant, White Bean and Tomato Sauce

Comforting white beans add protein to this vegetarian pasta sauce. Feta cheese complements the eggplant and makes a nice change from Parmesan.

- 1 (28-oz.) can whole plum tomatoes, drained
- 2 tablespoons olive oil
- 4 garlic cloves, thinly sliced
- 1/8 teaspoon crushed red pepper
- 1 (3/4-lb.) eggplant, cut into 1-inch cubes
- 1 (19-oz.) can cannellini beans, drained, rinsed
- 1/2 cup slivered fresh basil
- 1/4 teaspoon salt
- 1/4 teaspoon freshly ground pepper
- 1 (1-lb.) pkg. penne pasta
- 1 cup (4 oz.) crumbled feta cheese

❶ Pass tomatoes through food mill into medium bowl. In large saucepan, heat 1 tablespoon oil over low heat until hot. Add garlic and red pepper; cook 1 to 2 minutes or until tender and fragrant but not browned, stirring constantly. Add tomatoes; bring to a simmer. Reduce heat to low; simmer, covered, 10 minutes.

❷ Meanwhile, in large nonstick skillet, heat remaining 1 tablespoon oil over medium-high heat until hot. Add eggplant; cook 4 to 6 minutes or until tender and browned, turning occasionally. Add tomato sauce; reduce heat to low. Cover loosely with aluminum foil; simmer about 10 minutes or until eggplant is very tender. Add beans; simmer about 5 minutes or until heated through. Stir in basil, salt and pepper.

❸ Cook penne according to package directions. Drain, reserving 1/2 cup cooking water. Place pasta in a large warm bowl. Add eggplant sauce and enough cooking water to moisten; toss to coat. Sprinkle with feta cheese.

4 servings.

Preparation time: 25 minutes. Ready to serve: 50 minutes.

Per serving: 790 calories, 18 g total fat (7 g saturated fat), 35 mg cholesterol, 1555 mg sodium, 13.5 g fiber.

Farro Risotto with Asparagus and Lemon

Farro is a grain from Italy. It has a nutty flavor that is reminiscent of barley, a chewy texture similar to wheat kernels. Farro is great in soups or in a distinctive risotto like this one. This risotto makes a good accompaniment to salmon or chicken, but can also be served as a vegetarian main dish.

- 2 (14.5-oz.) cans reduced-sodium chicken broth
- 1 cup water
- 1 lb. asparagus, cut into 1-inch pieces
- 1 tablespoon olive oil
- 1/2 cup trimmed chopped scallions
- 1 cup farro
- 1/2 cup (2 oz.) freshly grated Parmesan cheese
- 1/4 cup chopped fresh chives
- 2 teaspoons grated lemon peel
- 1 tablespoon fresh lemon juice
- Dash of salt
- 1/4 teaspoon freshly ground pepper

❶ In medium saucepan, combine broth and water; bring to a simmer over medium heat. Drop in asparagus; cook, uncovered, 2 to 4 minutes or until just tender. With slotted spoon, transfer asparagus to plate; set aside. Reduce heat to low; keep broth at low simmer.

❷ In Dutch oven, heat oil over medium heat until hot. Add scallions; cook about 1 minute or until tender, stirring frequently. Add farro; cook 30 seconds, stirring constantly. Add about 1 cup of the hot broth; cook 1 to 1 1/2 minutes or until most of the liquid has been absorbed, stirring constantly. Continue to simmer and stir about 20 minutes, adding broth about 1/2 cup at a time and waiting until most of it has been absorbed before adding more, until farro is tender and risotto has creamy consistency.

❸ Add asparagus; stir about 1 minute or until heated through. Remove risotto from heat; stir in Parmesan cheese, chives, lemon peel, lemon juice, salt and pepper.

4 (1-cup) servings.

Preparation time: 15 minutes. Ready to serve: 55 minutes.

Per serving: 325 calories, 9.5 g total fat (3.5 g saturated fat), 10 mg cholesterol, 765 mg sodium, 9 g fiber.

CHEF'S NOTE:

- You can find farro in natural food stores and Italian markets, or through mail order sources. If it is not available, substitute quick-cooking barley. Reduce water to 3/4 cup and simmer risotto about 15 minutes.

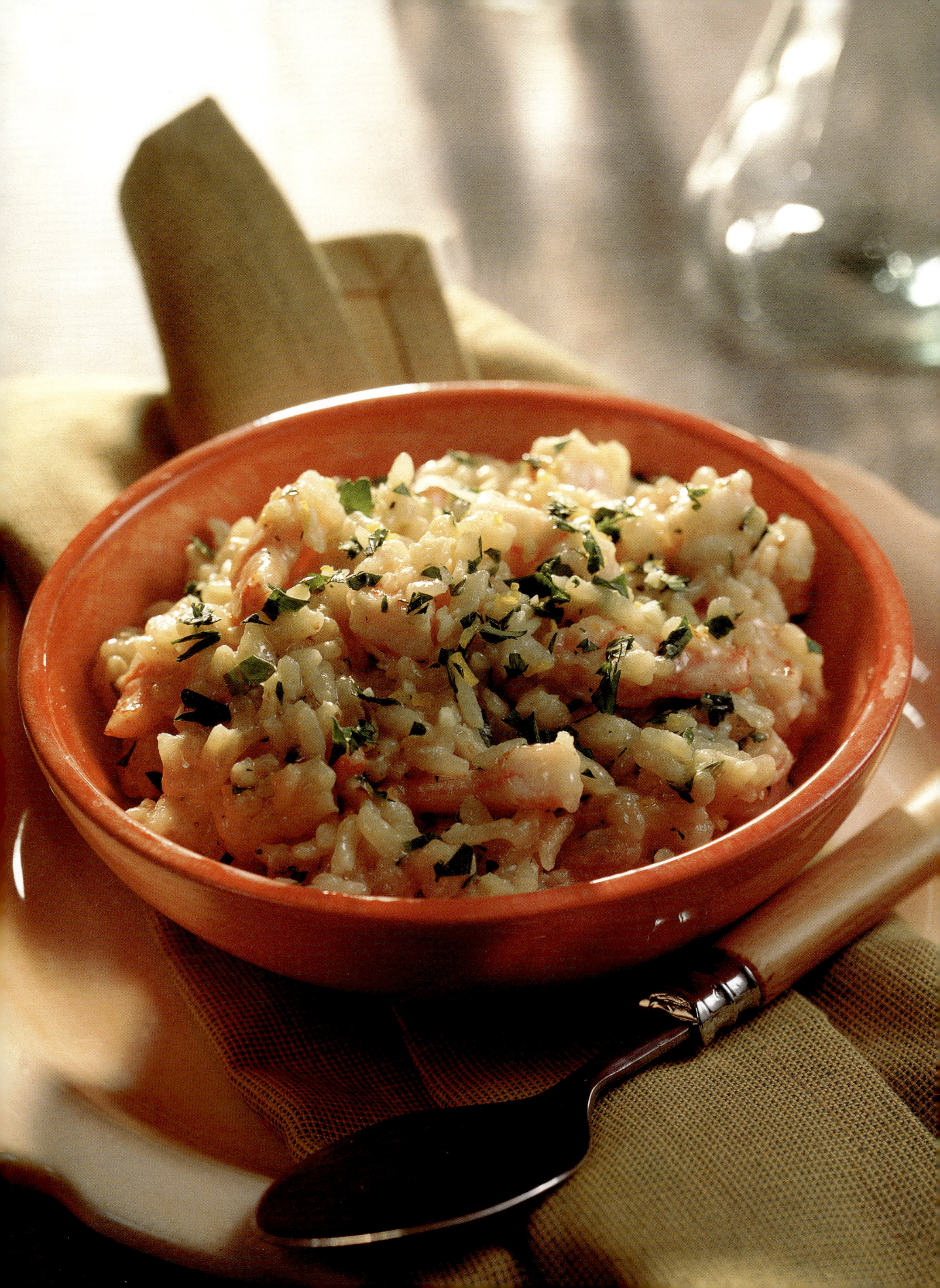

Shrimp Risotto with Gremolada

Here's one more example of how gremolada, the classic trio of parsley, lemon peel and garlic, gives a simple dish a special flourish.

- 1/3 cup chopped fresh Italian parsley
- 1 teaspoon freshly grated lemon peel
- 2 medium garlic cloves, minced
- 2 (14.5-oz.) cans reduced-sodium chicken broth
- 1/2 cup water
- 4 teaspoons olive oil
- 12 oz. shelled, deveined uncooked medium shrimp, each cut into 2 or 3 pieces
- 2 medium shallots, finely chopped
- Dash of crushed red pepper
- 1 cup Arborio rice
- 1/2 cup dry white wine
- 2 teaspoons fresh lemon juice
- 1/4 teaspoon freshly ground pepper

❶ In small bowl, combine parsley, lemon peel and garlic; toss with fork to mix.

❷ In large saucepan, combine chicken broth and water; bring to a simmer over medium heat. Reduce heat to low; keep broth at low simmer.

❸ In Dutch oven, heat 2 teaspoons oil over medium heat until hot. Add shrimp; cook about 2 minutes or until shrimp turn pink and opaque in center, stirring occasionally. Transfer to plate.

❹ Add remaining 2 teaspoons oil to Dutch oven. Add shallots and red pepper; cook 30 seconds to 1 minute or until shallots are tender, stirring constantly. Add rice; cook 30 seconds, stirring constantly. Add wine; cook about 30 seconds or until almost evaporated, stirring constantly. Add 1 cup of the hot broth; cook 1 to 2 minutes or until most of the liquid has been absorbed, stirring constantly. Continue to simmer 18 to 20 minutes, stirring frequently, adding broth about 1/2 cup at a time and waiting until most of it has been absorbed before adding more, until rice is just tender and risotto has a creamy consistency.

❺ Add shrimp; cook about 1 minute or until heated through. Remove risotto from heat. Stir in parsley mixture, lemon juice and pepper.

4 (1 1/4-cup) servings.

Preparation time: 15 minutes. Ready to serve: 40 minutes.

Per serving: 335 calories, 7 g total fat (1.5 g saturated fat), 120 mg cholesterol, 570 mg sodium, 1 g fiber.

Pasta, Grains & Beans

Slow-Cooker Mexican Beans

Here is an easy way to cook basic beans to use for refried beans, soups or black beans and rice. The gentle, even heat of a slow cooker is ideal for beans and simulates an old-fashioned earthenware bean pot. There is a generous quantity of flavorful cooking broth to moisten refried beans or to cook rice.

- 2 cups black beans, rinsed
- 1 medium onion, chopped
- 2 garlic cloves, crushed, peeled
- 1 (4-inch-long) fresh epazote sprig or 1 teaspoon dried
- 5 cups boiling water
- 1½ teaspoons salt

❶ Place beans in large bowl; cover with cold water. Cover bowl; soak beans at room temperature at least 6 hours or overnight. (Or place beans in a large pot with enough water to cover by 2 inches. Bring to a boil over medium-high heat. Remove from heat and let stand 1 hour.)

❷ Drain beans and rinse thoroughly. Place in 3½-quart slow cooker. Add onion, garlic and epazote sprig. Add boiling water. Cook, covered, on High setting 3½ hours or until beans are almost tender.

❸ Add salt; cook an additional 15 to 30 minutes or until beans are tender. Remove and discard epazote sprig. (*Beans will keep, covered, in the refrigerator up to 3 days.*)

5 cups beans, 4 cups broth.

Preparation time: 10 minutes. Ready to serve: 4 hours, 10 minutes (not including soaking time).

Per ½-cup serving: 140 calories, 0.5 g total fat (0 g saturated fat), 0 mg cholesterol, 350 mg sodium, 7 g fiber.

CHEF'S NOTES:

- If you do not have a slow cooker, you can gently simmer the beans in a large heavy pot on the stovetop. Cook beans about 1½ hours, then add salt and simmer about 30 minutes longer.
- To make refried beans, soften some chopped onion and a few minced garlic cloves in a little canola oil in a large nonstick skillet. Add beans (with some of their broth) and cook, mashing with a wooden spoon until mixture has thickened. Serve, sprinkled with minced jalapeño chiles, slivered cilantro and crumbled farmer cheese. Accompany with toasted corn tortillas.

GREEN RICE

A rice pilaf seasoned with cilantro and mild chiles makes a perfect accompaniment to many Latin dishes.

- 2 teaspoons olive oil
- 1 medium onion, chopped
- 1 (4.5-oz.) can chopped green chiles
- 2 garlic cloves, minced
- 1 cup long-grain white rice
- 1 (14.5-oz.) can reduced-sodium chicken broth
- ¾ cup chopped fresh cilantro
- ½ cup chopped trimmed scallions
- 1 tablespoon fresh lime juice
- ⅛ teaspoon salt
- ⅛ teaspoon freshly ground pepper

❶ In medium saucepan, heat oil over medium heat until hot. Add onion; cook about 2 to 3 minutes or until tender, stirring frequently. Add chiles and garlic; cook 1 minute, stirring frequently. Add rice; cook 1 minute, stirring constantly, until well mixed. Add broth; bring to a simmer over medium heat. Reduce heat to low; simmer, covered, about 20 minutes or until rice is tender and liquid has been absorbed. Remove from heat. Add cilantro, scallions, lime juice, salt and pepper; fluff and mix gently with rubber spatula.

4 (1-cup) servings.

Preparation time: 10 minutes. Ready to serve: 40 minutes.

Per serving: 245 calories, 3.5 g total fat (0.5 g saturated fat), 0 mg cholesterol, 570 mg sodium, 2 g fiber.

Pasta, Grains & Beans

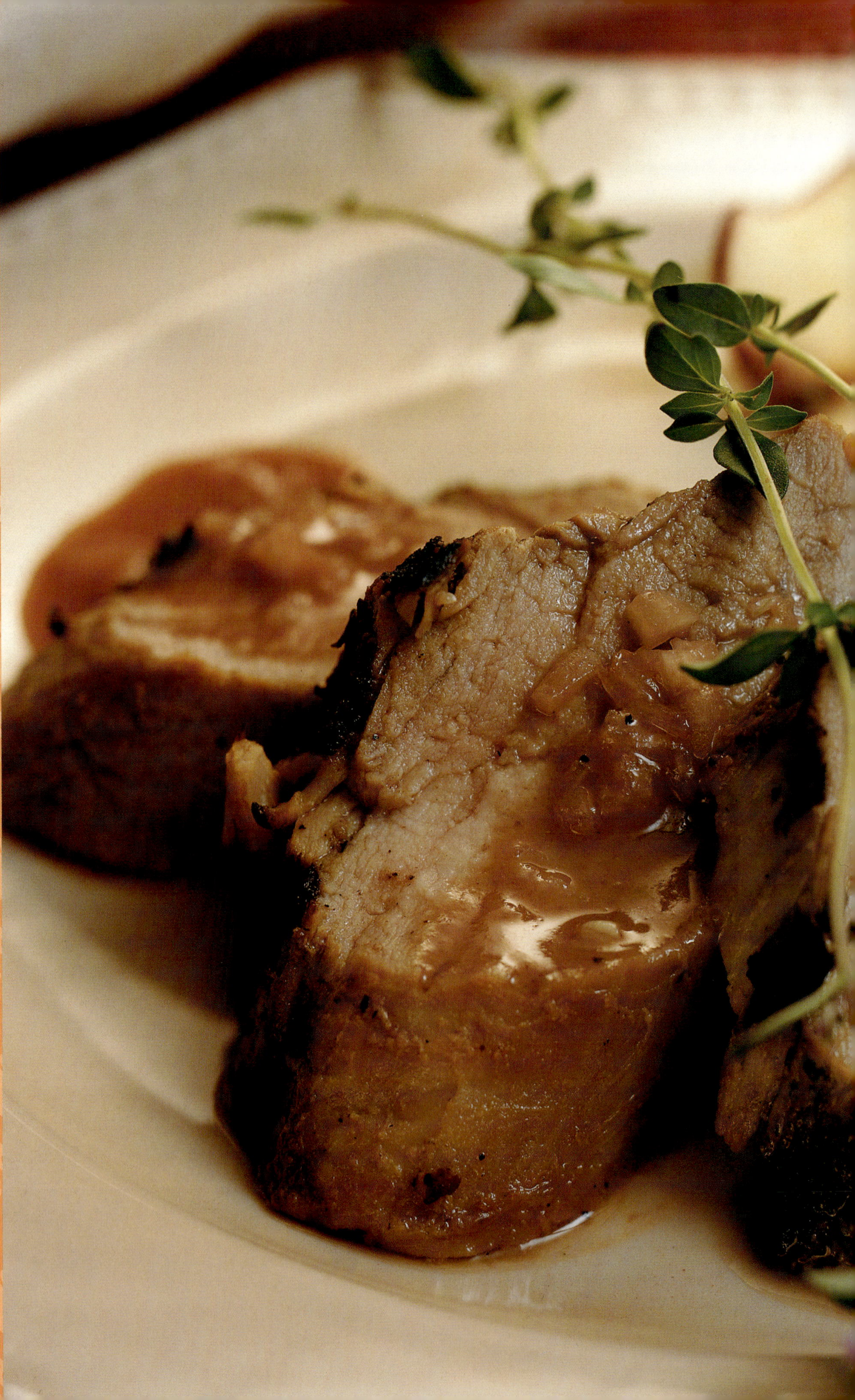

Meat, Poultry, Fish & Seafood

Whether you are roasting, grilling, braising or poaching, herbs are integral to enhancing meat, poultry, fish and seafood. This chapter covers the basic techniques.

Pork Tenderloin with Apple, Thyme and Mustard Marinade, page 122

Leg of Lamb with Herbes de Provence

Aromatic herbs, mustard and garlic make a delicious crust for a Sunday dinner lamb roast. Accompany with Herbed Goat Cheese Mashed Potatoes *(page 88) and steamed green beans.*

2 tablespoons grainy mustard	1 medium onion, sliced
2 tablespoons olive oil	1 medium carrot, sliced
2 tablespoons *Herbes de Provence* (page 14)	2/3 cup dry red wine
4 garlic cloves, minced	1 (14.5-oz.) can reduced-sodium chicken broth
1/2 teaspoon salt	1 tablespoon cornstarch
1/2 teaspoon freshly ground pepper	1 tablespoon water
1 (4 1/2- to 5 1/2-lb.) shank-half, bone-in leg of lamb	

❶ In small bowl, combine mustard, olive oil, *herbes de Provence*, garlic, salt and pepper; mix well. Rub mixture evenly over lamb. Place in shallow glass dish. Refrigerate, covered, at least 30 minutes or up to 4 hours.

❷ Heat oven to 425°F. Spray small roasting pan or large oven-safe skillet with nonstick cooking spray.

❸ Place onion and carrot slices in center of pan. Place lamb over vegetables. Bake 20 minutes. Reduce oven temperature to 350°F. Bake 45 minutes to 1 1/2 hours or until of desired doneness. Place lamb on cutting board; cover loosely with aluminum foil and let rest.

❹ Discard any charred vegetables. Place roasting pan with vegetables on stovetop over medium-high heat. Pour in wine; bring to a boil, stirring to scrape up any browned bits. Cook 2 to 3 minutes or until reduced by half. Add broth; bring to a boil. Cook 2 to 3 minutes to intensify flavor. Strain sauce into medium saucepan, Bring sauce to a simmer over medium-high heat. In small bowl, mix cornstarch and water; add to simmering sauce. Cook about 1 minute, whisking constantly, until slightly thickened. Keep warm. Carve lamb and serve with sauce.

6 servings.

Preparation time: 25 minutes. Ready to serve: 2 hours, 45 minutes.

Per serving: 445 calories, 22 g total fat (7 g saturated fat), 170 mg cholesterol, 535 mg sodium, 0.5 g fiber.

CHEF'S NOTE:
- Set the roast on a bed of sliced onions and carrots to make a vegetable "rack" that helps flavor the pan drippings for the pan sauce.

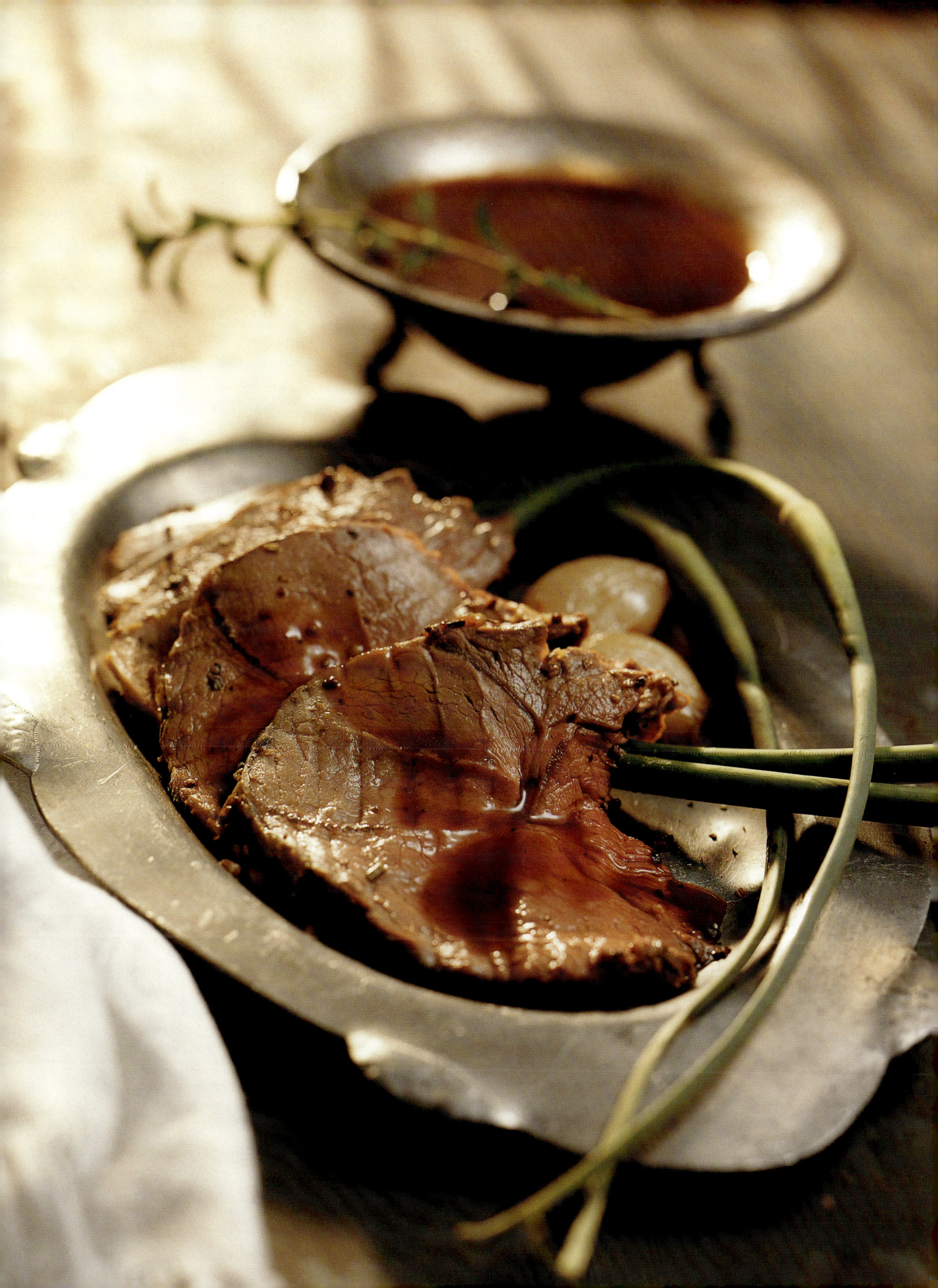

Chicken Saute with Tarragon

One my favorite dishes in the repertoire of classical French cooking is poulet a l'estragon. *Tarragon has a special affinity with chicken, and this timeless recipe is neither difficult to make nor excessively rich.*

4	chicken breast halves, bone-in (about 3 lb.)	1	fresh tarragon sprig
½	teaspoon salt	4	teaspoons cornstarch
¼	teaspoon freshly ground pepper	1	tablespoon water
1	tablespoon olive oil	¼	cup reduced-fat sour cream
¼	cup finely chopped shallots	4	teaspoons chopped fresh tarragon
½	cup dry white wine	1	tablespoon Dijon mustard
1	cup reduced-sodium chicken broth		

❶ Season chicken with salt and pepper. In large nonstick skillet, heat oil over medium-high heat until hot. Add chicken; cook about 3 minutes per side or until browned. Transfer chicken to plate. Add shallots to skillet; cook 30 to 60 seconds or until tender, stirring constantly. Add wine; cook about 1 minute or until slightly reduced. Add broth and tarragon sprig; bring to a simmer.

❷ Return chicken to skillet. Reduce heat to low. Cover and cook 25 to 30 minutes or until chicken juices run clear and internal temperature reaches 170°F. With tongs, transfer chicken to platter or individual plates; keep warm. Discard tarragon sprig.

❸ Increase heat under skillet to medium-high. Simmer cooking liquid 2 to 3 minutes until reduced slightly. In small bowl, mix cornstarch and water. Add to skillet; cook about 1 minute or until slightly thickened, whisking constantly. Add sour cream, chopped tarragon and mustard; whisk until heated through and smooth. Spoon sauce over chicken.

4 servings.

Preparation time: 20 minutes. Ready to serve: 1 hour.

Per serving: 315 calories, 15.5 g total fat (4 g saturated fat), 95 mg cholesterol, 555 mg sodium, 0.5 g fiber.

CHEF'S NOTE:
- In this dish, a whole sprig of tarragon is used to subtly infuse the sauce with tarragon flavor, while chopped fresh tarragon provides the final herbal finish.

ROSEMARY-SCENTED LAMB KABOBS

Rosemary, garlic and lamb make a magical trio. To accompany these Mediterranean-flavored kabobs, try Herbed Goat Cheese Mashed Potatoes *(page 88) and steamed green beans.*

- 2 tablespoons chopped fresh rosemary
- 4 garlic cloves, minced
- 3 tablespoons olive oil
- 1 tablespoon red wine vinegar
- 1 teaspoon Dijon mustard
- ½ teaspoon Worcestershire sauce
- ¾ teaspoon salt
- ½ teaspoon freshly ground pepper
- 2¼ lb. boneless leg of lamb, fat and membrane carefully trimmed, cut into 1¼-inch chunks
- 2 large red bell peppers, seeded, cut into 1¼-inch pieces
- Fresh rosemary sprigs

❶ In small bowl, whisk together chopped rosemary, garlic, oil, vinegar, mustard, Worcestershire sauce, salt and pepper. Place lamb in shallow glass dish. Pour rosemary marinade over lamb; turn to coat. Refrigerate, covered, at least 30 minutes or up to 2 hours, turning lamb occasionally.

❷ Heat grill. Thread 1 piece of lamb, followed by a piece of bell pepper and another piece of lamb, onto 10- or 12-inch skewer. Continue threading skewer, using a total of 5 pieces of lamb and 4 pieces of bell pepper. Repeat with remaining lamb and bell pepper to make a total of 6 kabobs.

❸ Lightly oil grill rack. Place kabobs on gas grill over high heat or on charcoal grill 4 to 6 inches from hot coals. Cover grill and cook 6 to 8 minutes or until lamb is browned and cooked to medium-rare, turning occasionally. Garnish with rosemary sprigs.

6 servings.

Preparation time: 25 minutes. Ready to serve: 1 hour, 10 minutes.

Per serving: 190 calories, 9.5 g total fat (3 g saturated fat), 75 mg cholesterol, 210 mg sodium, 1 g fiber.

CHEF'S NOTE:

- Because lamb leg needs to be carefully trimmed, this recipes makes allowance for loss during trimming. If your meat counter carries cubed, trimmed lamb for kabobs, 1½ pounds should be enough. What to do with the lamb trimmings? Make lamb broth by browning the trimmings, then simmering in water with several rosemary sprigs and garlic cloves for about 1 hour. Chill; skim off fat. Freeze for use later in lamb stew or gravy for roast lamb.

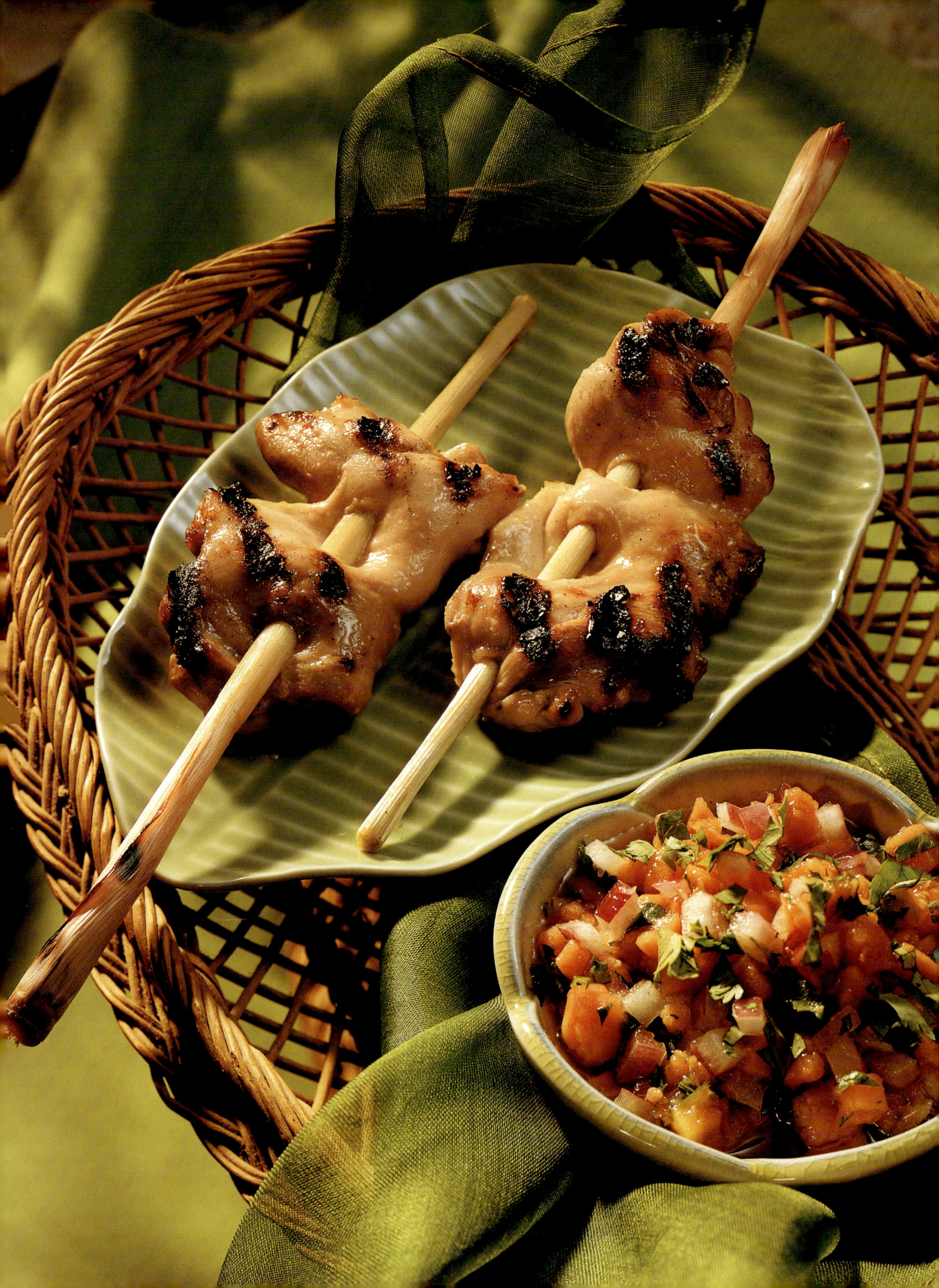

Vietnamese Grilled Chicken Thighs

Meaty chicken thighs are well suited to this intensely flavored Vietnamese marinade. You can certainly use bone-in chicken thighs (adjust cooking time accordingly — they will take 20 to 30 minutes) if you prefer, but boneless thighs are easy to eat and fun when they are secured on lemongrass "skewers" (page 19). Serve with steamed rice.

6 stalks fresh lemongrass	2 tablespoons fish sauce
2 serrano or jalapeño chiles, seeded, coarsely chopped	1 tablespoon canola oil
4 garlic cloves, crushed	8 boneless skinless chicken thighs (1¾ lb.), trimmed
2 tablespoons sugar	1 recipe *Papaya Relish* (page 157)
¼ cup fresh lime juice	Lime wedges

❶ Prepare 4 stalks lemongrass for lemongrass skewers (see page 19).

❷ Trim remaining 2 lemongrass stalks (see page 9); chop coarsely. In mini food processor, combine chopped lemongrass, chiles, garlic and sugar; pulse until finely chopped. Add lime juice, fish sauce and oil; process until mixture forms a chunky puree. Reserve ¼ cup of this mixture for basting.

❸ Place chicken in shallow glass dish. Add remaining lemongrass marinade; turn to coat. Refrigerate, covered, 30 minutes or up to 4 hours, turning occasionally.

❹ Meanwhile, prepare Papaya Relish.

❺ Heat grill. With metal skewer, poke 2 holes through each chicken thigh. Thread 2 chicken thighs onto each frozen lemongrass skewer. Strain reserved lemongrass mixture, pressing on solids to extract flavor; set aside for basting.

❻ Lightly oil grill rack. Place skewered chicken on gas grill over medium-high heat or on charcoal grill 4 to 6 inches from medium-hot coals. Cover grill and cook, turning once or twice and basting browned sides with reserved marinade, 12 to 15 minutes or until chicken is browned and no longer pink in center. Garnish with lime wedges. Serve with Papaya Relish.

4 servings.

Preparation time: 45 minutes. Ready to serve: 1 hour, 30 minutes.

Per serving: 280 calories, 10.5 g total fat (3 g saturated fat), 95 mg cholesterol, 345 mg sodium, 2 g fiber.

> **CHEF'S NOTE:**
> - This marinade is also delicious with quail. Split quail before marinating and grilling.

Meat, Poultry, Fish & Seafood

Greek Chicken Pie

The chicken filling for this impressive Greek phyllo pie is flavored with a tangy lemon-dill avgolemono sauce. The pie sports a special ruffled phyllo top crust. It makes an interesting presentation, but is actually easy to make. This is a great dish for entertaining because, although there is considerable preparation involved, it can be made in advance and reheated.

FILLING
- 2 teaspoons olive oil
- 4 cups thinly sliced leeks
- 2 (14.5-oz.) cans reduced-sodium chicken broth
- 1/2 cup long-grain white rice
- 4 medium carrots, cut into 1x1/4-inch sticks
- 1/4 cup all-purpose flour
- 1/2 cup fresh lemon juice
- 1 egg
- 3 1/2 cups shredded cooked chicken breasts
- 6 green onions
- 1/2 cup chopped fresh dill
- 3/4 teaspoon salt
- 1/2 teaspoon freshly ground pepper

CRUST
- Olive oil nonstick cooking spray
- 1/3 cup unseasoned dry bread crumbs
- 14 sheets phyllo dough*
- 2 teaspoons butter, melted

❶ Heat oil in large saucepan over medium heat until hot. Add leeks; cook 3 to 4 minutes or until tender, stirring frequently. (If necessary, add a little water to prevent sticking.)

❷ Add broth; bring to a boil. Add rice; boil 7 minutes. Add carrots; boil 3 minutes. Drain rice mixture; reserve broth. Measure 2 1/4 cups reserved broth; add water if necessary. Pour into large saucepan; bring to a boil over medium heat.

❸ Meanwhile, place flour in small bowl; gradually whisk in lemon juice. Beat egg in large bowl; set aside. Slowly add lemon mixture to broth, whisking constantly. Bring to a boil; boil 1 to 2 minutes or until sauce thickens slightly. Gradually add hot sauce to egg, whisking constantly.

❹ In large bowl, combine rice mixture, chicken, sauce, green onions, dill, salt and pepper. (*Filling can be made up to 24 hours before baking. Cover and refrigerate.*)

❺ Place oven rack in lower third of oven; heat to 375°F. Spray 12-inch tart pan* with nonstick cooking spray; sprinkle lightly with bread crumbs.

❻ Place 1 sheet phyllo in tart pan. Spray with nonstick cooking spray; sprinkle with bread crumbs. Repeat with 7 sheets phyllo, angling each sheet to form a rough circle to cover bottom and sides of pan. Trim overhang to 1/2 inch; fold inside to form neat rim. Spread filling over phyllo.

7 To make ruffled top, place 1 sheet phyllo on work surface. Spray with nonstick cooking spray; sprinkle with bread crumbs. Cut phyllo in half lengthwise. Starting at long side, roll each piece into 1/2-inch-thick rope. Arrange over filling along edge of tart. Repeat with remaining 5 sheets phyllo to cover top of tart. Brush with butter. Set tart pan on baking sheet. Bake 50 to 60 minutes or until crust is golden brown. Remove sides of tart pan; place on serving platter. (*Pie can be baked up to 24 hours ahead. Cover and refrigerate. Reheat in 350°F oven 25 to 30 minutes or until filling is hot.*)

TIP *Recipe can be assembled in 13x9-inch pan. Bake as directed.

8 servings.

Preparation time: 1 hour, 45 minutes. Ready to serve: 2 hours, 45 minutes.

Per serving: 375 calories, 7.5 g total fat (2 g saturated fat), 75 mg cholesterol, 675 mg sodium, 4 g fiber.

CHEF'S NOTE:
- If using frozen phyllo, let thaw in refrigerator at least 12 hours.

Meat, Poultry, Fish & Seafood

PORK TENDERLOIN WITH APPLE, THYME AND MUSTARD MARINADE

A little sweetness in a marinade enhances flavors and promotes browning. In this marinade, apple juice concentrate provides the sweet element and offers a good fruity complement to the thyme. The marinade is also good with chicken.

PORK AND MARINADE
- ¼ cup frozen apple juice concentrate, thawed
- 2 tablespoons Dijon mustard
- 2 tablespoons chopped fresh thyme or 2 teaspoons dried
- 1 tablespoon olive oil
- 4 garlic cloves, minced
- 1 teaspoon black peppercorns, crushed
- 1½ lb. pork tenderloin

PORT VINAIGRETTE
- 3 tablespoons port wine
- 2 tablespoons balsamic vinegar
- 1 tablespoon extra-virgin olive oil
- 1½ teaspoons Dijon mustard
- 2 tablespoons finely chopped shallot
- ¼ teaspoon salt
- ⅛ teaspoon freshly ground pepper

❶ In small bowl, whisk apple juice concentrate, 2 tablespoons mustard, thyme, 1 tablespoon oil, garlic and peppercorns. Reserve ¼ cup of mixture for basting. Place tenderloins in shallow glass dish. Pour remaining marinade over pork; turn to coat. Refrigerate, covered, at least 30 minutes or up to 8 hours, turning several times.

❷ Heat grill. In small bowl, make port vinaigrette: combine port, vinegar, 1 tablespoon oil, 1½ teaspoons mustard, shallot, salt and pepper; whisk to blend.

❸ Lightly oil grill rack. Place tenderloins on gas grill over medium-high heat or on charcoal grill 4 to 6 inches from medium-hot coals. Cover grill and cook 20 to 25 minutes, turning occasionally and basting with reserved marinade until tenderloins are browned and internal temperature reaches 150°F. Transfer tenderloins to clean cutting board. Cover tenderloins loosely with aluminum foil; let rest 5 to 10 minutes.

❹ Carve tenderloins into ½-inch slices. Serve with port vinaigrette.

6 servings.

Preparation time: 20 minutes. Ready to serve: 1 hour, 20 minutes.

Per serving: 215 calories, 9 g total fat (2 g saturated fat), 70 mg cholesterol, 200 mg sodium, 0.5 g fiber.

CHEF'S NOTE:
- Substitute chopped fresh rosemary for fresh thyme.

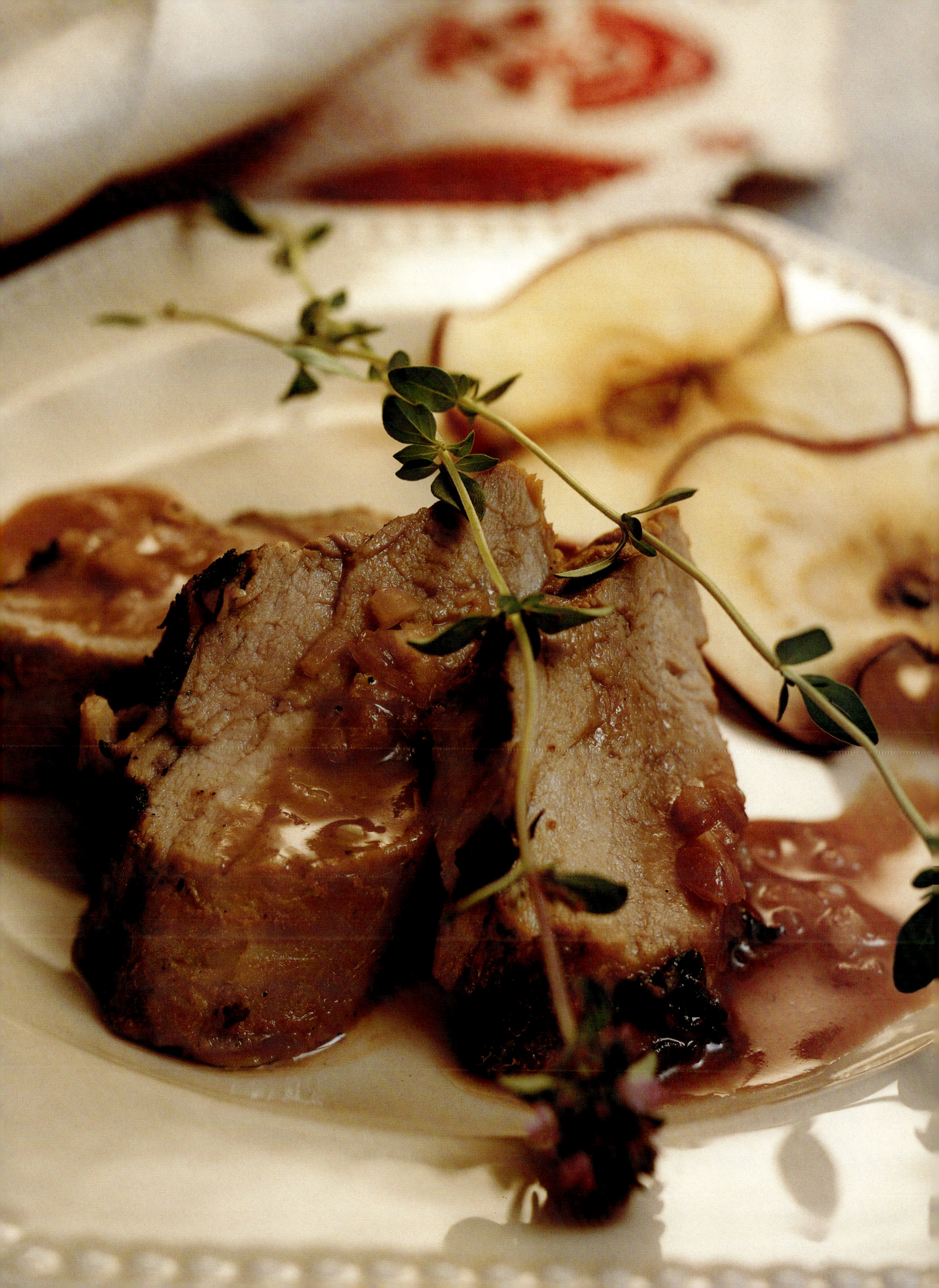

Stuffed Chicken Breasts with Herbed Goat Cheese

A stuffing of flavorful herbed goat cheese and savory olive paste is an easy way to dress up a basic chicken breast. Round out this simple, elegant dish with roasted red potatoes and steamed green beans.

3 tablespoons *Herbed Goat Cheese Spread* (page 61)	2 teaspoons Dijon mustard
4 (4- to 6-oz.) boneless chicken breast halves	2 teaspoons fresh lemon juice
2 tablespoons black olive spread (olivada)* or finely chopped pitted ripe olives	1 teaspoon honey
2 teaspoons chopped fresh rosemary	½ teaspoon salt
	½ teaspoon freshly ground pepper
	1 tablespoon olive oil

❶ Prepare Herbed Goat Cheese Spread.

❷ Create a pocket by cutting a 3-inch horizontal slit in each chicken breast half. Place ¼ of black olive spread in each pocket. Close pockets; secure with toothpicks. Place chicken on plate. Refrigerate, covered, at least 30 minutes or up to 8 hours.

❸ Heat oven to 375°F. In small bowl, combine rosemary, mustard, lemon juice and honey; mix well.

❹ Sprinkle chicken with salt and pepper. Heat oil in large ovenproof skillet over medium-high heat until hot. Add chicken; cook 2 to 3 minutes or until lightly browned. Turn chicken; brush tops with rosemary mixture.

❺ Place skillet in oven. Bake about 20 minutes or until chicken is tender and juices run clear. Remove toothpicks before serving.

TIP *Black olive spread is made from pureed ripe olives and olive oil. You can find it in specialty food stores as well as Italian and Greek markets.

4 servings.

Preparation time. 30 minutes. Ready to serve: 1 hour, 20 minutes.

Per serving: 290 calories, 17.5 g total fat (5.5 g saturated fat), 90 mg cholesterol, 530 mg sodium, 0.5 g fiber.

CHEF'S NOTE:

- Boneless chicken breasts with skin on combine the advantages of traditional bone-in, skin-on chicken breasts and the boneless, skinless variety. Boneless chicken breasts cook quickly and are easy to eat, but the skin helps protect the meat from drying out during cooking. If your supermarket does not carry boneless chicken breast halves with skin, you may be able to purchase bone-in chicken breasts and ask the meat department to bone them for you, leaving the skin on.

Grilled Chicken with Parsley-Caper Sauce

A piquant herb sauce enlivens simple grilled chicken breasts. This recipe is a good choice for a simple late summer dinner; serve with grilled zucchini, roasted potatoes and sliced tomatoes.

- 1 recipe *Parsley-Caper Sauce* (page 167)
- 4 boneless skinless chicken breast halves
- 2 teaspoons olive oil
- 1/2 teaspoon salt
- 1/4 teaspoon freshly ground pepper
- 8 fresh sage leaves

❶ Heat grill. Prepare Parsley-Caper Sauce; set aside.

❷ Brush chicken with oil; sprinkle with salt and pepper. Press 1 sage leaf onto each side of chicken breasts.

❸ Place chicken on gas grill over medium-high heat or on charcoal grill 4 to 6 inches from medium-hot coals. Cover grill and cook 10 to 12 minutes or until juices run clear, turning once. Serve with Parsley-Caper Sauce.

4 servings.

Preparation time: 15 minutes. Ready to serve: 30 minutes.

Per serving: 225 calories, 10.5 g total fat (2 g saturated fat), 70 mg cholesterol, 805 mg sodium, 1.5 g fiber.

CHEF'S NOTES:

- When you are grilling skinless chicken breasts that have not been marinated, protect them by sticking a whole herb leaf on the surface.

Meat, Poultry, Fish & Seafood

Chicken, Prosciutto and Sage Kabobs

In addition to flavoring the chicken, a delicate wrapper of sage leaves and sliced prosciutto helps keep it moist and tender. Serve these Italian-inspired kabobs with rice pilaf, sautéed spinach and grilled cherry tomatoes.

- 3 tablespoons fresh lemon juice
- 3 tablespoons olive oil
- 2 garlic cloves, minced
- ½ teaspoon freshly ground pepper
- 1¾ lb. boneless skinless chicken breast halves, cut into 1¼-inch chunks
- 1 recipe *Shallot-Mustard Herb Butter* (page 163)
- 4 oz. thinly sliced prosciutto
- 30 fresh sage leaves

❶ In small bowl, whisk lemon juice, olive oil, garlic and pepper. Place chicken in shallow glass baking dish. Pour lemon marinade over chicken; turn to coat. Refrigerate, covered, at least 20 minutes or up to 2 hours, turning chicken occasionally.

❷ Meanwhile, prepare Shallot-Mustard Herb Butter.

❸ Heat grill. Cut prosciutto slices in half lengthwise, then in thirds crosswise to make pieces about 3x1½ inches. Place one piece of prosciutto on cutting board. Center a sage leaf on top. Place one piece of chicken on sage leaf; fold up edges of prosciutto to partially enclose chicken. Thread onto 10- or 12-inch skewer. Repeat with remaining prosciutto, sage and chicken; continue threading skewers with 3 or 4 additional pieces until 6 kabobs are prepared.

❹ Lightly oil grill rack. Place kabobs on gas grill over medium heat or on charcoal grill 4 to 6 inches from medium coals. Cover grill and cook, turning occasionally, 8 to 10 minutes or until browned and chicken is no longer pink. Serve with Mustard-Shallot Herb Butter.

6 servings.

Preparation time: 30 minutes. Ready to serve: 1 hour.

Per serving: 360 calories, 24.5 g total fat (8 g saturated fat), 105 mg cholesterol, 335 mg sodium, 0.5 g fiber.

Fillet of Sole with Tarragon Mayonnaise

Round out this simple fish supper with boiled red potatoes and steamed asparagus.

TARRAGON MAYONNAISE
- ½ cup reduced-fat mayonnaise
- ¼ cup reduced-fat plain yogurt
- 2 tablespoons fresh lemon juice
- 1 teaspoon Dijon mustard
- Dash of cayenne pepper
- 2 tablespoons finely chopped shallot
- 2 tablespoons chopped fresh tarragon

SOLE
- ¼ cup all-purpose flour
- ½ teaspoon salt
- ¼ teaspoon freshly ground pepper
- 1 lb. sole, turbot or flounder fillets
- 2 tablespoons olive oil
- 1 lemon, cut into wedges

❶ In small bowl, whisk mayonnaise, yogurt, lemon juice, mustard and cayenne until smooth. Stir in shallot and tarragon. *(Mayonnaise can be made ahead. Cover and refrigerate up to 2 days).*

❷ In 9-inch pie plate, mix flour, salt and pepper. Dredge fillets in flour mixture; discard remaining mixture.

❸ In large nonstick skillet, heat oil over medium-high heat until hot. Add fillets; cook 3 to 4 minutes per side or until golden and opaque in the center. Serve with Tarragon Mayonnaise.

4 servings.

Preparation time: 30 minutes. Ready to serve: 40 minutes.

Per serving: 250 calories, 15 g total fat (2.5 g saturated fat), 65 mg cholesterol, 490 mg sodium, 0.5 g fiber.

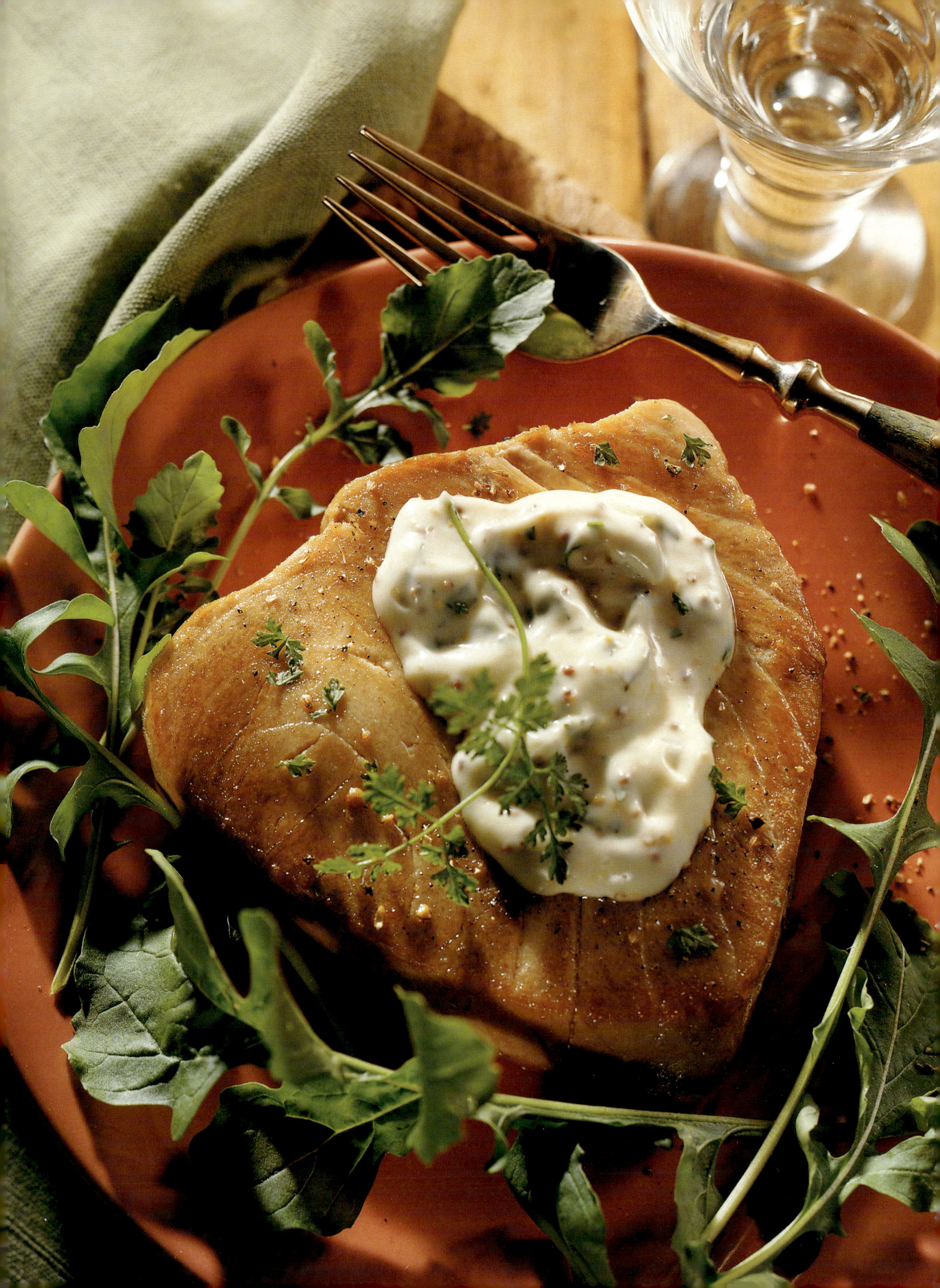

Grilled Salmon with Mint and Ginger Chutney

Accompany the salmon with a basmati rice pilaf and green peas simmered with scallions.

- 1 recipe *Mint and Ginger Chutney* (page 161)
- 4 (5-oz.) salmon fillets (1 inch thick)
- 2 teaspoons canola oil
- 3/4 teaspoon salt
- 1/2 teaspoon freshly ground pepper
- 4 fresh mint leaves
- Fresh mint sprigs
- Lime wedges

❶ Prepare Mint and Ginger Chutney; set aside.

❷ Heat grill. Brush salmon with oil; sprinkle with salt and pepper. Press 1 mint leaf onto curved skinless side of each piece of salmon.

❸ Place salmon, skin side up, on gas grill over medium-high heat or on charcoal grill 4 to 6 inches from medium-hot coals. Cover grill and cook, turning once, 8 to 10 minutes or until fish just begins to flake. Garnish with fresh mint and lime wedges. Serve with Mint and Ginger Chutney.

4 servings.

Preparation time: 20 minutes. Ready to serve: 30 minutes.

Per serving: 240 calories, 9.5 g total fat (2 g saturated fat), 80 mg cholesterol, 670 mg sodium, 1 g fiber.

CHEF'S NOTE:
- Mint leaves pressed on the salmon help protect the delicate fillet from the heat of the grill. The mint adds a subtle fragrance as well.

Swordfish Souvlaki

Oregano-laced Greek souvlaki is usually associated with lamb, but souvlaki made with swordfish is popular throughout Greece. Bay leaves dress up the skewers and contribute a subtle fragrance.

20 to 24	fresh or dried bay leaves
3	tablespoons fresh lemon juice
3	tablespoons dry white wine
1	tablespoon extra-virgin olive oil
1½	tablespoons chopped fresh oregano or 1½ teaspoons dried
1	garlic clove, minced
½	teaspoon salt
⅛	teaspoon freshly ground pepper
1¼	lb. swordfish steak (1¼ inches thick), skin removed, cut into 1¼-inch chunks
	Lemon wedges

❶ If using dried bay leaves, soak in water 30 minutes.

❷ In small bowl, whisk lemon juice, wine, oil, oregano, garlic, salt and pepper. Reserve 3 tablespoons of this mixture for basting. Place swordfish in shallow glass dish. Add remaining marinade; turn to coat. Refrigerate, covered, 20 to 30 minutes, turning occasionally.

❸ Heat grill. Thread swordfish onto 4 (10- or 12-inch) skewers, placing one bay leaf between each piece of swordfish.

❹ Lightly oil grill rack. Place skewers on gas grill over medium-high heat or charcoal grill over medium-hot coals. Cover grill and cook, turning occasionally and basting with reserved marinade, 8 to 12 minutes or until swordfish is opaque in center. Garnish with lemon wedges.

4 servings.

Preparation time: 20 minutes. Ready to serve: 40 minutes.

Per serving: 185 calories, 8 g total fat (2 g saturated fat), 75 mg cholesterol, 215 mg sodium, 0 g fiber.

CHEF'S NOTES:
- You can also use this souvlaki marinade with fresh tuna, lamb, chicken or pork.

Oven-Poached Salmon with Fines Herbes

Salmon fillets are wonderfully moist and succulent when they are poached in the oven with a little wine and shallots and then topped with a deceptively rich-tasting sauce. Serve the fillets on a bed of sautéed spinach accompanied by rice pilaf.

1	lb. salmon fillet, cut into 4 pieces
2	tablespoons dry white wine
1/4	teaspoon salt
1/4	teaspoon freshly ground pepper
2	tablespoons finely chopped shallot
1	recipe *Springtime Sauce with Fines Herbes* (page 171)
	Fresh chervil or parsley sprigs
	Lemon wedges

❶ Heat oven to 425°F. Spray 9-inch glass pie plate with cooking spray.

❷ Place salmon, skin side down, in pie plate. Sprinkle with wine, salt, pepper and shallots. Cover with aluminum foil. Bake 15 to 25 minutes or just until salmon is opaque and begins to flake.

❸ Meanwhile, make Springtime Sauce; keep warm.

❹ When salmon is done, transfer pieces to dinner plates. Stir remaining liquid from pie plate into sauce; spoon sauce over salmon. Garnish with chervil sprigs and lemon wedges.

4 servings.

Preparation time: 15 minutes. Ready to serve: 35 minutes.

Per serving: 195 calories, 9.5 g total fat (2.5 g saturated fat), 75 mg cholesterol, 280 mg sodium, 0 g fiber.

Meat, Poultry, Fish & Seafood

PROVENCAL BEEF STEW WITH OLIVES

Here is a robust, make-ahead stew you can proudly serve to company. Accompany with egg noodles. And don't forget to pick up some good crusty bread to soak up the delicious sauce.

- 1 (3½-lb.) beef chuck roast, trimmed, cut into 1¾-inch pieces
- 1 (750-ml) bottle dry red wine
- 1 teaspoon black peppercorns, crushed
- 8 fresh thyme sprigs or 1 teaspoon dried
- 8 fresh Italian parsley stems (reserve leaves for garnish)
- 2 (2x½-inch) strips orange peel
- 1 bay leaf
- 2 tablespoons olive oil, divided
- 2 cups chopped onions
- 1 cup chopped carrots
- 4 garlic cloves, minced
- 1 (28-oz.) can plum tomatoes, drained
- ¼ teaspoon freshly ground pepper
- ⅔ cup niçoise olives, pitted
- ¼ teaspoon salt, if desired
- ½ cup chopped fresh Italian parsley

❶ In large resealable plastic bag, combine beef, wine and peppercorns; seal bag. Refrigerate at least 2 hours or overnight.

❷ Heat oven to 300°F. With butcher's twine, tie thyme, parsley, orange peel and bay leaf together in piece of cheesecloth to make a bouquet garni. Set aside.

❸ Drain beef, reserving marinade. Dry beef with paper towels. Heat oil in nonreactive Dutch oven over medium-high heat until hot. Brown beef in batches 2 to 4 minutes or until well-browned on all sides. Remove from Dutch oven; set aside.

❹ Add onions and carrots to Dutch oven; cook 4 to 6 minutes or until tender and lightly browned, stirring frequently. Add garlic; cook and stir about 30 seconds. Add reserved marinade. Bring to a boil, stirring to scrape up any browned bits. Add beef, tomatoes, pepper and bouquet garni. Bring to a boil over medium-high heat.

❺ Bake, covered, 2½ hours or until beef is almost tender.

❻ Add olives to stew; bake an additional 20 to 30 minutes or until beef is very tender.

❼ With slotted spoon, transfer beef and olives to serving dish; keep warm. Discard bouquet garni. Skim fat from top of sauce with paper towels. If desired, boil sauce over high heat 5 to 10 minutes to intensify flavor and thicken slighlty. Add salt. Pour sauce over beef and olives. (*Stew can be made up to 2 days ahead. Cover and refrigerate. Reheat gently on stovetop before serving.*) Garnish with parsley.

6 (1¼-cup) servings.

Preparation time: 45 minutes. Ready to serve: 6 hours.

Per serving: 550 calories, 30.5 g total fat (10.5 g saturated fat), 140 mg cholesterol, 485 mg sodium, 3.5 g fiber.

CHEF'S NOTES:

- A *bouquet garni* is an essential flavoring element in long-simmered meat stews. In addition to the standard parsley, thyme and bay leaf, this bouquet includes orange peel, which gives this stew a distinctive Provençal flavor.
- Tangy and delicate, niçoise olives are small, dark brownish-purple brine-cured olives from France. Look for them in specialty stores.

Meat, Poultry, Fish & Seafood

SPRING ROLLS WITH SHRIMP AND RICE NOODLE FILLING

These lively and light Vietnamese spring rolls make ideal hot-weather fare. Cilantro and mint provide a fresh contrast to the spicy dipping sauce.

DRESSING
- 1/2 cup pineapple juice
- 2 tablespoons low-sodium soy sauce
- 1 tablespoon fish sauce
- 2 tablespoons rice vinegar
- 1 tablespoon canola oil
- 1 teaspoon Thai green curry paste
- 1 teaspoon packed brown sugar
- 3 tablespoons coarsely chopped fresh ginger
- 2 medium garlic cloves, crushed

SPRING ROLLS
- 2 oz. thin rice noodles or rice sticks
- 12 rice-paper wrappers
- 12 large leaves Boston lettuce
- 1 lb. shelled, deveined cooked medium shrimp, tails removed
- 3/4 cup grated carrots (2 to 3 medium)
- 3/4 cup finely diced fresh pineapple
- 3/4 cup slivered fresh cilantro
- 3/4 cup slivered fresh mint

❶ In blender, combine pineapple juice, soy sauce, fish sauce, rice vinegar, oil, curry paste, brown sugar, ginger and garlic; process until well blended. (*Dressing can be made ahead. Cover and refrigerate up to 2 days.*)

❷ In large bowl, cover rice noodles with boiling water; stir to immerse and separate strands. Let soak 5 minutes. Drain noodles; rinse with cold water. Drain again, shaking colander to release excess water. Return noodles to bowl. Add 2 tablespoons of the dressing; toss to coat.

❸ Shortly before serving, assemble spring rolls. Set all prepared filling ingredients out on counter. Set out large bowl of warm water, baking sheet, serving platter and damp kitchen towel. Working with 2 rice paper wrappers at a time, dip into warm water 10 to 20 seconds or until softened. Shake off moisture and lay out on baking sheet. Place one lettuce leaf on bottom third of each wrapper. Top each lettuce leaf with about 2 tablespoons rice noodle mixture, 3 or 4 shrimp, generous 1 tablespoon carrot, generous 1 tablespoon pineapple, 1 tablespoon cilantro and 1 tablespoon mint. Fold bottom of wrapper over to partially cover filling. Fold sides over filling and continue to roll wrapper into a cylinder to seal.

❹ Place on platter. Cover with damp kitchen towel to prevent spring rolls from drying out. Repeat with remaining rice paper wrappers and filling ingredients. Serve with remaining dressing as dipping sauce.

6 servings.

Preparation time: 1 hour, 30 minutes. Ready to serve: 1 hour, 30 minutes.

Per serving: 210 calories, 3.5 g total fat (0.5 g saturated fat), 155 mg cholesterol, 490 mg sodium, 2 g fiber.

CHEF'S NOTES:
- Fish sauce, green curry paste, rice vermicelli and rice paper wrappers can be found in the Asian section of many supermarkets, health food stores, Asian markets.
- For an interesting presentation, wrap each spring roll with a chive ribbon (see page 16).
- Whole shrimp look attractive. But for easier wrapping, chop them coarsely and use about 2 tablespoons per roll.

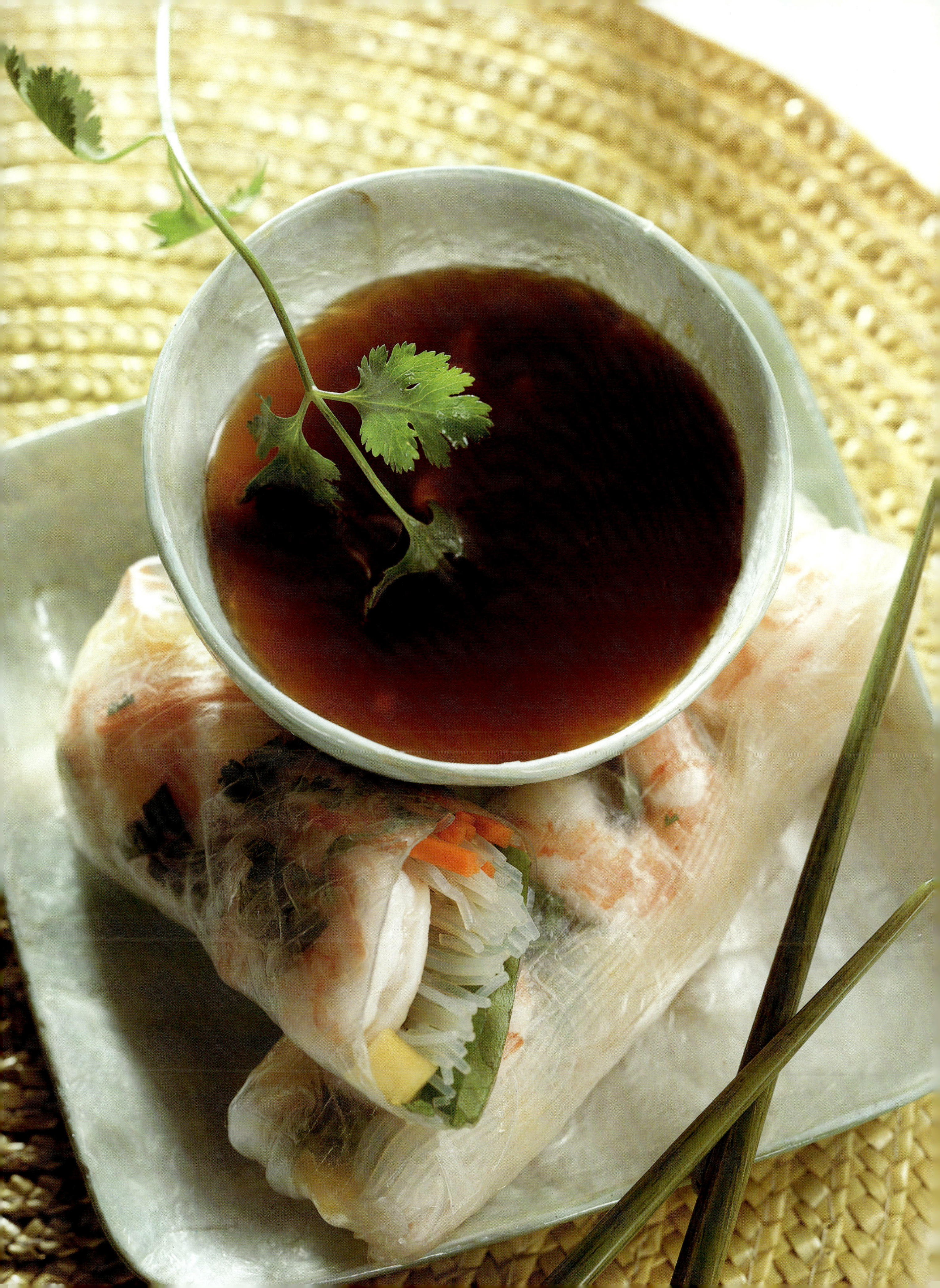

North African Tuna Kabobs

Lemon wedges give these kabobs an interesting presentation, but when the kabobs are cooked, the grilled lemon wedges can also be used for squeezing extra lemon juice over the tuna. Serve these kabobs over couscous and accompany with a selection of grilled vegetables.

½	cup chopped fresh cilantro	1½	teaspoons paprika
½	cup chopped fresh Italian parsley	¾	teaspoon salt
4	garlic cloves, minced	½	teaspoon freshly ground pepper
½	cup extra-virgin olive oil	1¾	lb. tuna steak (1¼-inch thick), cut into 1¼-inch chunks
⅓	cup fresh lemon juice		
2	teaspoons ground cumin	2	lemons, each cut into 6 wedges

❶ In small bowl, whisk together cilantro, parsley, garlic, olive oil, lemon juice, cumin, paprika, salt and pepper. Reserve ½ cup of this mixture to serve as sauce. Place tuna in a shallow glass dish. Pour remaining marinade over tuna; turn to coat. Refrigerate, covered, at least 20 minutes or up to 1 hour, turning occasionally. Cover and keep reserved sauce at room temperature.

❷ Heat grill. Thread 1 piece of tuna, 1 lemon wedge, 2 pieces of tuna, another lemon wedge and final piece of tuna onto 10- or 12-inch skewer. Repeat with remaining tuna and lemon wedges to make a total of 6 kabobs.

❸ Lightly oil grill rack. Place kabobs on gas grill over high heat or on charcoal grill 4 to 6 inches from hot coals. Cover grill and cook, turning occasionally, 7 to 9 minutes or until tuna is browned and just begins to flake. Serve with reserved sauce.

6 servings.

Preparation time: 30 minutes. Ready to serve: 1 hour.

Per serving: 300 calories, 20.5 g total fat (4 g saturated fat), 80 mg cholesterol, 295 mg sodium, 1 g fiber.

Aegean Halibut Stew

This fish stew is fragrant with the flavors of the Greek islands. It is a one-pot meal with a generous amount of lemon-dill avgolemono sauce. Serve with crusty bread to mop up the sauce.

- 2 teaspoons olive oil
- 1 medium onion, chopped
- 2 garlic cloves, minced
- 2½ cups reduced-sodium chicken broth
- 1 lb. Yukon Gold potatoes, cut into 2½ x ¾-inch wedges
- 6 medium carrots, cut into 2 x ½-inch sticks
- 1 lb. halibut fillet, skin removed, cut into 1¼-inch chunks
- 1 large egg
- 3 tablespoons fresh lemon juice
- ¼ cup chopped fresh dill
- ¼ teaspoon salt
- ⅛ teaspoon freshly ground pepper
- Lemon wedges
- Fresh dill sprigs

❶ In Dutch oven, heat oil over medium heat until hot. Add onion; cook about 2 minutes or until tender, stirring constantly. Add garlic; cook 30 seconds. Add broth; bring to a simmer. Add potatoes and carrots; return to a simmer. Cook, covered, about 15 minutes or until vegetables are tender. With slotted spoon, transfer vegetables to serving bowl. Cover and keep warm.

❷ Add halibut to Dutch oven. Reduce heat to medium-low; cook, covered, 5 to 7 minutes or until halibut is opaque and begins to flake. With slotted spoon, transfer fish to bowl with vegetables. Cover and keep warm.

❸ In medium bowl, whisk egg and lemon juice. Stir in chopped dill. Gradually whisk a little of the hot cooking liquid into egg mixture; pour egg mixture into remaining cooking liquid in Dutch oven. Cook, stirring constantly, over medium heat 2 to 3 minutes or until slightly thickened and temperature reaches 160°F. Season with salt and pepper. Spoon sauce over halibut and vegetables. Garnish with lemon wedges and fresh dill.

4 (1½-cup) servings.

Preparation time: 30 minutes. Ready to serve: 50 minutes.

Per serving: 320 calories, 6 g total fat (1.5 g saturated fat), 115 mg cholesterol, 605 mg sodium, 6 g fiber.

CHEF'S NOTES:

- You can also use halibut steaks. Just cut around the bones to separate fillet portions. Purchase about 1⅔ pounds halibut steaks to allow for loss during filleting and trimming.
- You can substitute other firm fish, such as monkfish or sea bass.

Meat, Poultry, Fish & Seafood

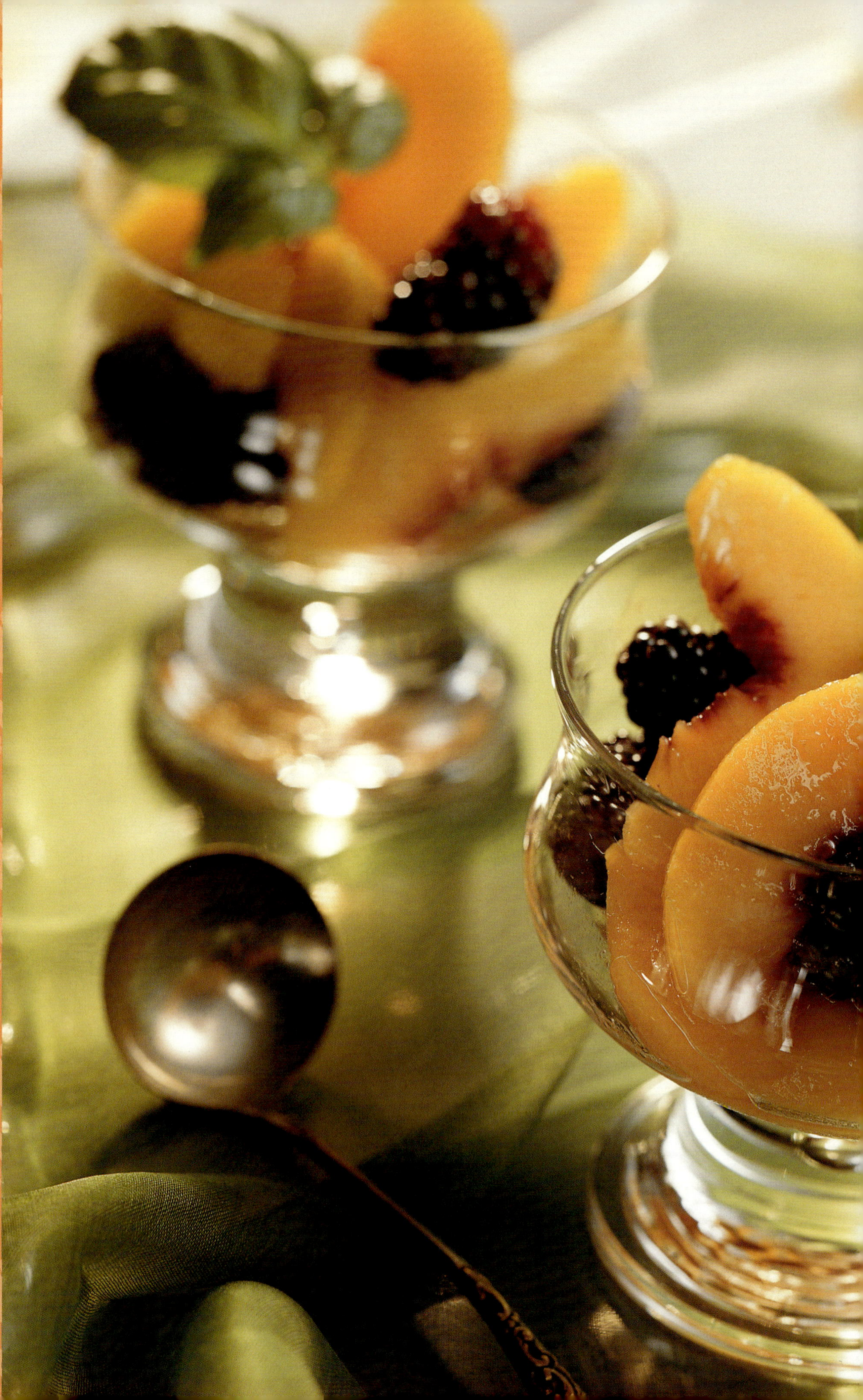

Desserts & Beverages

The only herb routinely paired with sweet flavors is mint. But some nontraditional dessert herbs, such as basil and rosemary, also complement fruit flavors in delightful ways. This chapter offers a selection of refreshing herbal beverages and fragrant sweet endings.

Peach-Blackberry Compote with Basil Syrup, page 145

ROSEMARY-SCENTED LEMON LOAF

Rosemary works well in sweet preparations and is a natural partner with lemon. Enjoy this fragrant loaf with afternoon tea.

2¼	cups all-purpose flour
1½	teaspoons baking powder
½	teaspoon baking soda
½	teaspoon salt
2	large eggs
1	cup sugar
⅓	cup butter, melted, or light olive oil
4	teaspoons chopped fresh rosemary
2	teaspoons freshly grated lemon peel
1	teaspoon vanilla
¾	cup buttermilk

❶ Heat oven to 350°F. Spray 9x5-inch loaf pan with cooking spray.

❷ In medium bowl, whisk flour, baking powder, baking soda and salt.

❸ In large bowl, combine eggs and sugar; beat at high speed 3 to 5 minutes or until pale in color and thickened. Add butter, rosemary, lemon peel and vanilla; beat at low speed just until blended. With rubber spatula, alternately fold in flour mixture and buttermilk, beginning and ending with flour. Spread batter evenly in pan.

❹ Bake 40 to 45 minutes or until golden and toothpick inserted near center comes out clean. Cool in pan on wire rack 5 minutes. Loosen edges; turn loaf out onto rack. Cool completely.

12 servings.

Preparation time: 25 minutes. Ready to serve: 1 hour, 45 minutes.

Per serving: 215 calories, 6.5 g total fat (3.5 g saturated fat), 50 mg cholesterol, 270 mg sodium, 0.5 g fiber.

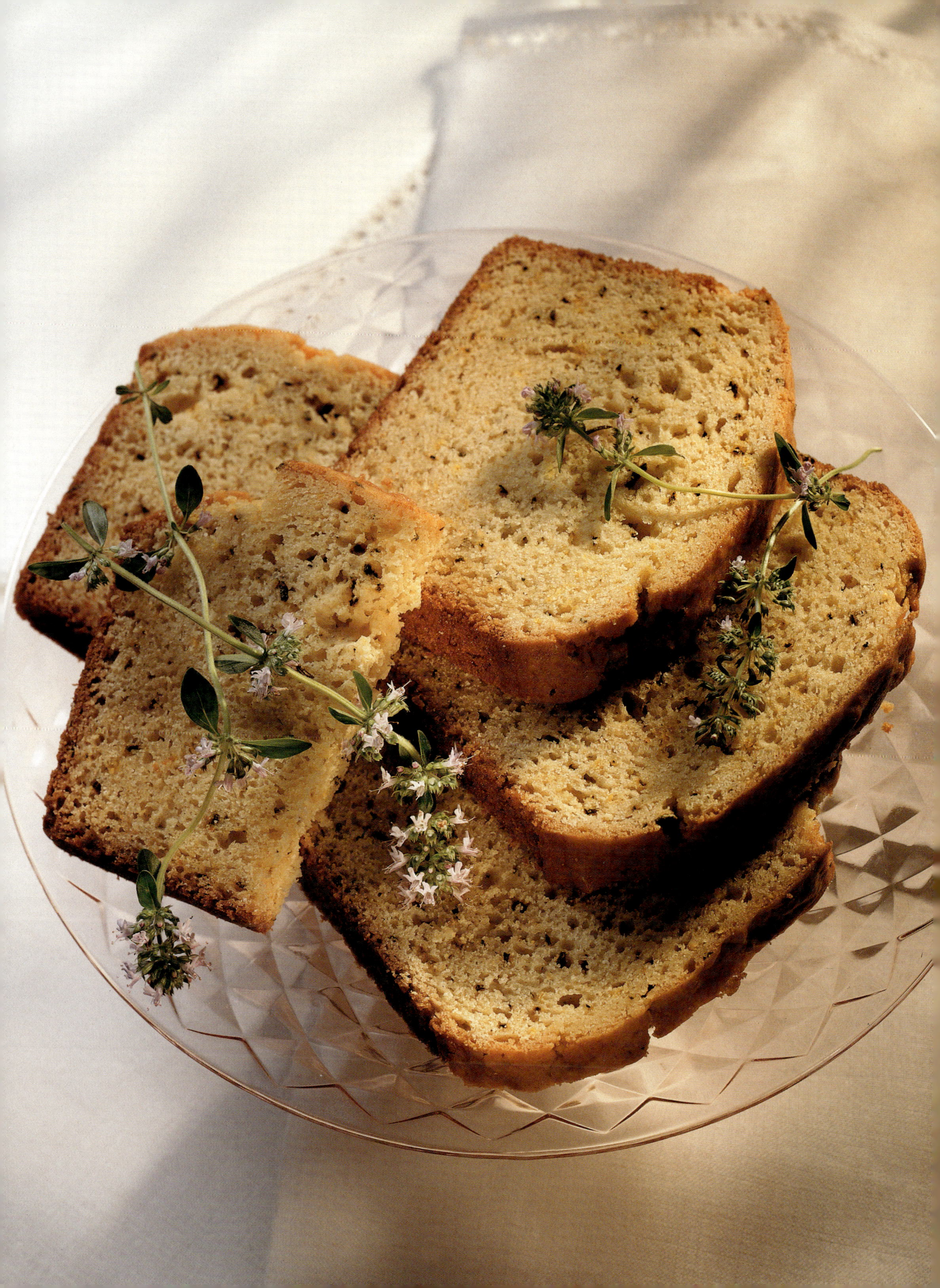

Bloody Mary Mix

This savory smoothie makes a healthful "pick-me-up" snack or delicious base for a vodka-laced Bloody Mary cocktail. In addition to the traditional Bloody Mary seasonings, it is doctored with fresh tomato and herbs.

1½	cups chilled tomato-vegetable juice blend
1	medium tomato, seeded, coarsely chopped
2	tablespoons coarsely chopped fresh lovage*
1	tablespoon fresh lime juice
1	teaspoon Worcestershire sauce
¼ to ½	teaspoon hot pepper sauce
2	ice cubes
	Fresh lovage sprigs

❶ In blender, combine tomato-vegetable juice, tomato, lovage, lime juice, Worcestershire sauce, hot pepper sauce and ice cubes. Cover and blend until smooth. Pour into glasses. Garnish each serving with fresh lovage.

3 (6-oz.) servings.

Preparation time: 15 minutes. Ready to serve: 15 minutes.

Per serving: 35 calories, 0.5 g total fat (0 g saturated fat), 0 mg cholesterol, 470 mg sodium, 1.5 g fiber.

CHEF'S NOTE:

- Lovage contributes a very distinctive and complementary celery-like flavor to this Bloody Mary Mix. Unfortunately, unless you are an avid gardener, lovage can be difficult to find. You can substitute Italian parsley or basil for lovage.

HERB CIDER

Infusing apple cider with thyme creates a hot beverage that combines the soothing qualities of herb tea and the warming properties of spiced apple cider.

- 8 fresh thyme sprigs
- 1/2 teaspoon black peppercorns
- 4 cups pasteurized apple cider

❶ Place thyme and peppercorns in tea infuser or tie in cheesecloth bag. In large saucepan, bring cider just to a simmer over medium-high heat. Remove from heat. Place tea infuser in cider; cover and steep 30 minutes. Remove infuser; reheat cider until steaming. Serve hot.

4 (1-cup) servings.

Preparation time: 5 minutes. Ready to serve: 35 minutes.

Per serving: 115 calories, 0.5 g total fat (0 g saturated fat), 0 mg cholesterol, 5 mg sodium, 0.5 g fiber.

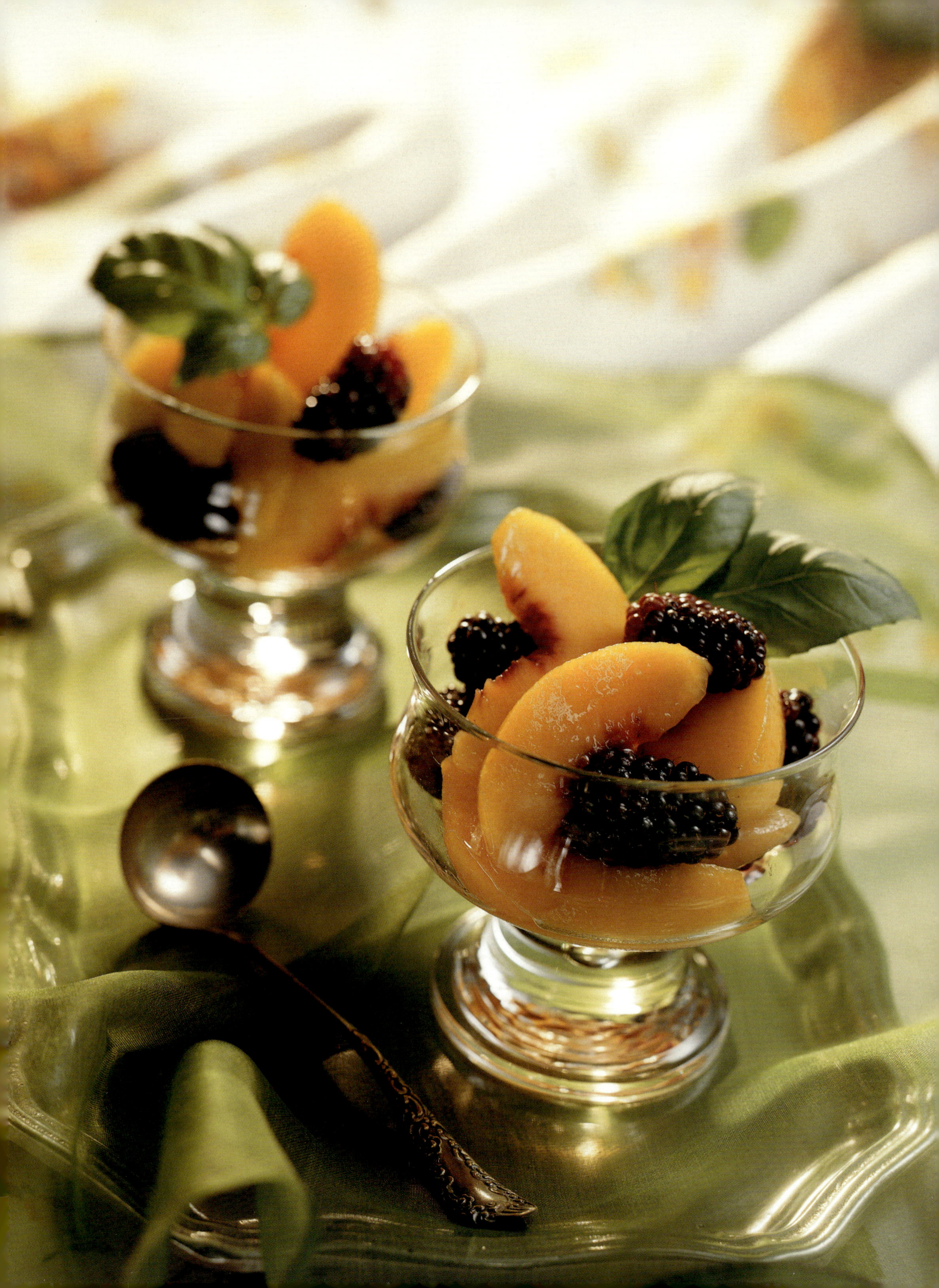

PEACH-BLACKBERRY COMPOTE WITH BASIL SYRUP

There is a secret ingredient in this sophisticated summer fruit compote — it is fresh basil, which has a special affinity with peaches. The basil garnish is a clue to the subtle — yet distinctive — flavor in the syrup.

- ¼ cup sugar
- 3 tablespoons dry white wine
- 3 fresh basil sprigs
- 2 (2-inch) strips orange peel (thin colored portion only)
- 3 cups sliced peeled peaches (1½ lb.)*
- 1 cup fresh blackberries, rinsed
- 1 tablespoon fresh lemon juice
- Fresh basil sprigs

❶ In small saucepan, simmer sugar and wine over medium heat. Remove from heat; stir in 3 basil sprigs and orange peel. Cover and steep 30 minutes.

❷ Strain syrup into small bowl, pressing on basil and orange peel to release flavor.

❸ In large bowl, combine peaches, blackberries and lemon juice. Add basil-infused syrup; toss gently to coat. Garnish with basil sprigs.

TIP *To peel peaches, dip them into boiling water for a few seconds, and then slip off skin.

4 (1-cup) servings.

Preparation time: 20 minutes. Ready to serve: 50 minutes.

Per serving: 125 calories, 0.5 g total fat (0 g saturated fat), 0 mg cholesterol, 0 mg sodium, 4.5 g fiber.

Desserts & Beverages

Honey-Lavender Plum Gratin

Infuse lavender blossoms into the milk for a delicate perfume. This honey-sweetened, lavender-scented custard marries well with summer plums. A quick pass under the broiler to caramelize the top creates a simple, elegant dessert. Note that because the custard is stabilized with cornstarch, you can let it reach a gentle simmer.

CUSTARD*
- 3/4 cup reduced-fat milk
- 3/4 teaspoon unsprayed fresh lavender blossoms or 1/4 teaspoon dried
- 2 egg yolks
- 2 tablespoons honey
- 1 teaspoon cornstarch
- 1/2 teaspoon vanilla**

FRUIT AND TOPPING
- 4 medium plums, quartered, pitted
- 2 tablespoons sugar

❶ In small saucepan, heat milk over medium heat until steaming. Remove from heat. Add lavender; cover and steep 30 minutes.

❷ Pass milk through fine sieve into medium bowl. Return strained milk to saucepan; reheat until steaming.

❸ In medium bowl, whisk egg yolks, honey and cornstarch until smooth. Gradually add hot milk, whisking until blended. Return mixture to saucepan over medium heat. Cook 1 1/2 to 2 minutes or until slightly thickened and starting to bubble gently, whisking constantly. Transfer to clean medium bowl; whisk in vanilla. Cover loosely; refrigerate at least 1 hour or until chilled. (*Custard can be made ahead. Cover and refrigerate up to 2 days.*)

❹ Heat broiler. Spray 11x7-inch oval gratin dish or 4 individual gratin dishes with cooking spray. Spoon custard evenly over bottom of gratin dishes. Arrange plums, skin side down, in single layer over custard. Sprinkle sugar evenly over plums. Broil 5 to 7 minutes or until plums are lightly caramelized. Serve immediately.

TIP *You can also use the custard as a sauce for fresh raspberries or figs.

TIP **If vanilla bean is available, this is a great opportunity to use it. Replace the vanilla extract with a 3-inch piece of vanilla bean. Make a lengthwise slit in the bean with tip of sharp knife, scrape out the seeds and drop the whole bean into milk along with the lavender in step 1; let steep.

4 servings.

Preparation time: 25 minutes. Ready to serve: 2 hours, 15 minutes.

Per serving: 150 calories, 4 g total fat (1.5 g saturated fat), 110 mg cholesterol, 25 mg sodium, 1 g fiber.

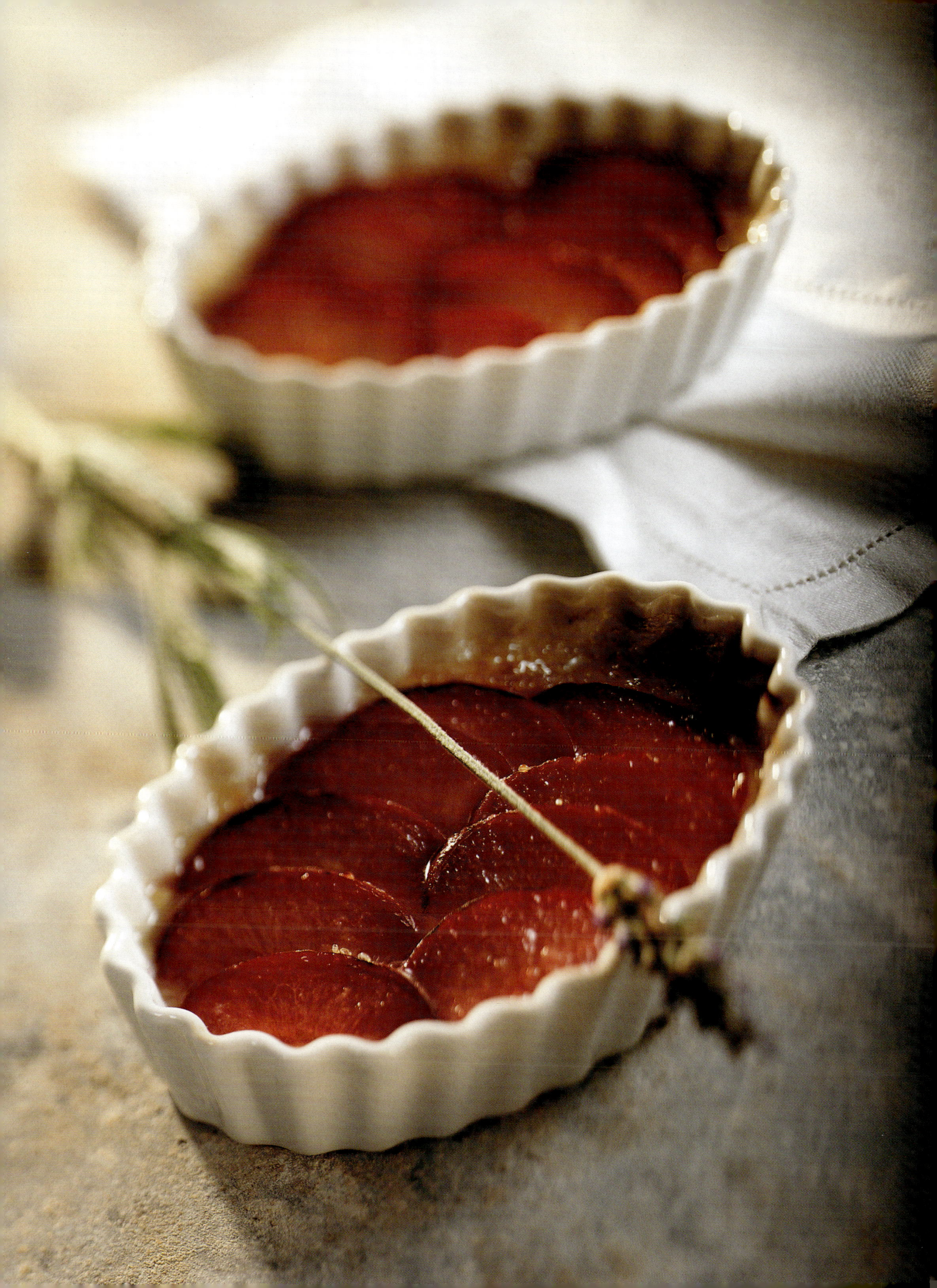

RHUBARB FOOL WITH ANGELICA

Vanilla yogurt and a touch of whipped cream enrich a tart rhubarb compote in this old-fashioned fool. Angelica, which is traditionally used to mellow and enhance rhubarb, contributes a pleasant herbal note.

- 1 lb. fresh rhubarb, stem ends trimmed, cut into 1/2-inch lengths (3 1/2 cups)
- 1/3 cup sugar
- 2 tablespoons fresh orange juice
- 2 tablespoons finely diced angelica stems*
- 1 1/4 cups low-fat vanilla yogurt
- 1/3 cup whipping cream
- 6 strawberries, hulled, sliced
- Fresh mint sprigs

❶ In medium saucepan, combine rhubarb, sugar, orange juice and angelica. Cook over medium heat 7 to 9 minutes, stirring frequently, until rhubarb is tender and mixture has broken down into chunky puree. Transfer puree to medium bowl; cover loosely and refrigerate about 2 hours or until completely cooled.

❷ Line sieve or colander with cheesecloth; set over medium bowl at least 1/2 inch from bowl. Spoon yogurt into sieve. Cover; drain in refrigerator 1 1/2 to 2 hours.

❸ Meanwhile, place small bowl and beaters in freezer to chill.

❹ Discard whey that has drained from yogurt. Add drained yogurt to rhubarb; mix gently with rubber spatula. In chilled bowl, whip cream to soft peaks. Add to rhubarb-yogurt mixture; fold gently to mix, leaving distinct swirls. Spoon into 6 dessert glasses or bowls. (*Dessert can be made ahead. Cover and refrigerate up to 1 day.*) Garnish each serving with strawberry slices and mint sprigs.

6 (1/2-cup) servings.

Preparation time: 20 minutes. Ready to serve: 2 hours, 30 minutes.

Per serving: 145 calories, 4.5 g total fat (3 g saturated fat), 15 mg cholesterol, 35 mg sodium, 1 g fiber.

CHEF'S NOTE:

- Angelica is a delightful addition to any rhubarb dish, but it is not terribly common or easy to find. If it is not available, just leave it out; add an extra tablespoon of sugar instead.

TUNISIAN MINT TEA

While traveling in Tunisia, I discovered this delightful way to serve tea. Green tea is infused with mint leaves and served in a pretty glass. The special Tunisian touch is a garnish of pine nuts. The result is pure refreshment.

- 2 green tea bags
- 1/3 cup fresh mint sprigs
- 5 cups boiling water
- 1 tablespoon pine nuts, toasted (see TIP, page 54)
- Fresh mint sprigs
- Sugar, if desired

❶ Warm teapot by rinsing with boiling water. Place tea bags and 1/3 cup mint sprigs in teapot; pour in 5 cups boiling water. Cover and steep 5 minutes. Pour tea into individual glasses. Float a few pine nuts in each glass. Garnish each serving with mint sprigs. Sweeten with sugar.

6 (3/4-cup) servings.

Preparation time: 10 minutes. Ready to serve: 15 minutes.

Per serving: 9 calories, 1 g total fat (0 g saturated fat), 0 mg cholesterol, 5 mg sodium, 0 g fiber.

Desserts & Beverages

Strawberry Shortcakes with Lemon Verbena Cream

Here is a lightened-up version of a classic. Instead of straight whipped cream, the topping is made from vanilla yogurt and just enough real whipped cream to lighten the texture and contribute a luxurious taste. A whisper of lemon verbena adds a sophisticated and elegant note.

LEMON-VERBENA CREAM
- 1½ cups low-fat vanilla yogurt
- ½ cup whipping cream
- 4 teaspoons very finely chopped fresh lemon verbena

SHORTCAKES
- 2 cups all-purpose flour
- 2 tablespoons plus 2 teaspoons sugar
- 1 tablespoon baking powder
- ½ teaspoon baking soda
- ½ teaspoon salt
- 6 tablespoons butter, cut into small pieces
- 1 cup buttermilk
- 2 teaspoons reduced-fat milk

STRAWBERRY FILLING
- 6 cups (1½ lb.) strawberries, hulled, sliced
- 2 tablespoons sugar
- Fresh lemon verbena sprigs

❶ Line sieve or colander with cheesecloth; set over medium bowl at least ½ inch from bottom. Spoon yogurt into sieve. Cover; drain in refrigerator 1½ hours. Meanwhile, place small bowl and beaters in freezer to chill. In chilled bowl with chilled beaters, whip cream to soft peaks. Push to one side of bowl. Discard whey that has drained from yogurt. Add drained yogurt and lemon verbena to whipped cream. With rubber spatula, fold gently to mix. (*Cream can be made ahead. Cover and refrigerate up to 8 hours.*)

❷ Heat oven to 425°F. Spray baking sheet with cooking spray.

❸ In large bowl, combine flour, 2 tablespoons sugar, baking powder, baking soda and salt; whisk to blend. Using pastry blender or fingertips, cut in butter until mixture crumbles. Make a well in center of flour mixture; add buttermilk, stirring with fork, just until dough clumps together. Turn out onto lightly floured surface; knead several times. Roll or pat dough ¾ inch thick. Using a 3- or 3½-inch round cutter, cut out circles. Arrange shortcakes 1 inch apart on baking sheet. Gather scraps; reroll. Brush tops with milk; sprinkle with remaining 2 teaspoons sugar.

❹ Bake shortcakes 15 to 20 minutes or until golden brown. Transfer to wire rack; cool at least 10 minutes. Meanwhile, in medium bowl, combine strawberries and 2 tablespoons sugar; toss gently to coat. Let stand about 20 minutes or until strawberries give off juice.

❺ Just before serving, assemble shortcakes: Using serrated knife, split 6 shortcakes horizontally. Place shortcake bottoms on individual plates. Spoon about ⅓ cup strawberries and juice over each shortcake bottom. Top each with scant ¼ cup lemon verbena cream. Replace shortcake tops. Place dollop of the remaining cream on each shortcake. Spoon remaining strawberries and juice over top. Garnish with lemon verbena sprigs.

6 servings.

Preparation time: 50 minutes. Ready to serve: 2 hours, 30 minutes.

Per serving: 455 calories, 20 g total fat (12 g saturated fat), 60 mg cholesterol, 700 mg sodium, 3 g fiber.

Desserts & Beverages **151**

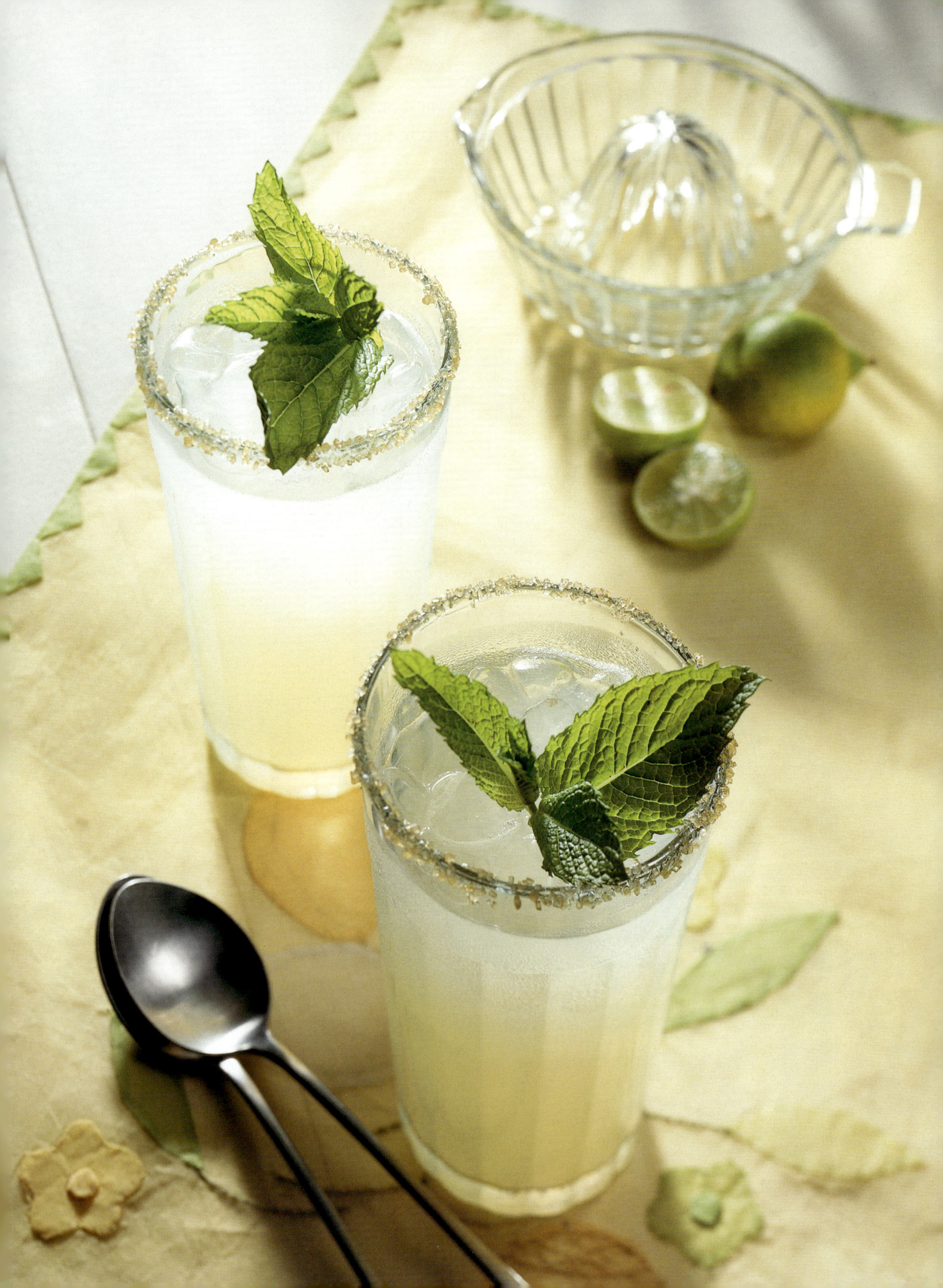

Sparkling Mint Limeade

For pure refreshment, nothing beats homemade limeade or lemonade. In this version, the citrus base is infused with herbs and diluted with sparkling water for a lively finish.

- 1 cup fresh mint sprigs, plus more for garnish
- 1¼ cups fresh lime juice
- ⅔ cup sugar
- Ice cubes
- 3 cups (750 ml) chilled sparkling seltzer or soda water

❶ In medium bowl, bruise mint with pestle or wooden spoon to release fragrance. Add lime juice and sugar; stir to dissolve sugar. Cover and refrigerate at least 2 hours or up to 8 hours.

❷ Strain lime juice mixture, pressing on mint sprigs to extract flavor. To serve, place several ice cubes in each of 4 tall glasses. Pour ⅓ cup lime juice mixture into each glass; top off with ¾ cup sparkling water. Garnish each serving with a mint sprig.

4 (1-cup) servings.

Preparation time: 20 minutes. Ready to serve: 2 hours, 20 minutes.

Per serving: 145 calories, 0 g total fat (0 g saturated fat), 0 mg cholesterol, 55 mg sodium, 0.5 g fiber.

CHEF'S NOTES:
- To make lemonade, substitute rosemary sprigs for mint, lemon juice for lime juice, and reduce sugar to ½ cup. Garnish with rosemary sprigs.
- Whether you're serving lemonade or limeade, dip the edge of each glass in honey, then sugar.

Desserts & Beverages

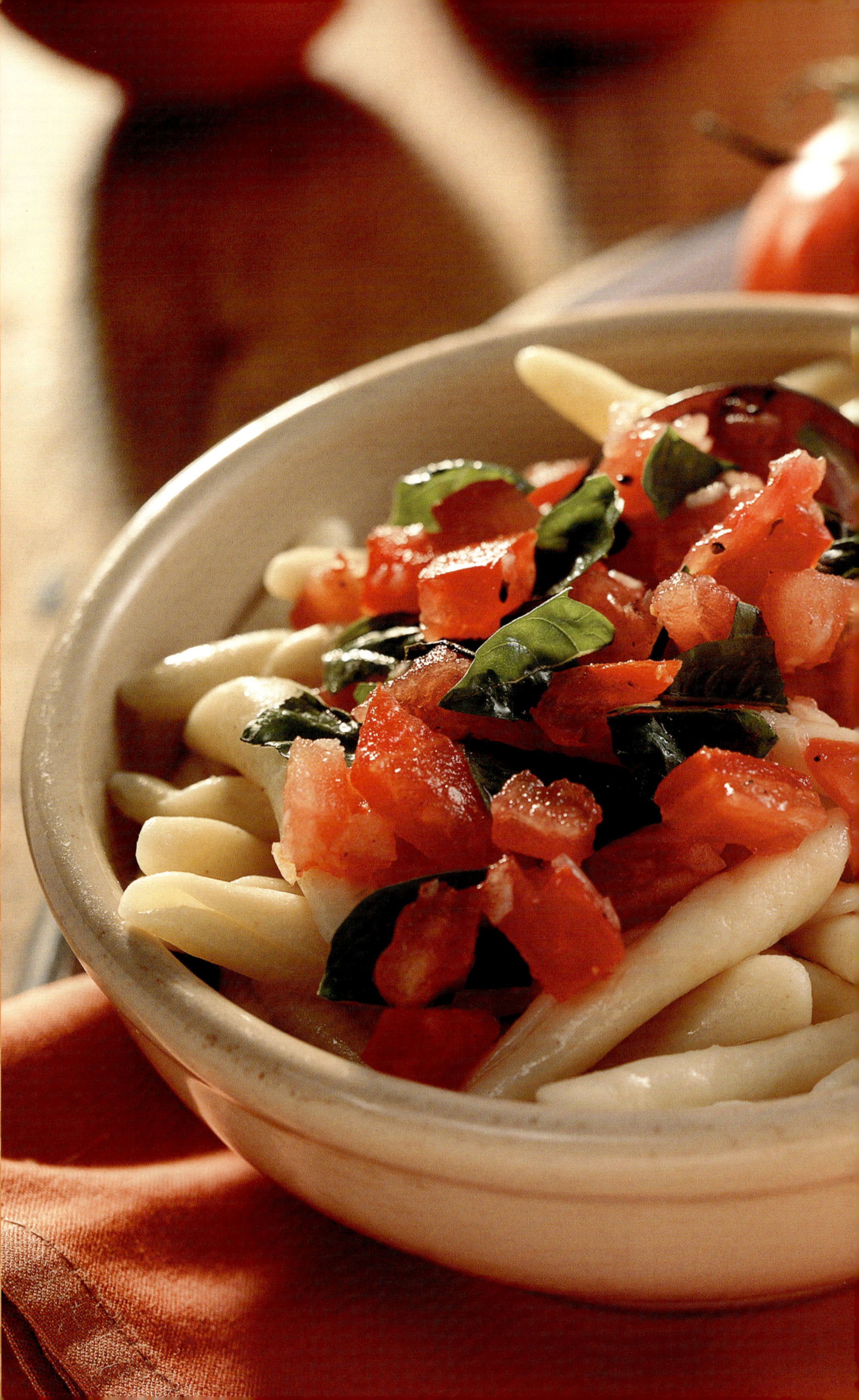

Sauces & Condiments

Herbs build terrific flavor, so it is not surprising that they play a key role in a wide variety of sauces and condiments. This chapter serves as a handy reference, providing a selection of pestos, compound butters, mayonnaise-based sauces and relishes to brighten your meals.

No-Cook Summer Tomato Sauce, page 168

Health-Conscious Basil Pesto

Silken tofu is an effective replacement for much of the olive oil in a traditional pesto. Sneaking some tofu into a pesto is an easy way to include more beneficial soy protein in your diet.

- 1 large garlic clove, crushed
- ½ teaspoon salt
- 1½ cups lightly packed fresh basil leaves
- ¼ cup pine nuts, toasted (see TIP, page 54)
- ⅛ teaspoon freshly ground pepper
- Dash of crushed red pepper
- ½ cup reduced-fat firm silken tofu
- 1 tablespoon extra-virgin olive oil
- ¼ cup (1 oz.) freshly grated Parmesan cheese

❶ Using mortar and pestle or side of chef's knife, mash garlic and salt into a paste. Transfer to food processor. Add basil, pine nuts, ground pepper and red pepper; process until finely chopped. Add tofu and oil; process until smooth and creamy. Add Parmesan cheese; pulse several times to blend. (*Pesto can be made ahead. Place sheet of plastic wrap directly on surface to prevent discoloration; refrigerate up to 2 days or freeze up to 6 months.*)

¾ cup.

Preparation time: 10 minutes. Ready to serve: 10 minutes.

Per tablespoon: 45 calories, 4 g total fat (1 g saturated fat), 2 mg cholesterol, 290 mg sodium, 0.5 g fiber.

Traditional Basil Pesto

Pesto has become a standby in American kitchens. A stash of pesto in the freezer is one of the best ways to preserve the taste of summer. Use it as a stuffing for boneless chicken breasts, toss it with pasta or top a pizza with it.

- 4 cups lightly packed fresh basil leaves
- 1/2 cup pine nuts, toasted (see TIP, page 54)
- 3 garlic cloves, crushed
- 1/2 teaspoon salt
- 1/4 teaspoon freshly ground pepper
- 1/4 cup extra-virgin olive oil
- 3/4 cup (3 oz.) freshly grated Parmesan cheese

CHEF'S NOTE:
- If using pesto for grilled pizza, bring to room temperature before spreading over crust.

❶ In food processor, combine basil, pine nuts, garlic, salt and pepper; process until pine nuts are ground. With motor running, gradually add oil through feed tube, processing until mixture forms a paste. Add Parmesan cheese; pulse until blended. (*Pesto can be made ahead. Place sheet of plastic wrap directly on surface to prevent discoloration; refrigerate up to 2 days or freeze up to 6 months.*)

1 1/3 cups.

Preparation time: 10 minutes. Ready to serve: 10 minutes.

Per tablespoon: 60 calories, 5.5 g total fat (1.5 g saturated fat), 5 mg cholesterol, 135 mg sodium, 0.5 g fiber.

Papaya Relish

Here's a refreshing accompaniment to Asian grilled fare. Substitute mango for papaya, if you like.

- 2 garlic cloves, crushed
- 2 teaspoons sugar
- 1/4 teaspoon salt
- 2 tablespoons rice vinegar
- 1/2 teaspoon hot pepper sauce
- 1 firm papaya, seeded, diced
- 1/2 cup diced red onion
- 1/2 cup slivered fresh cilantro

❶ Using mortar and pestle or with side of chef's knife, mash garlic, sugar and salt into a paste; transfer to medium bowl. Whisk in vinegar and hot pepper sauce. Add papaya, onion and cilantro; toss gently to mix. Serve within 1 hour.

1 1/2 cups.

Preparation time: 20 minutes. Ready to serve: 20 minutes.

Per (1/4-cup) serving. 35 calories, 0 g total fat (0 g saturated fat), 0 mg cholesterol, 100 mg sodium, 1 g fiber.

QUICK TOMATO SAUCE

This basic tomato sauce is so easy, it is hard to imagine why anyone would bother with prepared sauces that are frequently too sweet and "cooked" tasting. Peppery marjoram gives a basic tomato sauce character and a meaty taste. Use this sauce for pizzas and pasta, or serve with fish. Note that if you are making the sauce to use in a dish that highlights other herbs, omit the marjoram.

- 1 tablespoon olive oil
- 4 garlic cloves, minced
- 1/8 teaspoon crushed red pepper
- 2 (14.5-oz.) cans diced tomatoes, undrained
- 1 to 2 tablespoons chopped fresh marjoram or 1 to 2 teaspoons dried, if desired
- Dash of salt
- 1/8 teaspoon freshly ground pepper

❶ In large saucepan, heat oil over medium-low heat until warm. Add garlic and red pepper; cook 30 seconds to 1 minute or until tender and fragrant but not colored, stirring constantly. Add tomatoes and 1 tablespoon marjoram; mash with potato masher. Bring to a simmer. Cook, uncovered, 20 to 25 minutes or until thickened, stirring and mashing occasionally. Season with salt and pepper. Taste and add more marjoram, if desired (*Sauce can be made ahead. Cover and refrigerate up to 4 days or freeze up to 3 months.*)

2 1/4 cups.

Preparation time: 10 minutes. Ready to serve: 35 minutes.

Per 1/4 cup serving: 35 calories, 1.5 g total fat (0 g saturated fat), 0 mg cholesterol, 175 mg sodium, 1 g fiber.

CHEF'S NOTE:
- If marjoram is not available, substitute oregano. You can also flavor the sauce with 1/3 cup slivered fresh basil, added at the end of cooking.

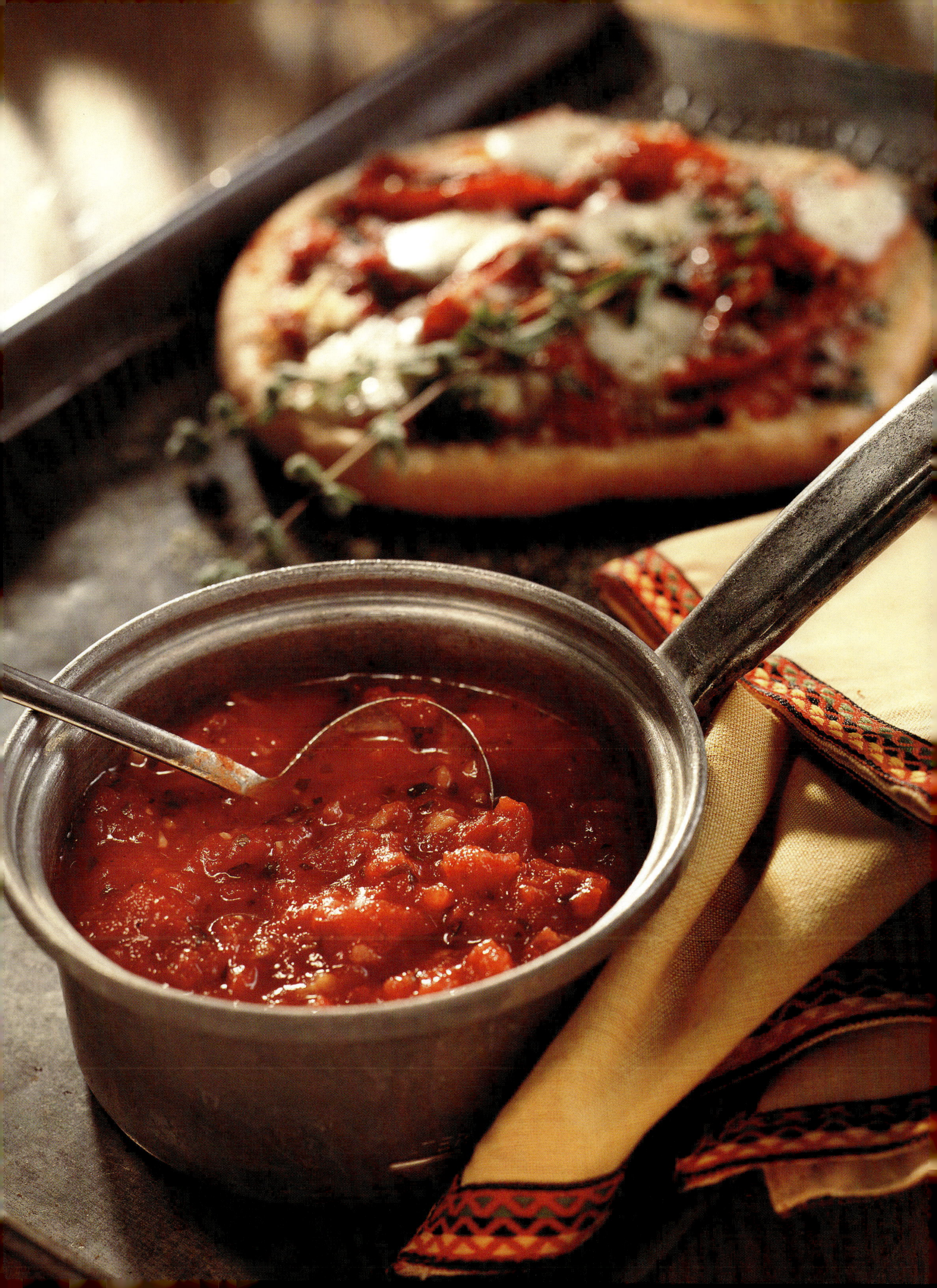

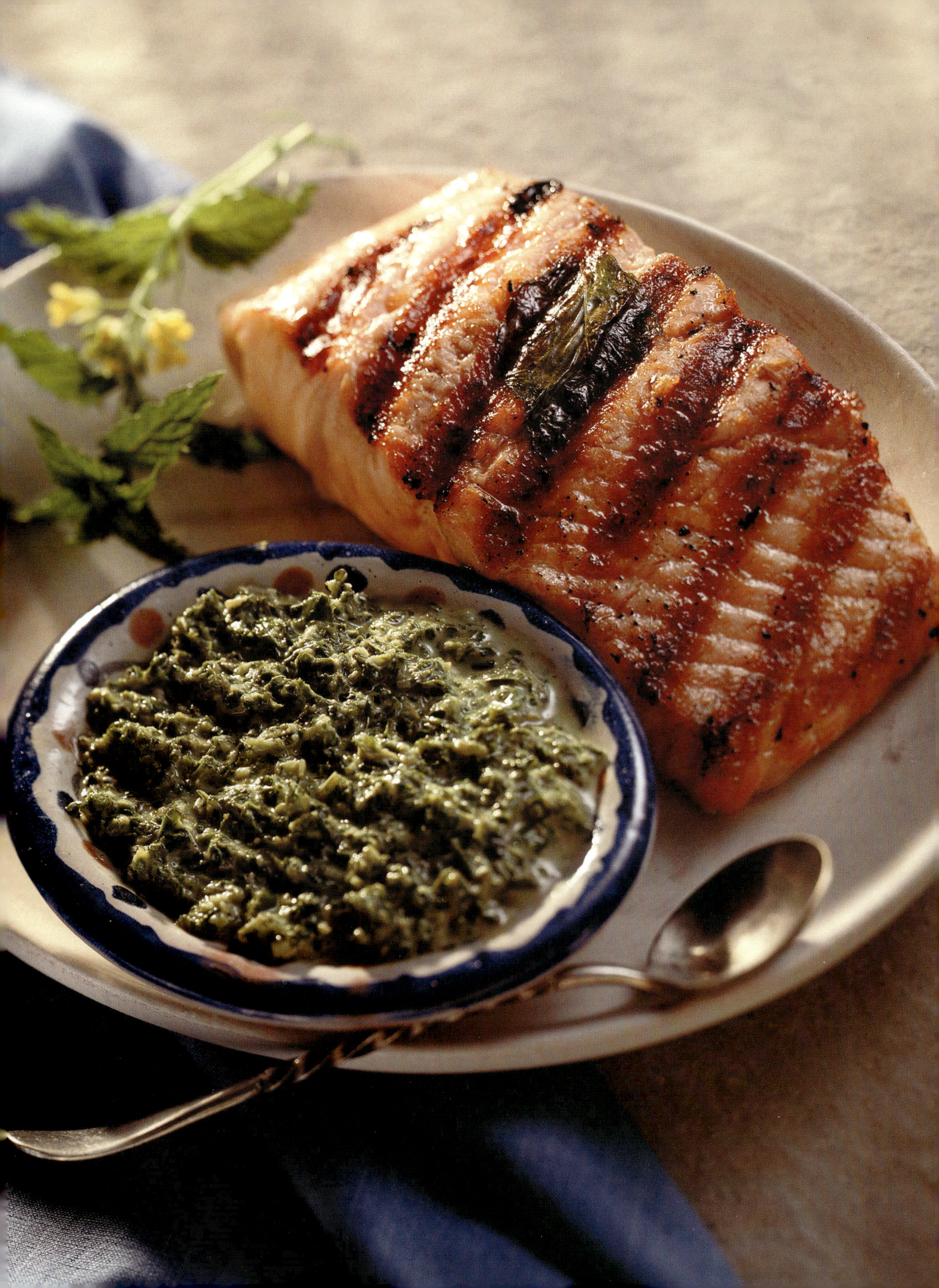

MINT AND GINGER CHUTNEY

If mint is taking over your garden, take advantage and make up a batch of this bright, lively herb chutney. Serve with salmon, lamb chops or as an accompaniment to curries.

- 3 cups lightly packed fresh mint leaves
- 1 medium jalapeño chile, seeded, coarsely chopped
- 4 teaspoons coarsely chopped fresh ginger
- 1 tablespoon sugar
- ½ teaspoon salt
- 2 garlic cloves, crushed
- ⅓ cup plain nonfat yogurt
- 3 tablespoons rice vinegar

❶ In food processor, combine mint, chile, ginger, sugar, salt and ½ teaspoon salt; process until finely chopped. Add yogurt and vinegar; process until mixture forms a creamy sauce, stopping to scrape down sides of bowl several times. (*Sauce can be made ahead. Place sheet of plastic wrap directly on surface to prevent discoloration; refrigerate up to 2 days.*) Serve at room temperature.

¾ cup.

Preparation time: 10 minutes. Ready to serve: 10 minutes.

Per tablespoon: 15 calories, 0 g total fat (0 g saturated fat), 0 mg cholesterol, 105 mg sodium, 0 g fiber.

Sauces & Condiments

PARSLEY-WALNUT PESTO

Requiring just a few basic ingredients you may have on hand, this easy sauce for pasta makes a handy standby for busy nights when the refrigerator seems bare. The proportion of nuts to herbs is higher than a traditional basil pesto. When this pesto is thinned with some pasta cooking water, it becomes a delicious garlicky walnut cream. This recipe makes about the right amount for 12 ounces of pasta.

- 1 cup lightly packed fresh Italian parsley leaves
- 3/4 cup walnuts, toasted*
- 2 garlic cloves, crushed
- 1/4 teaspoon salt
- 1/4 teaspoon freshly ground pepper
- 1/4 cup extra-virgin olive oil
- 1/2 cup (2 oz.) freshly grated Parmesan cheese

❶ In food processor, combine parsley, walnuts, garlic, salt and pepper; process until walnuts are ground. With motor running, gradually add oil, processing until mixture forms a paste. Add Parmesan cheese; pulse several times until blended. (Pesto can be made ahead. Place sheet of plastic wrap directly on surface to prevent discoloration; refrigerate up to 2 days or freeze up to 6 months.)

TIP *To toast walnuts, spread on baking sheet; bake at 375°F for 7 to 10 minutes or until fragrant. Transfer to small bowl to cool. Or in small dry skillet, toast walnuts over medium-low heat 3 to 4 minutes or until fragrant, stirring constantly. Transfer to small bowl to cool.

3/4 cup.

Preparation time: 20 minutes. Ready to serve: 20 minutes.

Per tablespoon: 105 calories, 10 g total fat (2 g saturated fat), 5 mg cholesterol, 190 mg sodium, 0.5 g fiber.

SHALLOT-MUSTARD HERB BUTTER

Compound butters are one of the simplest and most satisfying ways to embellish grilled foods. Traditional recipes use all butter, but I have found that I can lighten the butter by whipping in an equal proportion of flavorful olive oil, thereby improving the ratio of healthful mono-unsaturated fats to saturated fats. Serve with grilled fish steaks, veal or lamb chops, or beef steaks.

- ¼ cup butter, softened
- ¼ cup extra-virgin olive oil
- 2 tablespoons Dijon mustard
- 4 teaspoons fresh lemon juice
- 2 tablespoons finely chopped shallot
- 2 tablespoons chopped fresh Italian parsley
- ¼ teaspoon freshly ground pepper

CHEF'S NOTES:
- One of the easiest ways to preserve fresh herbs is to make up a batch of compound butter and freeze it in small portions. Place a portion of compound butter in a sheet of plastic wrap, roll into a cylinder and secure the plastic wrap.
- For basil butter: Substitute basil for parsley and orange juice for lemon juice.
- For tarragon butter: Substitute tarragon for parsley.
- For *fines herbes* butter: Substitute *fines herbes* (page 13) for parsley.

❶ In medium bowl, beat butter at medium speed until smooth and creamy. Gradually add oil, beating until well blended. Beat in mustard and lemon juice. Stir in shallots, parsley and pepper. Serve at room temperature. (*Butter can be made ahead. Cover and refrigerate up to 4 days or freeze up to 6 months.*)

⅔ cup.

Preparation time: 10 minutes. Ready to serve: 10 minutes.

Per tablespoon: 90 calories, 10 g total fat (3.5 g saturated fat), 10 mg cholesterol, 70 mg sodium, 0 g fiber.

Sauces & Condiments

Cilantro Pesto

Fresh chopped chiles and lime juice give a pleasant kick to cilantro pesto. Serve with tortilla chips or use to top burgers or grilled fish.

- 2 cups lightly packed fresh cilantro leaves
- 1/4 cup slivered almonds, toasted*
- 1 jalapeño chile, seeded, coarsely chopped
- 2 garlic cloves, crushed
- 1/4 teaspoon salt
- 1/4 cup vegetable oil
- 1 tablespoon fresh lime juice
- 1/4 teaspoon freshly ground pepper

1 In food processor, combine cilantro, almonds, chile, garlic and salt; process until finely chopped. With motor running, gradually add oil through feed tube, processing until mixture forms a paste. Add lime juice and pepper; process to mix. (*Pesto can be made ahead. Place sheet of plastic wrap directly on surface to prevent discoloration; refrigerate up to 2 days or freeze up to 6 months.*)

TIP *In small, dry skillet, toast slivered almonds over medium-low heat 3 to 4 minutes or until light golden and fragrant, stirring constantly. Transfer to small bowl to cool.

2/3 cup.

Preparation time: 15 minutes. Ready to serve: 15 minutes.

Per tablespoon: 70 calories, 7 g total fat (1 g saturated fat), 0 mg cholesterol, 60 mg sodium, 0.5 g fiber.

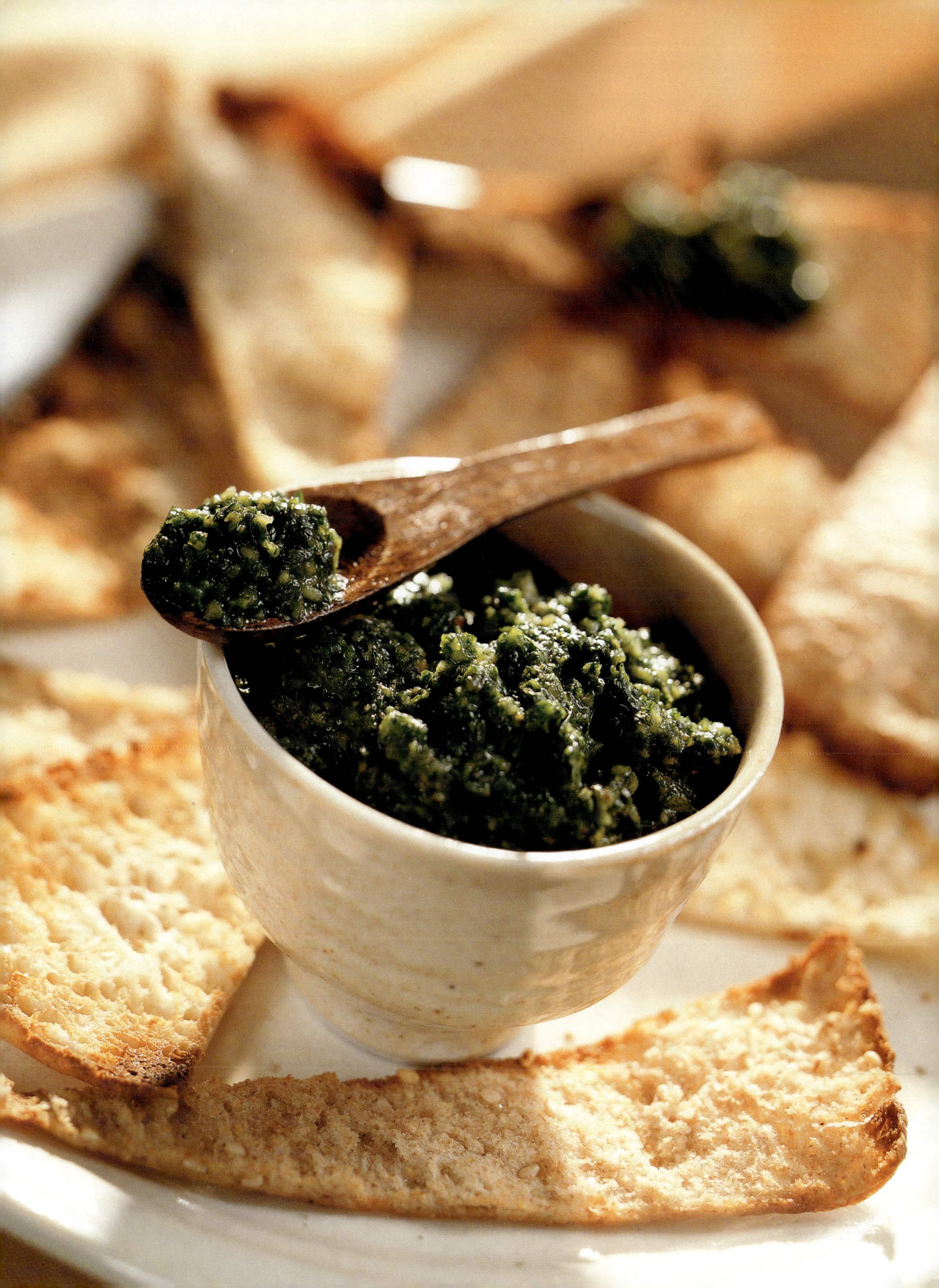

Moroccan Charmoula Sauce

This versatile sauce from North Africa complements grilled fish and poultry. It can also jazz up vegetarian entrées.

1½	cups lightly packed fresh cilantro leaves
1½	cups lightly packed fresh Italian parsley leaves
3	garlic cloves, crushed
1	tablespoon ground cumin
2	teaspoons paprika
¾	teaspoon salt
	Dash of cayenne pepper
½	cup vegetable or reduced-sodium chicken broth
⅓	cup reduced-fat firm silken tofu
2	tablespoons fresh lemon juice
1	tablespoon extra-virgin olive oil

❶ In food processor, combine cilantro, parsley, garlic, cumin, paprika, salt and cayenne; pulse until finely chopped. Add broth, tofu, lemon juice and oil; process until mixture forms creamy sauce, stopping to scrape down sides of bowl several times. (*Sauce can be made ahead. Place sheet of plastic wrap directly on surface to prevent discoloration; refrigerate up to 2 days.*) Just before serving, heat sauce over medium heat, stirring until heated through but not boiling.

1 cup.
Preparation time: 15 minutes. Ready to serve: 15 minutes.

Per tablespoon: 20 calories, 1.5 g total fat (0 g saturated fat), 0 mg cholesterol, 130 mg sodium, 0.5 g fiber.

PARSLEY-CAPER SAUCE

This piquant green sauce is an Italian classic. It provides a perfect flourish for grilled chicken or turkey cutlets, fish steaks or veal chops.

- 2 cups lightly packed fresh Italian parsley leaves
- 1/4 cup drained capers, rinsed
- 3 garlic cloves, crushed
- 2 tablespoons vegetable or reduced-sodium chicken broth
- 1 tablespoon extra-virgin olive oil
- 1 tablespoon low-fat mayonnaise
- 1 tablespoon fresh lemon juice
- 1 teaspoon Dijon mustard
- 3/4 teaspoon anchovy paste

❶ In food processor, combine parsley, capers and garlic; pulse until finely chopped. Add broth, oil, mayonnaise, lemon juice, mustard and anchovy paste; process until mixture forms a creamy sauce, stopping to scrape down sides of bowl several times. (*Sauce can be made up ahead. Place sheet of plastic wrap directly on surface to prevent discoloration; refrigerate up to 2 days.*)

1/2 cup.

Preparation time: 10 minutes. Ready to serve: 10 minutes.

Per tablespoon: 30 calories, 2.5 g total fat (0.5 g saturated fat), 0 mg cholesterol, 175 mg sodium, 0.5 g fiber.

Sauces & Condiments

No-Cook Summer Tomato Sauce

Tomato season is all too short. Enjoy them every day in late summer. Here is an easy sauce that is only worth making with "real" tomatoes. Toss with hot pasta for a light summer supper. This is enough for about 12 ounces of uncooked pasta. Sprinkle with Parmesan if you like. Or you can use this sauce as a topping for bruschetta.

- 3 medium vine-ripe tomatoes, halved crosswise
- 3 garlic cloves, crushed,
- 1/2 teaspoon kosher (coarse) salt
- 1/8 teaspoon crushed red pepper
- 1 cup lightly packed fresh basil leaves, torn into 1/2-inch pieces
- 2 tablespoons extra-virgin olive oil
- 2 teaspoons balsamic vinegar, if desired
- 1/4 teaspoon freshly ground pepper

1. With fingers, remove tomato seeds into strainer set over small bowl. With rubber spatula, press on seeds to extract juice. Reserve juice; dice tomatoes.
2. Using mortar and pestle or with side of chef's knife, mash garlic, salt and red pepper into a paste.
3. In medium bowl, combine tomatoes, reserved juice, garlic mixture, basil, oil, vinegar and pepper; toss to mix gently. Serve shortly after making. Do not refrigerate.

3 cups.

Preparation time: 20 minutes. Ready to serve: 20 minutes.

Per (3/4-cup) serving: 85 calories, 7 g total fat (1 g saturated fat), 0 mg cholesterol, 200 mg sodium, 1.5 g fiber.

CHEF'S NOTE:
- Put away your knives when you are preparing the basil. Large pieces of casually torn basil leaves are nicest for this rustic sauce.

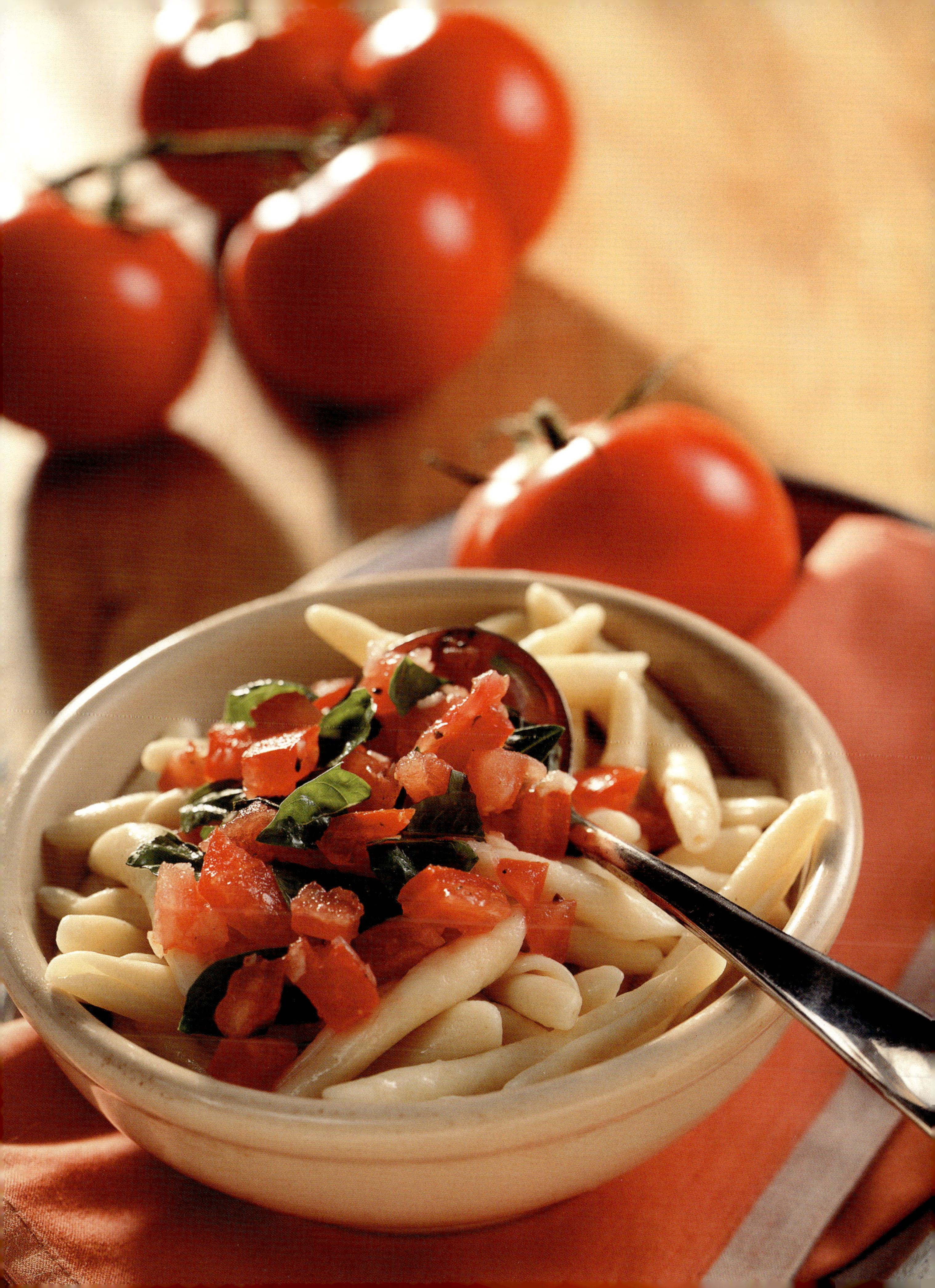

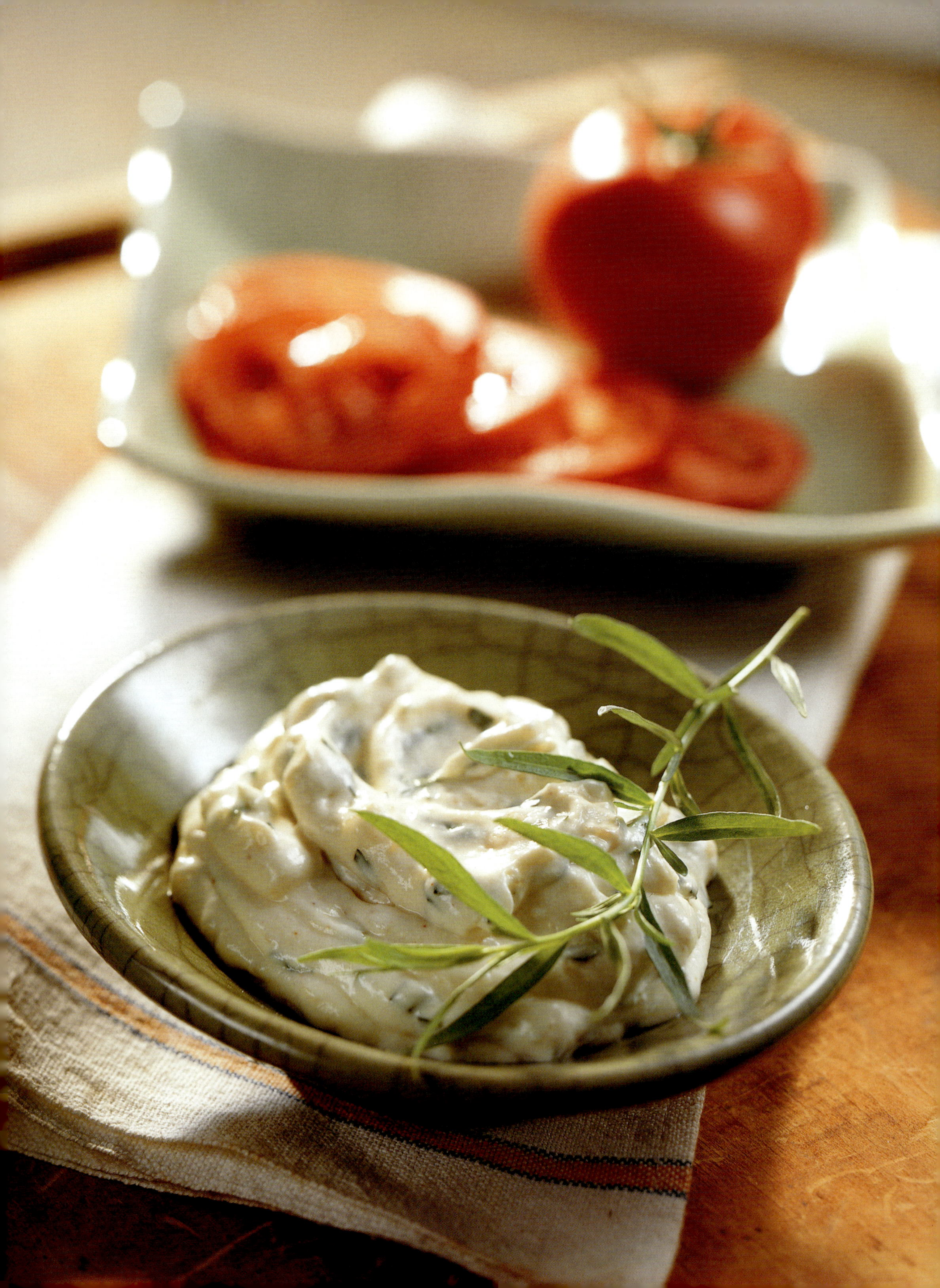

SPRINGTIME SAUCE WITH FINES HERBES

This sauce is similar to hollandaise, but it is much lighter and easier to make. The base is actually low-fat mayonnaise that is thinned with broth, warmed and finished with fresh herbs, mustard and lemon. The sauce is perfect with poached fish.

¼	cup reduced-fat mayonnaise
¼	cup vegetable or reduced-sodium chicken broth
1	tablespoon grainy mustard
1	tablespoon extra-virgin olive oil
1	tablespoon fresh lemon juice
2	tablespoons *fines herbes* (page 13)
¼	teaspoon freshly ground pepper

❶ Place mayonnaise in small saucepan. Gradually add broth, whisking until smooth. Set saucepan over medium-low heat; cook, whisking constantly 2 to 3 minutes or until mixture is heated through but not bubbling. Remove from heat. Stir in mustard, oil, lemon juice, *Fines Herbes* and pepper. Serve warm.

¾ cup.

Preparation time: 10 minutes. Ready to serve: 15 minutes.

Per tablespoon: 30 calories, 3 g total fat (0.5 g saturated fat), 0 mg cholesterol, 65 mg sodium, 0 g fiber.

CHEF'S NOTE:

- If more convenient, use just one or two of the herbs in the *fines herbes* mixture. Or use 2 tablespoons chopped fresh dill.

Sauces & Condiments

RECIPE INDEX

This index lists every recipe in **Celebrating Herbs** *by name. If you're looking for a specific recipe but can't recall the exact name, turn to the General Index that starts on page 173.*

Aegean Halibut Stew, 137
Asparagus Salad with Mint and Almonds, 89
Baked Eggs with Tarragon, 50
Bloody Mary Mix, 142
Butternut Squash Gratin, 81
Butternut Squash Ravioli, 102
Caramelized Red Onion, Olive and Goat Cheese Galette, 64
Cauliflower and Spinach Curry, 85
Cherry Tomatoes Filled with Pesto Cream Cheese, 54
Chicken Sauté with Tarragon, 116
Chicken, Prosciutto and Sage Kabobs, 126
Cilantro Pesto, 164
Couscous Salad with Apricots, Pine Nuts and Mint, 90
Couscous with Grilled Vegetables and Charmoula Sauce, 101
Edamame with Shiso-Sesame Salt, 62
Farro Risotto with Asparagus and Lemon, 107
Fillet of Sole with Tarragon Mayonnaise, 127
Greek Chicken Pie, 120
Greek Lentil Salad, 79
Green Bean and Fresh Cranberry Bean Salad, 80
Green Rice, 111
Grilled Chicken with Parsley-Caper Sauce, 125
Grilled Salmon with Mint and Ginger Chutney, 129
Harvest "Thyme" Squash Soup, 82
Health-Conscious Basil Pesto, 156
Herb Cider, 143
Herb Garden Salad, 87
Herbed Goat Cheese Mashed Potatoes, 88
Herbed Goat Cheese Spread, 61
Herbed Pinwheel Biscuits, 66
Herbed Potato Bread, 68
Herbed Tomato Gratin, 72
Honey-Lavender Plum Grain, 146
Leg of Lamb with Herbs De Provence, 114
Lentil-Orzo Stew, 104
Mexcian Potato Omelet, 51
Middle Eastern Bean Spread, 63
Mint and Ginger Chutney, 161
Moroccan Charmoula Sauce, 166
Mushroom-Marjoram Lasagna, 98
No-Cook Summer Tomato Sauce, 168
North African Tuna Kabobs, 136
Oven-Poached Salmon with Fines Herbes, 131
Papaya Relish, 157
Parsley-Caper Sauce, 167
Parsley-Walnut Pesto, 162
Peach-Blackberry Compote with Basil Syrup, 145
Peanut Noodles, 96
Penne with Eggplant, White Bean and Tomato Sauce, 106
Penne with Pesto, Potatoes and Green Beans, 94
Pizza with Potato-Rosemary Topping, 67
Pork Tenderloin with Apple, Thyme and Mustard Marinade, 122
Provençal Beef Stew with Olives, 132
Quick Tomato Sauce, 158
Quick Whole Wheat Pizza Dough, 59
Rhubarb Fool with Angelica, 148
Root Vegetable and Barley Soup, 73
Rosemary-Scented Lamb Kabobs, 117
Rosemary-Scented Lemon Loaf, 140
Savory Noodle Kugel, 95
Semolina Focaccia with Olives and Rosemary, 58
Shallot-Mustard Herb Butter, 163
Shrimp Risotto with Gremolada, 109
Slow-Cooker Mexican Beans, 110
Smoked Salmon Canapes, 52
Southwestern Hominy Soup, 76
Sparkling Mint Limeade, 153
Spinach and Sorrel Soup, 84
Spring Rolls with Shrimp and Rice Noodle Filling, 134
Springtime Sauce with Fines Herbes, 171
Strawberry Shortcakes with Lemon Verbena Cream, 150
Stuffed Chicken Breasts with Herbed Goat Cheese, 124
Swordfish Souvlaki, 130
Thai Chicken Soup, 74
Tortellini in Rosemary-Scented Broth, 77
Traditional Basil Pesto, 157
Tunisian Mint Tea, 149
Turkish Pide with Feta and Dill Filling, 57
Vietnamese Grilled Chicken Thighs, 119
White Bean Spread with Rosemary, 55

General Index

Three ways to use this index. Find recipes by name. Or look up a main ingredient or herb and see related recipes listed. Or check out a chapter category (such as soups & stews) and see those recipes listed.

A

Aegean Halibut Stew, 137
Angelica
   description, traditional use and storage, 22
   Rhubarb Fool with Angelica, 148
Anise
   herbes de Provence, 14
Appetizers
   Cherry Tomatoes Filled with Pesto Cream Cheese, 54
   Herbed Goat Cheese Spread, 61
   Middle Eastern Bean Spread, 63
   Smoked Salmon Canapes, 52
   Spring Rolls with Shrimp and Rice Noodle Filling, 134
   White Bean Spread with Rosemary, 55
Asparagus
   Asparagus Salad with Mint and Almonds, 85
   Farro Risotto with Asparagus and Lemon, 107
Asparagus Salad with Mint and Almonds, 89

B

Basil
   Cauliflower and Spinach Curry, 85
   Cherry Tomatoes Filled with Pesto Cream Cheese, 54
   chiffonade, 9
   cleaning, 8
   description, traditional use and storage, 23
   Health-Conscious Basil Pesto, 156
   herbes de Provence, 14
   herb-infused vinegar, 12
   No-Cook Summer Tomato Sauce, 168
   Peach-Blackberry Compote with Basil Syrup, 145
   Penne with Eggplant, White Bean and Tomato Sauce, 106
   refrigeration of, 8
   slivering, 9
   stripping leaves from stems, 9
   tearing, 9
   timing use of, 18
   Traditional Basil Pesto, 157
Bay Leaf
   bouquet garni, 13
   description, traditional use and storage, 24
   herb bouquet, 16
   herbes de Provence, 14
   Lentil-Orzo Stew, 104
   Provençal Beef Stew with Olives, 132–133

   Swordfish Souvlaki, 130
   timing use of, 18
Beans, Dry
   Greek Lentil Salad, 79
   Lentil-Orzo Stew, 104
   Penne with Eggplant, White Bean and Tomato Sauce, 106
   Slow-Cooker Mexican Beans, 110
   White Bean Spread with Rosemary, 55
Beans, Green
   Edamame with Shiso-Sesame Salt, 62
   Green Bean and Fresh Cranberry Bean Salad, 80
   Penne with Pesto, Potatoes and Green Beans, 94
Beef
   Provençal Beef Stew with Olives, 132–133
Beverages
   Bloody Mary Mix, 142
   Herb Cider, 143
   Sparkling Mint Limeade, 153
   Tunisian Mint Tea, 149
Blanching herbs, 10–11
Bloody Mary Mix, 142
Borage
   edible flower of, 17
bouquet garni, 13
Bread, Quick, Sweet or Flatbread
   Caramelized Red Onion, Olive and Goat Cheese Galette, 64
   Greek Chicken Pie, 120–121
   Herbed Pinwheel Biscuits, 66
   Pizza with Potato-Rosemary Topping, 67
   Rosemary-Scented Lemon Loaf, 140
   Semolina Focaccia with Olives and Rosemary, 58
   Strawberry Shortcakes with Lemon Verbena Cream, 150–151
   Turkish Pide with Feta and Dill Filling, 57
Bread, Yeast
   Herbed Potato Bread, 68–69
   Quick Whole Wheat Pizza Dough, 59
Burnet
   description, traditional use and storage, 25
   herb-infused vinegar, 12
Butter
   freezing, 10
   preserving herbs through, 10
   Shallot-Mustard Herb Butter, 163
Butternut Squash Gratin, 81
Butternut Squash Ravioli, 102–103

C

Caramelized Red Onion, Olive and Goat Cheese Galette, 64
Cauliflower and Spinach Curry, 85
Cheese
   Caramelized Red Onion, Olive and Goat Cheese Galette, 64
   Cherry Tomatoes Filled with Pesto Cream Cheese, 54
   Herbed Goat Cheese Mashed Potatoes, 88
   Herbed Goat Cheese Spread, 61
   Mushroom-Marjoram Lasagna, 98–99
   Penne with Eggplant, White Bean and Tomato Sauce, 106
   Stuffed Chicken Breasts with Herbed Goat Cheese, 124
   Turkish Pide with Feta and Dill Filling, 57
   Cherry Tomatoes Filled with Pesto Cream Cheese, 54
Chervil
   description, traditional use and storage, 26
   fines herbes, 13
   snipping, 9
   Spinach and Sorrel Soup, 84
Chicken. *See* Poultry
Chicken, Prosciutto and Sage Kabobs, 126
Chicken Sauté with Tarragon, 116
Chiffonade, 9
Chives
   chive ribbons, 16
   description, traditional use and storage, 27
   edible flowers, 17
   fines herbes, 13
   Herbed Goat Cheese Mashed Potatoes, 88
   snipping, 9
   tearing, 9
Cilantro
   chiffonade, 9
   Cilantro Pesto, 164
   cleaning, 8
   description, traditional use and storage, 28
   Green Rice, 111
   Mexican Potato Omelet, 51
   Middle Eastern Bean Spread, 63
   Moroccan Charmoula Sauce, 166
   North African Tuna Kabobs, 136
   Papaya Relish, 157
   Peanut Noodles, 96
   slivering, 9
   Southwestern Hominy Soup, 76
   Spring Rolls with Shrimp and Rice Noodle Filling, 134

stripping leaves from stems, 9
Thai Chicken Soup, 74
timing use of, 18
Cilantro Pesto, 164
Couscous
   Couscous Salad with Apricots, Pine Nuts and Mint, 90
   Couscous with Grilled Vegetables and Charmoula Sauce, 101
Couscous Salad with Apricots, Pine Nuts and Mint, 90
Couscous with Grilled Vegetables and Charmoula Sauce, 101

D
Dehydrator, 11
Dessert
   Honey-Lavender Plum Gratin, 146
   Peach-Blackberry Compote with Basil Syrup, 145
   Rhubarb Fool with Angelica, 148
   Rosemary-Scented Lemon Loaf, 140
   Strawberry Shortcakes with Lemon Verbena Cream, 150–151
Dill
   Aegean Halibut Stew, 137
   cleaning, 8
   description, traditional use and storage, 29
   Greek Chicken Pie, 120–121
   Greek Lentil Salad, 79
   Herbed Pinwheel Biscuits, 66
   herb-infused vinegar, 12
   Middle Eastern Bean Spread, 63
   Root Vegetable and Barley Soup, 73
   Savory Noodle Kugel, 95
   Smoked Salmon Canapes, 52
   stripping leaves from stems, 9
   timing use of, 18
   Turkish Pide with Feta and Dill Filling, 57
Dressing/Vinaigrette
   Asparagus Salad with Mint and Almonds, 89
   Greek Lentil Salad, 79
   Green Bean and Fresh Cranberry Bean Salad, 80
   Herb Garden Salad, 87
   Pork Tenderloin with Apple, Thyme and Mustard Marinade, 122
   Spring Rolls with Shrimp and Rice Noodle Filling, 134
Drying Herbs, 11–12
   in dehydrator, 11
   by hanging, 11
   storing dried herbs, 12

E
Edamame with Shiso-Sesame Salt, 62
Edible Flowers, 17
   Herb Garden Salad, 87
Egg Dishes
   Baked Eggs with Tarragon, 50
   Mexican Potato Omelet, 51
Eggplant
   Couscous with Grilled Vegetables and Charmoula Sauce, 101
   Penne with Eggplant, White Bean and Tomato Sauce, 106
Epazote
   description, traditional use and storage, 30
   Slow-Cooker Mexican Beans, 110

F
Farro Risotto with Asparagus and Lemon, 107
Fillet of Sole with Tarragon Mayonnaise, 127
fines herbes, 13
   Oven-Poached Salmon with Fines Herbes, 131
   Springtime Sauce with Fines Herbes, 171
Fish and Seafood
   Aegean Halibut Stew, 137
   Fillet of Sole with Tarragon Mayonnaise, 127
   Grilled Salmon with Mint and Ginger Chutney, 129
   North African Tuna Kabobs, 136
   Oven-Poached Salmon with Fines Herbes, 131
   Shrimp Risotto with Gremolada, 109
   Smoked Salmon Canapes, 52
   Spring Rolls with Shrimp and Rice Noodle Filling, 134
   Swordfish Souvlaki, 130
Freezing Herbs, 10–11
   by blanching method, 10–11
   butters, 10
   by ice cube method, 11
   pesto, 10
Frosted herb sprigs, 17

G
Garlic
   Asparagus Salad with Mint and Almonds, 89
   Butternut Squash Gratin, 81
   Butternut Squash Ravioli, 102–103
   Caramelized Red Onion, Olive and Goat Cheese Galette, 64
   Cherry Tomatoes Filled with Pesto Cream Cheese, 54
   Chicken, Prosciutto and Sage Kabobs, 126
   Cilantro Pesto, 164
   Couscous Salad with Apricots, Pine Nuts and Mint, 90
   Greek Lentil Salad, 79
   Green Rice, 111
   gremolada, 15
   Harvest "Thyme" Squash Soup, 82
   Health-Conscious Basil Pesto, 156
   Herbed Goat Cheese Mashed Potatoes, 88
   Herbed Goat Cheese Spread, 61
   Herbed Pinwheel Biscuits, 66
   Herbed Tomato Gratin, 72
   Herb Garden Salad, 87
   infusion, 18
   Middle Eastern Bean Spread, 63
   Moroccan Charmoula Sauce, 166
   No-Cook Summer Tomato Sauce, 168
   North African Tuna Kabobs, 136
   Papaya Relish, 157
   Parsley-Caper Sauce, 167
   Parsley-Walnut Pesto, 162
   Peanut Noodles, 96
   Penne with Eggplant, White Bean and Tomato Sauce, 106
   persillade, 15
   Pork Tenderloin with Apple, Thyme and Mustard Marinade, 122
   Provençal Beef Stew with Olives, 132–133
   Quick Tomato Sauce, 158
   Root Vegetable and Barley Soup, 73
   Rosemary-Scented Lamb Kabobs, 117

Shrimp Risotto with Gremolada, 109
Slow-Cooker Mexican Beans, 110
Southwestern Hominy Soup, 76
Spring Rolls with Shrimp and Rice Noodle Filling, 134
Swordfish Souvlaki, 130
Thai Chicken Soup, 74
tips for using, 47
Tortellini in Rosemary-Scented Broth, 77
Traditional Basil Pesto, 157
White Bean Spread with Rosemary, 55
Garnishes
   chive ribbons, 16
   edible flowers, 17
   fried parsley, 16
   frosted herb sprigs, 17
   herb bouquets, 16
Grains
   Couscous Salad with Apricots, Pine Nuts and Mint, 90
   Couscous with Grilled Vegetables and Charmoula Sauce, 101
   Farro Risotto with Asparagus and Lemon, 107
   Green Rice, 111
   Shrimp Risotto with Gremolada, 109
Greek Chicken Pie, 120–121
Greek Lentil Salad, 79
Green Bean and Fresh Cranberry Bean Salad, 80
Green Rice, 111
Gremolada, 15
Grilled Chicken with Parsley-Caper Sauce, 125
Grilled Salmon with Mint and Ginger Chutney, 129
Grilling
   add aroma to fire, 19
   Chicken, Prosciutto and Sage Kabobs, 126
   creative kabobs, 19
   Grilled Salmon with Mint and Ginger Chutney, 129
   herbal protection, 19
   lemongrass skewers, 19
   North African Tuna Kabobs, 136
   Pork Tenderloin with Apple, Thyme ad Mustard Marinade, 122
   Rosemary-Scented Lamb Kabobs, 117
   Swordfish Souvlaki, 130
   tips for, 19
   Vietnamese Grilled Chicken Thighs, 119

H
Harvest "Thyme" Squash Soup, 82
Health-Conscious Basil Pesto, 156
Herb Bouquet, 16
Herb Cider, 143
Herbed Goat Cheese Mashed Potatoes, 88
Herbed Goat Cheese Spread, 61
   Stuffed Chicken Breasts with Herbed Goat Cheese, 124
Herbed Pinwheel Biscuits, 66
Herbed Potato Bread, 68–69
Herbed Tomato Gratin, 72
Herbes de Provence, 14
   Herbed Tomato Gratin, 72
   Leg of Lamb with Herbes De Provence, 114
Herb Garden Salad, 87
Herb infusions, 12, 18
Herb Tips and Techniques
   chopping, 9

174

classic herb combos, 13–15
cleaning, 8
drying, 11–12
freezing, 10–11
grilling tips, 18
harvesting, 10
herb garnishes, 16–17
herb infusions, 18
preserving through pesto or compound butter, 10
short-term storage, 8
slivering, 9
snipping, 9
stripping leaves from stems, 9
tearing, 9
timing cooking tip, 18
use quickly, 9
Honey-Lavender Plum Gratin, 146

I
Infusions, 12, 18

L
Lamb
Leg of Lamb with Herbes De Provence, 114
Rosemary-Scented Lamb Kabobs, 117
Lavender
description, traditional use and storage, 31
herbes de Provence, 14
Honey-Lavender Plum Gratin, 146
Leg of Lamb with Herbes De Provence, 114
Lemon Balm
description, traditional use and storage, 32
Lemongrass
description, traditional use and storage, 33
skewers for grilling, 19
Thai Chicken Soup, 74
Vietnamese Grilled Chicken Thighs, 119
Lemon Verbena
description, traditional use and storage, 34
frosted herb sprigs, 17
Strawberry Shortcakes with Lemon Verbena Cream, 150–151
Lentil-Orzo Stew, 104
Lovage
Bloody Mary Mix, 142
description, traditional use and storage, 35

M
Marjoram
description, traditional use and storage, 36
herbes de Provence, 14
Mushroom-Marjoram Lasagna, 98–99
Quick Tomato Sauce, 158
Mexican Potato Omelet, 51
Middle Eastern Bean Spread, 63
Mint
Asparagus Salad with Mint and Almonds, 89
chiffonade, 9
Couscous Salad with Apricots, Pine Nuts and Mint, 90
description, traditional use and storage, 37
Grilled Salmon with Mint and Ginger Chutney, 129
herb-infused vinegar, 12
Middle Eastern Bean Spread, 63
Mint and Ginger Chutney, 161
Peanut Noodles, 96

Rhubarb Fool with Angelica, 148
slivering, 9
Sparkling Mint Limeade, 153
Spring Rolls with Shrimp and Rice Noodle Filling, 134
Tunisian Mint Tea, 149
Mint and Ginger Chutney, 161
Grilled Salmon with Mint and Ginger Chutney, 129
Moroccan Charmoula Sauce, 166
Mushroom-Marjoram Lasagna, 98–99

N
Nasturtium flowers, 17
No-Cook Summer Tomato Sauce, 168
North African Tuna Kabobs, 136
Nuts
Cherry Tomatoes Filled with Pesto Cream Cheese, 54
Cilantro Pesto, 164
Couscous Salad with Apricots, Pine Nuts and Mint, 90
Health-Conscious Basil Pesto, 156
Parsley-Walnut Pesto, 162
Peanut Noodles, 96
Traditional Basil Pesto, 157

O
Oil, herb-infused, 12
Oregano
description, traditional use and storage, 38
drying, 11–12
Southwestern Hominy Soup, 76
Swordfish Souvlaki, 130
timing use of, 18
Oven-Poached Salmon with Fines Herbes, 131

P
Papaya Relish, 157
Vietnamese Grilled Chicken Thighs, 119
Parsley
bouquet garni, 13
cleaning, 8
description, traditional use and storage, 39
fines herbes, 13
fried parsley, 16
gremolada, 15
Herbed Goat Cheese Mashed Potatoes, 88
Herbed Goat Cheese Spread, 61
Herbed Pinwheel Biscuits, 66
Herb Garden Salad, 87
Lentil-Orzo Stew, 104
Moroccan Charmoula Sauce, 166
North African Tuna Kabobs, 136
Parsley-Caper Sauce, 167
Parsley-Walnut Pesto, 162
persillade, 15
Provençal Beef Stew with Olives, 132–133
Savory Noodle Kugel, 95
Shallot-Mustard Herb Butter, 163
Shrimp Risotto with Gremolada, 109
Spinach and Sorrel Soup, 84
stripping leaves from stems, 9
timing use of, 18
Parsley-Caper Sauce, 167
Grilled Chicken with Parsley-Caper Sauce, 125
Parsley-Walnut Pesto, 162
Pasta
Butternut Squash Ravioli, 102–103

Lentil-Orzo Stew, 104
Mushroom-Marjoram Lasagna, 98–99
Peanut Noodles, 96
Penne with Eggplant, White Bean and Tomato Sauce, 106
Penne with Pesto, Potatoes and Green Beans, 94
Savory Noodle Kugel, 95
Tortellini in Rosemary-Scented Broth, 77
Peach-Blackberry Compote with Basil Syrup, 145
Peanut Noodles, 96
Penne with Eggplant, White Bean and Tomato Sauce, 106
Penne with Pesto, Potatoes and Green Beans, 94
Persillade, 15
Pesto
Cherry Tomatoes Filled with Pesto Cream Cheese, 54
Cilantro Pesto, 164
freezing, 10
Health-Conscious Basil Pesto, 156
Parsley-Walnut Pesto, 162
Penne with Pesto, Potatoes and Green Beans, 94
preserving herbs through, 10
Traditional Basil Pesto, 157
Pies, Main Dish
Greek Chicken Pie, 120–121
Pizza
Pizza with Potato-Rosemary Topping, 67
Quick Whole Wheat Pizza Dough, 59
Pizza with Potato-Rosemary Topping, 67
Pork Tenderloin with Apple, Thyme and Mustard Marinade, 122
Potatoes
Aegean Halibut Stew, 137
Herbed Goat Cheese Mashed Potatoes, 88
Herbed Potato Bread, 68–69
Mexican Potato Omelet, 51
Penne with Pesto, Potatoes and Green Beans, 94
Pizza with Potato-Rosemary Topping, 67
Poultry
Chicken, Prosciutto and Sage Kabobs, 126
Chicken Sauté with Tarragon, 116
Greek Chicken Pie, 120–121
Grilled Chicken with Parsley-Caper Sauce, 125
Southwestern Hominy Soup, 76
Stuffed Chicken Breasts with Herbed Goat Cheese, 124
Thai Chicken Soup, 74
Vietnamese Grilled Chicken Thighs, 119
Preserving Herbs
bouquet of flower method, 8
butters, 10
drying, 11–12
freezing, 10–11
herb-infused vinegar, 12
pesto, 10
plastic food bag method, 8
short-term, 8
Provençal Beef Stew with Olives, 132–133

Q
Quick Tomato Sauce, 158
Quick Whole Wheat Pizza Dough, 59

General Index **175**

R

Recipe Potpourri, 64
  Baked Eggs with Tarragon, 50
  Caramelized Red Onion, Olive and Goat Cheese Galette, 64
  Cherry Tomatoes Filled with Pesto Cream Cheese, 54
  Edamame with Shiso Sesame Salt, 62
  Herbed Goat Cheese Spread, 61
  Herbed Pinwheel Biscuits, 66
  Herbed Potato Bread, 68–69
  Mexican Potato Omelet, 51
  Middle Eastern Bean Spread, 63
  Pizza with Potato-Rosemary Topping, 67
  Quick Whole Wheat Pizza Dough, 59
  Semolina Focaccia with Olives and Rosemary, 58
  Smoked Salmon Canapes, 52
  Turkish Pide with Feta and Dill Filling, 57
  White Bean Spread with Rosemary, 55
Rhubarb Fool with Angelica, 148

Rice
  Green Rice, 111
  Shrimp Risotto with Gremolada, 109

Risotto
  Farro Risotto with Asparagus and Lemon, 107
  Shrimp Risotto with Gremolada, 109
Root Vegetables and Barley Soup, 73

Rosemary
  Butternut Squash Ravioli, 102–103
  Caramelized Red Onion, Olive and Goat Cheese Galette, 64
  description, traditional use and storage, 40
  drying, 11–12
  frosted herb sprigs, 17
  herb bouquet, 16
  Herbed Potato Bread, 68–69
  herbes de Provence, 14
  infusion, 18
  Pizza with Potato-Rosemary Topping, 67
  Rosemary-Scented Lamb Kabobs, 117
  Rosemary-Scented Lemon Loaf, 140
  Semolina Focaccia with Olives and Rosemary, 58
  Stuffed Chicken Breasts with Herbed Goat Cheese, 124
  timing use of, 18
  Tortellini in Rosemary-Scented Broth, 77
  White Bean Spread with Rosemary, 55
Rosemary-Scented Lamb Kabobs, 117
Rosemary-Scented Lemon Loaf, 140

S

Sage
  Chicken, Prosciutto and Sage Kabobs, 126
  description, traditional use and storage, 41
  drying, 11–12
  Grilled Chicken with Parsley-Caper Sauce, 125
  herb bouquet, 16
  Herbed Potato Bread, 68–69
  herbes de Provence, 14

Salads
  Asparagus Salad with Mint and Almonds, 89
  Couscous Salad with Apricots, Pine Nuts and Mint, 90
  Greek Lentil Salad, 79
  Green Bean and Fresh Cranberry Bean Salad, 80
  Herb Garden Salad, 87

Sauces and Condiments
  Cilantro Pesto, 164
  Couscous with Grilled Vegetables and Charmoula Sauce, 101
  Fillet of Sole with Tarragon Mayonnaise, 127
  Grilled Chicken with Parsley-Caper Sauce, 125
  Health-Conscious Basil Pesto, 156
  Mint and Ginger Chutney, 161
  Moroccan Charmoula Sauce, 166
  No-Cook Summer Tomato Sauce, 168
  Papaya Relish, 157
  Parsley-Caper Sauce, 167
  Parsley-Walnut Pesto, 162
  Pork Tenderloin with Apple, Thyme ad Mustard Marinade, 122
  Quick Tomato Sauce, 158
  Shallot-Mustard Herb Butter, 163
  Springtime Sauce with Fines Herbes, 171
  Traditional Basil Pesto, 157

Savory
  description, traditional use and storage, 42
  Green Bean and Fresh Cranberry Bean Salad, 80
  Herbed Goat Cheese Spread, 61
  herbes de Provence, 14
  Savory Noodle Kugel, 95

Seafood. *See* Fish and seafood
Semolina Focaccia with Olives and Rosemary, 58

Sesame Seeds
  Edamame with Shiso-Sesame Salt, 62
  zatar, 15
Shallot-Mustard Herb Butter, 163
  Chicken, Prosciutto and Sage Kabobs, 126

Shiso
  description, traditional use and storage, 43
  Edamame with Shiso-Sesame Salt, 62
Shrimp Risotto with Gremolada, 109

Side Dishes
  Butternut Squash Gratin, 81
  Cauliflower and Spinach Curry, 85
  Couscous with Grilled Vegetables and Charmoula Sauce, 101
  Herbed Goat Cheese Mashed Potatoes, 88
  Herbed Tomato Gratin, 72
  Slow-Cooker Mexican Beans, 110
  Smoked Salmon Canapes, 52

Sorrel
  description, traditional use and storage, 44
  Spinach and Sorrel Soup, 84

Soups and Stews
  Aegean Halibut Stew, 137
  Harvest "Thyme" Squash Soup, 82
  herb infusions, 18
  Lentil-Orzo Stew, 104
  Provençal Beef Stew with Olives, 132–133
  Root Vegetables and Barley Soup, 73
  Southwestern Hominy Soup, 76
  Spinach and Sorrel Soup, 84
  Thai Chicken Soup, 74
  Tortellini in Rosemary-Scented Broth, 77
Southwestern Hominy Soup, 76
Sparkling Mint Limeade, 153

Spinach
  Cauliflower and Spinach Curry, 85
  Spinach and Sorrel Soup, 84

Spreads
  Herbed Goat Cheese Spread, 61
  Middle Eastern Bean Spread, 63
  White Bean Spread with Rosemary, 55
Spring Rolls with Shrimp and Rice Noodle Filling, 134
Springtime Sauce with Fines Herbes, 171
  Oven-Poached Salmon with Fines Herbes, 131

Squash
  Butternut Squash Gratin, 81
  Butternut Squash Ravioli, 102–103
  Harvest "Thyme" Squash Soup, 82
Stews. *See* Soups and stews
Storing Herbs. *See* Preserving herbs
Strawberry Shortcakes with Lemon Verbena Cream, 150–151
Stuffed Chicken Breasts with Herbed Goat Cheese, 124

Sumac
  zatar, 15
Swordfish Souvlaki, 130

T

Tarragon
  Baked Eggs with Tarragon, 50
  Chicken Sauté with Tarragon, 116
  description, traditional use and storage, 45
  Fillet of Sole with Tarragon Mayonnaise, 127
  fines herbes, 13
  herb-infused vinegar, 12
  timing use of, 18
Thai Chicken Soup, 74

Thyme
  bouquet garni, 13
  Caramelized Red Onion, Olive and Goat Cheese Galette, 64
  description, traditional use and storage, 46
  drying, 11–12
  Harvest "Thyme" Squash Soup, 82
  herb bouquet, 16
  Herb Cider, 143
  Herbed Potato Bread, 68–69
  herbes de Provence, 14
  Lentil-Orzo Stew, 104
  Pork Tenderloin with Apple, Thyme ad Mustard Marinade, 122
  Provençal Beef Stew with Olives, 132–133
  zatar, 15

Tomatoes
  Cherry Tomatoes Filled with Pesto Cream Cheese, 54
  Herbed Tomato Gratin, 72
  No-Cook Summer Tomato Sauce, 168
  Quick Tomato Sauce, 158
Tortellini in Rosemary-Scented Broth, 77
Traditional Basil Pesto, 157
Tunisian Mint Tea, 149
Turkish Pide with Feta and Dill Filling, 57

V

Vietnamese Grilled Chicken Thighs, 119
Vinaigrette. *See* Dressing/Vinaigrette
Vinegar, herb-infused, 12

W

White Bean Spread with Rosemary, 55

Z

Zatar, 15